THEOLOGY AND MEDIA(TION)

THEOLOGY AND MEDIA(TION)

Rendering the Absent Present

Stephen Okey
Katherine G. Schmidt
Editors

THE ANNUAL PUBLICATION
OF THE COLLEGE THEOLOGY SOCIETY
2023
VOLUME 69

Maryknoll, New York 10545

Founded in 1970, Orbis Books endeavors to publish works that enlighten the mind, nourish the spirit, and challenge the conscience. The books published reflect the views of their authors and do not represent the official position of the Maryknoll Society. To learn more about Maryknoll and Orbis Books, please visit our website at www.orbisbooks.com.

Published by Orbis Books, Box 302, Maryknoll, NY 10545-0302.

Manufactured in the United States of America

Library of Congress Cataloging-in-Publication Data

Names: Okey, Stephen, editor. | Schmidt, Katherine G. (Katherine Gail), 1985- editor.
Title: Theology and media(tion) : rendering the absent present / Stephen Okey, Katherine G. Schmidt, editors.
Other titles: Theology and mediation
Description: Maryknoll, NY : Orbis Books, [2024] | Series: The annual publication of the College Theology Society ; volume 69, 2023 | Includes bibliographical references.
Identifiers: LCCN 2023052521 (print) | LCCN 2023052522 (ebook) | ISBN 9781626985681 (trade paperback) | ISBN 9798888660249 (epub)
Subjects: LCSH: Marginality, Social—Religious aspects—Christianity. |
Mass media—Religious aspects—Christianity. | Digital media—Religious aspects—Christianity. | Religion and sociology. | Art and religion.
Classification: LCC BR115.S56 T44 2024 (print) | LCC BR115.S56 (ebook) | DDC 261.5/2—dc23/eng/20240202
LC record available at https://lccn.loc.gov/2023052521
LC ebook record available at https://lccn.loc.gov/2023052522

Contents

Mediation and Place

Mediation and Art

Introduction

Stephen Okey
and Katherine G. Schmidt

The word "media" conjures a range of emotional and ideological responses in the context of the United States today. The common way it's used mostly refers to mass media, with a dash of new media, and involves the ridiculously fast news cycle, mostly related to celebrities and politics.

This volume is not unrelated to this understanding of media, but it seeks to expand the notion to include all of the ways in which we engage with methods, objects, and structures that "go between." Media are those various means by which individuals connect to individuals, individuals connect to communities, and particularly relevant for this volume, individuals and communities connect to the transcendent. This echoes Birgit Meyer's definition of media, which includes "both new and old mass media, as well as objects, sacred spaces and the human body" and makes up that which has been "authorized within particular religious traditions as suitable for humans to link up, in one way or another, with the divine or spiritual."[1]

But Meyer's definition raises many questions, and this volume is an effort to both tease these questions out and to provide some responses from theology and religious studies. As central as media are to any religious tradition, they can be messy—fraught with all of the problems of the human experience. It is telling that Meyer uses the word "authorized," as authority is a crucial element of

[1]Birgit Meyer, "Medium," in *Key Terms in Material Religion*, ed. Brent S. Plate (London: Bloomsbury, 2015), 140.

mediation in religious traditions. Who develops the various media we employ in our religious lives? Who sanctions certain media and disqualifies others? What happens when the authorities making these decisions become unreliable judges of the ways in which we are meant to connect to one another and to God?

Religious traditions in general are well suited for questions of mediation if we imagine media in Meyer's terms. For example, the paradox of presence and absence is at the heart of many religious traditions, as they move constantly within the often uncomfortable but inevitable space between the immanent and the transcendent. This dynamic is at the heart of Christianity: "No one comes to the Father except through me" (John 14:6). From the beginning, Christian thought has wrestled with questions of mediation. Following his death, resurrection, and ascension, how is Christ made present to the world today? How are distant communities held together in communion? What means should Christians use to spread the word of God?

Gospel narratives of Mary Magdalene and the Gardener or the Road to Emmaus point to the challenge of how to navigate the relationship between presence and absence. Mediation has, in fact, been a consistent and underlying concern of Christian theology, through Christ, the church, liturgy, scripture, tradition, ethics, and pedagogy. These questions have been amplified in new ways through the rise of digital technology and culture, posing challenges to traditional perspectives on embodiment, ritual, sociality, and aesthetics. More recently, the global pandemic of 2020–2022 has shown many ways that the relationship of presence and absence underlies our relationships within families, religious communities, universities, and more.

In the Catholic tradition, the church has been officially commenting on media (in a narrow sense) from at least 1766, when they warned against mass-produced paperback novels and other printed materials that "pollute the pure waters of belief and destroy the foundations of religion."[2] The height of its commentary on mass media was during the 1930s, when it was instrumental in developing the Motion Picture Production Code, more com-

[2]Pope Clement XIII, *Christianae Reipublicae: On the Dangers of Anti-Christian Writings*, 1766.

monly known as the Hays Code, for Hollywood, drastically changing both the form and content of modern films and laying the groundwork for contemporary rating systems still in use in the United States.

Several authors in this volume pick up on this understanding of media, focusing on "old media" such as print (Dulle) and new media such as TikTok (Sloan Peters). But we intentionally wanted to take Meyer's cue and broaden the notion of media to include a wide variety of understandings of media and mediation.

Meyer gives us a starting point but only does so to the extent that she can analyze the "material turn" within religious studies as an academic discipline. The present volume approaches the question of media/mediation from a variety of perspectives, reflecting on the complexities and considerations of what it might mean to "link up to the divine" and to one another in view of this link to the divine.

We begin with the first part, "Mediation and Bodies." Hanna Reichel pushes the conversation about authority forward and beyond the bounds of the church, inviting us to consider different understandings of belonging. Reichel raises interesting points about our current ideological identities, which are often mediated by a divisive and violent political discourse across various media. Most notably, Reichel ends with a reflection on the Body of Christ that turns our attention to considering the "misfit" as normative for this ecclesiology.

Trevor Williams's essay draws on French phenomenologist Emmanuel Falque's discussion of "animality" to highlight the centrality of the body in the divine-human relationship. Amy Maxey engages with Luce Irigaray and Audre Lorde to push against formulations of mystical eros that overly focus on the unconscious, arguing instead for a view of mystical eros that engenders both self-consciousness and responsible engagement with society. Laura Taylor highlights the role of using sources in theology and how these can render particular voices absent or present within theological discourse. She then focuses in particular on depictions of key Christian symbols in feminist visual culture as efforts to envision a more inclusive and less oppressive world.

Matthew Gummess considers how Catholic theology might respond to transgender persons if it were to assume, a priori, the validity of their claims about their bodies. From this, he engages with the theology of the body of John Paul II, arguing that the commensuration of body and soul in Thomistic thought does not require a binary view of gender. Jacob Kohlhaas draws on the thought and the style of Bruno Latour to consider the meaning of parenthood in Catholic thought, arguing that the particular and transformative character of being a parent can be illustrative of the transformative encounter with the sacraments.

The second part, "Mediation and Place," begins with the plenary address from Joseph Flipper. His essay introduces us to the community of his upbringing in Idaho. Flipper considers the role of the land as mediator in the complex history of the Indigenous Numipunm Wéetespe people and their relationship to Catholicism in the context of colonization.

Deepan Rajaratnam enters into contemporary discussions around synodality by arguing that the *sensus fidei* is better understood by considering the culture and practice of local churches rather than the typical, universalized tripartite structure of the sense of the bishops, of the theologians, and of the church as a whole. Christopher Denny argues for an approach to ecotheology that prioritizes praxis over theory, seeing the former as both more effective for responding to ecological problems and for emphasizing the embodied reality of the human relationship to the world.

Timothy Hanchin takes Pope Francis's call for ecological conversion and applies it to the campuses of Catholic colleges and universities, arguing that the decisions these institutions make about landscaping and architecture play a pedagogical role in forming students and in fulfilling institutional mission. Ethan Vander Leek brings together the philosophy of William Desmond and Rowan Williams. Through these two thinkers, he provides a theological account of mediation drawing on the classical doctrines of creation and incarnation.

The third part, "Mediation and Art," considers various ways that absence and presence are engaged through music, visual arts, and new media. Tim Dulle considers the work of mid-century American artist Corita Kent. Dulle places her work in the context of Marshall McLuhan's well-known "medium is the message," and discusses both in the context of Vatican II–era shifts in understandings of the media and the sacred. Charles Gillespie brings us into the world of Hildegard of Bingen, the twelfth-century Benedictine abbess known for her visions. Gillespie focuses on Hildegard's use of music (and the spaces between) to bring herself and her community into an encounter with God.

Jane Sloan Peters brings the discussion of media into the present moment, focusing her work on the social media platform of TikTok. She argues that TikTok offers a way for Gen Z to try to make sense of suffering and provides evidence from her own experience as a theological educator. Dennis Wieboldt offers a historical account of American Catholic use of mass media, specifically focusing on Fulton Sheen's *Catholic Hour* and its role in presenting natural law to the laity. Vicente Chong proposes art's capacity to mediate divine revelation. Drawing on Karl Rahner's theological understanding of symbol, he shows how the art of Sammy Chong can disclose the image of God as servant.

In the part titled "Mediation and Responsibility," the volume concludes with our first plenary address from the Convention, Robert Orsi's "Religion(s) in the Ruins of the Temples." Orsi centers his discussion on the ongoing sexual abuse crisis, inviting us to consider the church's role as mediator broadly. This gets to the heart of the question of authority/authorization, giving voice to the silenced and marginalized in the church. By closing with this essay, we mean to bring the conversation back to the messiness of mediation (to say the least) and to lift up the voices of victims and survivors.

By offering a broad consideration of media(tion) in this volume, we hope to present a picture of the robust discussions we had in the summer of 2023 and to inspire ongoing conversation about the relationship of theology to the media landscapes in which we always find ourselves, no matter the point in history.

MEDIATION AND BODIES

On Be/longing

Eschatological Mediations

Hanna Reichel

All of my life I have searched for a place of belonging, a place that would become home.

—bell hooks

Longing for Belonging: A Public Feeling?

Home. The very idea evokes and directs emotion. Home galvanizes longing, a longing to belong, to have a place of one's own, where one could fit in, be accepted, fully be oneself, be supported and protected and nourished, safe and secure, at peace, in harmony between the social, the ecological, and the intergenerational, a place that would be, as hooks says, "whole and holy."[1] Home, as the place of belonging, is a deeply romantic idea—in an everyday sense, but also in the technical sense. That is: The term "home" projects the source of aesthetic experience for the individual in its social and ecological nucleus, it imbues the simple and everyday with an aura, it chases fragments and glimpses of an idea that is marked by nostalgia as much as aspiration.

Home is primarily what is not. hooks writes, "Home was the place I longed for, it was *not* where I lived."[2] Home is not a place, but it is also not a people; home is a bundle of ideas, practices,

[1]bell hooks, *Belonging: A Culture of Place* (New York: Routledge, 2008), 53.

[2]hooks, *Belonging*, 215.

and attachments that mediate our experience of longing to belong. Whether we project the idea of home onto physical or social location, onto buildings or geographies or communities or institutions, "home" is marked by absence, memory or longing, nostalgia or projection, or both. Even where we do claim to have found it, it is haunted by this feeling of fleetingness, ephemerality, mortality: On the one hand, home is that which we never completely attain; on the other hand, home is that which you already miss while you are there. It is either already lost or never fully realized. We were never home, and most likely, we never will be on this earth.

In theological projects, too, the notion of "home" mostly appears marked by a negative—by feelings of absence, loss, and longing. "Home" is invoked in discourses of exile and diaspora, in talk of sin as estrangement and alienation, and in an eschatological "eternal home" as a counter-vision to earthly existence's restlessness, yearning, and transitoriness. All these descriptions have a powerful affective dimension and they are marked by a certain negativity, a "-lessness": restlessness, unsettledness, homelessness. It is easier to define *longing* than to pinpoint what constitutes *belonging*.

Home is neither a reality that exists, nor is it a simple absence. All its iterations are marked by a double negative, a longing for belonging: (1) a perceived lack or absence, (2) a negative affective response to this absence. In logic, a double negative makes a positive; in real life, things are more complicated, especially in relation to our affective orientations, and I want to lean a bit further into these complications, into the ambivalences both of the positive and of the negative valences of belonging with the help of affect theory.

The longing for belonging invokes feeling on two levels. First, the lack or absence that gets metabolized into a feeling of unbelonging, and second, an affective reaction to that unbelonging: the affective attachment to the absent object, the longing for belonging, the desire to belong. Two negatives, and two layers of feeling where feeling bad and feeling hopeful become almost indistinguishable.

In the past couple of decades, affect theorists such as Ann Cvetkovich, Lauren Berlant, and Sara Ahmed have questioned a clear-cut division between good and bad feelings and investigated the generativity and value of supposedly "bad feelings"—emotions like anxiety, anger, or moodiness. They have also pointed out the ambivalence of supposedly "good feelings" like happiness, belonging, and community as forms of "cruel optimism": objects of desire that are not only unachievable or disappointing, but the attachment to which is actually, and somewhat tragically, an obstacle to people's flourishing.[3] One aim of such critique has been to de-pathologize supposedly "bad feelings," turning them into a site of insight and critique by understanding them as "public feelings."

This approach draws on the traditional feminist conviction that "the personal is the political," in this case meaning that we need to consider that affect is much more than individual emotive or psychological states, which become explainable by personal experience or biochemical disbalances, but can also be symptoms of larger societal malaise that are in need of structural, social, and political rather than medical or therapeutic attention. In this vein, for example, depression has been diagnosed as a pervasive effect of neoliberal capitalism, and happiness has been closely identified with imperatives to cisheterormative reproduction.[4]

I want to propose that "belonging," or rather "the longing to belong" might be a site worthy of investigation in this vein, a structure of attachment, an indication of a certain historical atmosphere, a promise that motivates endurance and passivity as much as action, resistance, even revolution in diverse ways. With affect theory, we might want to dwell on the public feeling of unbelonging and ask what it can tell us about the realities we inhabit, materially, politically, culturally, as well as theologically.

Longing for Belonging: A Religious Sentiment?

It is not surprising that in a time of as much upheaval and transformation as ours (a time of trauma as much as of multiple

---

[3]Lauren Berlant, *Cruel Optimism* (Durham, NC: Duke University Press, 2011).

[4]Ann Cvetkovich, *Depression: A Public Feeling* (Durham, NC: Duke University Press, 2012); Sara Ahmed, *The Promise of Happiness* (Durham, NC: Duke University Press, 2010), and *What's the Use? On the Uses of Use* (Durham, NC: Duke University Press, 2019).

ongoing crises) that longings for belonging mark diverse public imaginaries, and can be found across all kinds of political, social, and theological divides. These longings for belonging get expressed in projects that might otherwise seem to be completely at odds with one another: We find them in private visions of "a place of one's own" as much as in agrarian and communitarian turns; they fuel projects of building "beloved community," of love and reconciliation in historically disenfranchised communities but also attend resurgences of diverse nationalisms and chauvinisms. I hope this list clarifies that I am for now utterly uninterested in judging such a longing for belonging and instead interested in marking it as utterly pervasive when I say that we are witnessing a rediscovery of community and place and space as mediation of the experience of salvation, and its name is "belonging."

What authorizes my claim—I am not a psychologist or cultural theorist—is that belonging has such strong religious overtones. In fact, in our times, religion is often the explicit site and name of projects of belonging, where we either envision or even attempt to (temporarily, transitorily, but yet) make the home that we fail to find in our families, in our social and political communities, in our societies, and in our world.

If there was a time and place (and we might associate this location with the church Catholic in all its magnificence), where the Christian religion understood itself primarily in terms of truth and doctrine, that is: *orthodoxy*, right ordering of thinking; if there was another time and place (and we might associate this location with Immanuel Kant's famous critiques, and with diverse branches of Neo-Protestantism as much as Liberation Theologies) where the Christian religion understood itself primarily in terms of right ordering of doing, that is *orthopraxy*, or ethics. We might argue that more recently, we can see a shift toward right ordering of relationships, I would call this *orthosocy*. In our time and place, what we conceive as religious then might be oriented less by doctrinal or ethical projects and more by projects of belonging.

This typology, I'll admit, is quite Eurocentric and Protestant, and I am not overly invested in it. But I do think we witness a tendency on the rise in our time to look to "the church" and "the faith," to religious communities, religious practices, and religious life, not primarily as an institution of truth and not primarily as an institution of morality but as a place of belonging. And we find that theologians today are explicitly taking up the language of belonging in order to reflect on our world as well as to conceptualize the work of reforming our institutions and practices, our ecclesial communities, and our sites of theological formation.[5] These are very important projects, and I resonate with them profoundly.

Such a shift to belonging might partially be a response to the moral crises of the pursuit of "truth" and "right thinking," and the epistemological crises of the pursuit of "ethics" and "right doing," and their historical disappointments and disillusionments in the past decades and centuries. Such a shift might also be a response to the erosion of belonging in our local, national, and global communities at large, to which religion then presents itself as a remedy. We know that religion has always had significant compensatory functions, or, if we want it to put it more positively, religion has always been a site of prophetic and priestly imaginaries, a place where we lean into the promise of a different world, and a laboratory of countercultural indication. And in our time, I would argue, "belonging" marks this promise like little else, and it is much more widespread than organized religion or reflective theology. It can be found in diverse "secular" and post-secular movements, well outside the realms of organized religion or of what would be framed as "religious" by most theories.

And yet through a theological lens I would claim that we might frame this longing for belonging as the transposition of a characteristically religious sentiment surrounding salvation into a different register. Individual and collective longings for belonging mediate and express—maybe implicitly, maybe inchoately—both a deep insight into the present unredeemed state of the world as well as a longing for redemption, including an intuition about their salvageability. The taste of a different world that is real *and therefore* must be possible, therefore becomes an object of longing. But what does salvation consist in, and how is it mediated, and by whom, and who gets to achieve it? In our times, these

[5]John Swinton, "From Inclusion to Belonging: A Practical Theology of Community, Disability and Humanness," *Journal of Religion, Disability & Health* 16, no. 2 (2012): 172–90; Willie James Jennings, *After Whiteness: An Education in Belonging* (Grand Rapids, MI: Eerdmans, 2020); Keri Day, *Azusa Reimagined: A Radical Vision of Religious and Democratic Belonging* (Redwood City, CA: Stanford University Press, 2022).

almost uncannily religious questions haunt all kinds of pursuits of belonging both within and beyond the church.

Previous generations might have articulated their sense of the unredeemed state of the world primarily as alienation, or guilt, or oppression. They might have arrived at such characterizations by way of transcendental introspection, existential analysis, or material critique. They have sought epistemic, dogmatic, cosmological, ethical, or aesthetical solutions. Our age, it seems to me, experiences the unredeemed state of the world to a significant extent mediated through feelings of *unbelonging*.

So as other sites of belonging break down or corrode, religion (whether in institutionalized or much more diffuse forms) becomes one site of hope for community and kinship, a sense of belonging in a world of unbelonging. Other visions of belonging are constructed outside of religious institutions and outside of theological reflection, and they are often quite secular but also become quickly imbued with an almost religious aura, or marked by a certain resurging interest in religion (see in the present volume, the contribution by Robert Orsi). In this sense, "belonging" has long become a theologically highly evocative category. It is also constantly in constant danger of what Linn Tonstad calls "projective correctionism"—a mechanism that often obtains when real or perceived social ills become the site where theology is generated.[6] Notions of God effectively become articulated as a remedy and correction to such malaise, constructed to solve our burning issues, and the insight that "only God can save" becomes indistinguishable from ideology.

Against the Romances of Be/longing: A Theological Analysis

Be/longing as a Site of Theological Investigation

This, then is, where the theologian comes in, if as part of the task and labor of theology we assume the labor of self-critical reflection on the structures, content, and effects of Christian

[6]Linn Marie Tonstad, *God and Difference: The Trinity, Sexuality, and the Transformation of Finitude* (New York: Taylor & Francis, 2015).

faith claims. If there is something religious about contemporary longings for belonging that are articulated both within religious communities and far outside them, then the theologian might not only have a professional responsibility to critique what is going on, but they might also have conceptual resources to offer for its theorization.

For starters, like the affect theorist, the theologian might be in a unique place not to judge these feelings, not to pathologize them, not to try, at least not immediately, to *resolve* them by whatever political or ecclesial programming. The theologian can recognize in our collective longings, whatever directly occasions them, utterly accurate and legitimate expressions of the unredeemed state of the world as sketched above.

Theologically speaking, the negativity of these feelings has twofold epistemic value: It both points us to "what actually is the case" in the state of the world as we find it, and, almost in spite of itself, carries within itself a profound "optimism." I am using the term "optimism" in a very particular sense here, one that I inherit from Lauren Berlant. In Berlant's theory, optimism is not about the expectation of a positive outcome; it is an affective structure of attachment that manifests itself in continuing to revisit the site of promise. The theologian might say it is a faithfulness to the possibility of a different world which is present in, with, and under the negativity of the negative affect of unbelonging. In its very negativity, the longing for belonging fiercely insists that another world is possible, is *necessary*, is just around the corner, in fact, might even be the *ultimate* reality, even as it remains painfully absent, unrealized, deferred to an eschatological horizon.

Second, the theologian might recognize in the *form* of this attachment a particular eschatological grammar, that of already-and-not-yet. In it is the tension between the experience of real moments of grace and revelation in the here and now, and the promise of their fuller realization as in the here and now they always remain anticipatory, partial, and elusive.

Third, the theologian, who has for centuries critically parsed through Christian promises of salvation, has a rich toolbox for navigating the peculiar impasse of the already-and-not-yet structure of our collective longings for belonging. In particular, the doctrinal history of eschatology alerts us that there are two possibilities of one-sidedly collapsing a certain intrinsic tension, two romanticizations that we recognize as theologically problematic, but for our intents and purposes in our present moment, they also have problematic political and social effects.

"Heaven on Earth"?

On the one hand, there is the corrective projectionism to the perceived lack that results in an overdetermination of our earthly dwellings and relationships. I want to call this romanticization of belonging the "heaven on earth" version: a socially, politically, or aesthetically realized eschatology. We are all familiar with this particular romance of belonging because our culture bombards us with visions of advertisements that show red-cheeked kids playing in sunny meadows, perfect meals prepared by a loving homemaker, and friends cozying up around an open fireplace. Belonging is this wholesome vision of safety and comfort, and a blissful detemporalization that seems to demand slow motion. As with any romantic vision, you might feel a warm fuzzy feeling—or you might feel your teeth put on edge.

Tolstoy famously opens *Anna Karenina* by saying, "*All happy families* are alike; each unhappy family is unhappy in its own way."[7] That might be true, but it is of course true because the happy family does not exist; it is an ideality. The cherished vision of belonging as heaven on earth *seems* like a vision of the good life, but it is never *there*. Instead, all families are different, and all families are unhappy in their own way.

Home, everyone has one—until we don't. But then again, most of us never did. Nomads, for starters. Migrants, exiles, displaced populations. Unhoused people in cityscapes. And then there are the many more who can't afford their own, or who have not fully paid off the mortgage. And then there are those who live in houses that never feel like home, that rather feel like prisons and entrapments and closets. Home—this supposed universality—is something that even at its best only a small elite enjoys only ever temporarily, and at a price that both those who find themselves on its inside and those who find themselves on the outside of this vision have to pay. A home is a privilege: a material, social,

[7]Leo Tolstoy, *Anna Karenina* (New Haven, CT: Yale University Press, 2014), xxiv.

and emotional one. For most of us, heaven on earth has never materialized, and for everyone, it comes with the accompanying vision of hell.

For all of us, this home is always already under threat. Even if there are moments of belonging and material designs, social arrangements, and patterns of consumption that we associate with it, this home is always already under threat because we have never truly *possessed* it. It is already filled with nostalgia and slipping from our grasp in the brief moments that we come close to experiencing it. We always already sense with dread that the warm fuzzy feeling will not last, that the lovingly prepared dinner will not be appreciated by the in-laws, that we can't buy the kids' affections or secure their sheltered innocence as they grow up and turn into *ungrateful brats*; we fear that the loving wife will leave us for a *feminist lesbian witch*, that immigrants will take our jobs, that the neighborhood will be gentrified to the point that it will look at *us* as less than respectable contenders for these holy grounds.

You might recognize these affective invocations of a sense of threat that both is diffuse and also tends to become projected onto specific bodies and ways of life all too predictably. They generate powerful emotive reactions, public feelings of anxiety, envy, and resentment, and political movements. We see them at work in the doubling down on the traditional family and its supposed values, in Christian nationalism, in white supremacy, in homophobia, xenophobia, and patriarchy at large as well as in institutional cultures of orthodoxy and purity. All of them overdetermine home into something that is always under threat and therefore must be protected. "A gentleman's home is his castle" and *woe to those* who dare invade it—or change its interior decorations. Home thus becomes a prized bourgeois possession, a shelter of the privileged, that produces neighborhood watches and security cameras, stand your ground laws and police states, white picket fences and border walls.

Of course, some might want to disarm such a possessive account of home and counter, "Home is where the heart is": It is not just a material space that can easily be fortified into a fortress of a territory that needs to be defended. Or, we might continue piously, "Home is not a place; it's a people." But other people, as not only Sartre knew, can also be hell. Those who grow up in houses that never felt like home, due to estrangement, emotional disconnect, abuse, violence, rejection, know this very well. Recalibrating belonging by shifting from place to community gives no respite from violent consequences. As it needs to *contain* these people, pinpointing belonging in terms of people rather than place will simply turn these *people* rather than the place into possessions of this vision, pressed into normative molds (the loving housewife, the red-cheeked child, the providing father). And *woe to those* who feel confined by this vision, who are not always loving, self-sacrificial, community-oriented, useful, industrious, and productive of "good feelings" because, say, they are old, queer, disabled, moody, or in some other way "anti-social." Some always belong more than others, some will be seen as disrupting the romance, and thus become subject to either fixing or excision from the "wholesome" vision. This vision of belonging is also the vision of a unity that comes at a high price, its nostalgic invocation is a deeply reactionary and potentially oppressive aspiration, one that engenders violence in its defense. As Chantal Mouffe asserts, "An organic unity can never be attained, and there is a heavy price to be paid for such an impossible vision."[8]

In our families, in our institutions, in our communities, we should distrust the romance of belonging as "heaven on earth." What is it trying to compensate for? What is it trying to cover up? Who must be cleaned up for the picture, what must be swept under the rug, who must be buried in the basement, and who must be kept away by all means from the premises to allow for this perfect moment to gain eternity, and for grace to be turned into a possession that must be defended?

"No Abiding City"?

The second romance of belonging ensues when one gives up trying to bring heaven onto earth, possibly in light of these problematic effects, and instead projects home onto a transcendent horizon. This, too, is a deeply theological orientation. If "home is where the heart is," St. Augustine can voice our second romantic variation on belonging as "restless is our heart, until it finds rest

---

[8]Chantal Mouffe, ed., *Dimensions of Radical Democracy: Pluralism, Citizenship, Community* (New York: Verso, 1992), 5.

in you."[9] Projecting home into a future—and ultimately into a beyond which we also never reach—will keep your gaze fixed to the horizon rather than to a nostalgic vision of an imaginary past. Its theological orientation is that of Hebrews 14: "We have here no lasting city, but we are looking for the city that is to come." Other biblical accounts celebrate our status as merely guests in this world and as pilgrims toward heaven. We might experience glimpses of belonging, this second theological romance of the home whispers, but our eternal home lies beyond, lies with God.

Such an orientation can be very effective in affectively immunizing us against the necessary disappointments of any actually existent communities, allowing us to survive them and keep us going. We do not only find it in otherworldly visions alone. We also find it in cultural forms of detachment and, ironically, in the many invocations and celebrations of "hopelessness" that have become fashionable once more, today. Whether oriented toward a material afterlife, articulated in more elusive eschatological orientations, or even when turning into complete nihilism, this is the romanticization in belonging that always *transcends* any actualizations.

Yes, these forms can prevent us from avoiding "cruel optimism." Yes, they can keep us from forming the sort of strong attachments that so easily pivot into violences when the vision slips from grasp. They might not always be conducive to quietism, but sometimes even to radical politics, as they can engender some solidarity with other dwellers in our shared predicament. But they also come at a cost, the cost of relativizing our existence here and now because of "what it is not," and potentially sacrificing it for either a future or transcendent vision.

Throughout history and into the present day, people have critiqued such a transcendent theological education as making Christians indifferent toward suffering in the here and now or even valorizing it into a price to pay for an eternal reward. Karl Marx and Ludwig Feuerbach—or in our days, Martha Nussbaum and Martin Hägglund—provide versions of such a critique, claiming that only by giving up the romantic idea of a "life to come" will we really be able to commit to the struggles of "this life" and truly seek the flourishing of earthly creatures, both ourselves

---

[9]Augustine, *Confessions* (New York: Penguin, 1961), 1.

and those around us.[10] This second romance of the home thus is also a utopian imagination, an eschatological aspiration, and one which—thus the theological suspicion—tends to engender a certain relativization of and disregard for this life in its pursuit, a disregard that might have just as much blood on its hands as the first one.

As a theologian, I would argue that *both* of these romances, whether in explicit doctrinal garb or in the many romanticizations of belonging we see in contemporary culture, are one-sided and should be critiqued as theologically problematic. The idea of the kingdom of God on earth as its immanent realization and the idea of a great-beyond are both central to Christian eschatology. However, the better versions of the former will insist that it is God who does the realizing and not us, and the better versions of the latter will remind us that the new creation is the fulfillment of this creation, not its leaving behind. Both visions become problematic when they fail to honor what is most crucial in Christian eschatology, namely the internal tension between the "already" and the "not yet." A robust fleshing out of an alternative eschatological vision as well as what it means for our affective attachments and investments in the here and now might take more time. Let me, however, provide three theological leads at least: the transfiguration, the Gentile church, and a "misfit" epistemology that resonates with the category of judgment in Christian eschatology.

Slippery Mountains, Monstrous Bodies, and Misfitting Judgments: Toward a Political Eschatology of Un/Belonging

First, as those who work toward community and belonging in academia and church, we might find our patron saint and our warning sign in the apostle Peter. At the scene of Transfiguration,

[10]Karl Marx, *Critique of Hegel's "Philosophy of Right,"* ed. Joseph O'Malley, trans. Annette Jolin (Cambridge: Cambridge University Press, 1977); Ludwig Feuerbach, *The Essence of Christianity* (New York: Ungar, 1957); Martha C. Nussbaum, *Upheavals of Thought: The Intelligence of Emotions* (Cambridge: Cambridge University Press, 2003); Martin Hägglund, *This Life: Secular Faith and Spiritual Freedom* (New York: Anchor Books, 2020).

the momentary but nonetheless dazzling glimpses of truth, glory, and fullness experienced lead him to exclaim, "It is good to be here, let us set up our tents here" (Matt. 17:4).

The revelation is real, but mountains are slippery terrain. Sometimes it is just one step between sure footing and the abyss. Sometimes, it is just a few steps between "I belong here" and "this belongs to me," between "this is sacred ground" and "stand your ground laws." Maybe, as on that mountain slope, the desire to build abodes, to achieve belonging, and to claim and secure spaces of holiness and purity, is to some extent a temptation, a misdirected desire that overlooks where the journey of this God on this road is headed: "Get thee behind me, Satan!" is what Jesus tells Peter when he tries to stay the journey to Jerusalem—trying to safeguard the wholeness and holiness of the experience, trying to avoid its compromise and rupture at the cross (Matt. 16:23). Maybe the pursuit of achieving and safeguarding belonging is to some extent a desire of mastery over self and world, and to some extent a territorial and colonial desire that attempts to attain ownership and proprietary rights over God, as well as a covering up of the repressive costs of any such movements—all of which Christian institutions have done so many times.

In surrender to the God who learned to dwell with us, but who is also always on the move beyond us, and whose incarnation did not retain docetic purity or avoid pain and compromise, could we learn to inhabit spaces and build community with one another without establishing ownership and without building bigger and higher walls against those who are different, who remind us that we, too, never quite achieve our belonging, and can never ultimately secure it?

Second, an important spiritual discipline for the church might be to learn to remember that we are Gentiles. In all our attempts to build community and to achieve belonging, we are actually not in the position of the threatened insider who needs to hold on to their space. As we strive to belong, we must be mindful that this space was never ours to begin with. As Christians, we have to be returned to the insight that we are strangers and latecomers, that God loved others before God loved us, and that God will never belong to us, let alone exclusively. Yes, we are called here, we get to dwell and participate in this shared space, but we do not own the place, the land, the community, or the church, let alone God.

Even the post-Easter Body of Christ is not an organic unity in which everyone can find their place. It is a monstruous assemblage of limbs, and that, historically, is the possibility of *our own* inclusion in it in the first place: Christians, as Gentiles, have only been posthumously ingrafted into it, breaking open its historic unity and *disfiguring* it permanently into a state that can never be quite closed again. *We* are the impurity in the Body of Christ. What would it mean to re-conceive Christian self-understanding, Christian religious practice, Christian articulations of the truth of our faith, and Christian institutions if we took that memory seriously?

And third, before we too quickly jump to reform our communities and institutions of belonging—before we attempt to aim toward purer or more inclusive, more transcendent or more immanent visions thereof, or else throw up our hands in despair over this apparent impossibility to make a positive out of two negatives—it would be worth lingering with the tension that marks the public feeling of unbelonging in its twofold negativity: a feeling that something is missing and a negative affective reaction to that feeling.

Two negatives don't necessarily make for a positive, but they do make for a powerful heuristic—they direct our attention to specific sites, shapes, and experiences of unbelonging: "Those who are not quite at home," discerns queer feminist theorist Sara Ahmed, "have much to teach us about the way things are built."[11]

The critical epistemological value of the "not-quite-at-home" has particularly been lifted up by crip and queer theorists in describing the epistemological value of "misfitting." Misfitting, a notion coined by disability scholar Rosemarie Garland-Thomson, is an incongruence between persons and environments that shifts from perceiving the lack in the person and their characteristics to a failure of the environment. It is not the body that is unfit or a misfit, rather, "a misfit occurs when the environment does not sustain the shape and function of the body that enters it."[12] The category "reflects the shift in feminist theory from an emphasis on the discursive toward the material," but it does not assign materiality one-sidedly to the body but rather attends to the story

[11] Ahmed, *What's the Use? On the Uses of Use*, 19.

[12] Rosemarie Garland-Thomson, "Misfits: A Feminist Materialist Disability Concept," *Hypatia* 26, no. 3 (2011): 594.

that the material environment tells, too. And it insists on the crip agenda that "social and political access should be achieved by changing the shape of the world rather than changing the shape of our bodies."[13] Rather than molding bodies and souls by normativity, we might diversify our understandings of what comes into view as belonging.

What has been said about disability is also true about unbelonging: that it is precisely what cannot be unified, describes nothing shared, has no family resemblance, "no one form of embodiment or orientation of being in the world."[14] The victims of sexual abuse, economic exploitation, enslavement, and forced dislocation; the migrant, the queer, the trans, the old, and the crip have nothing essential in common. They experience unbelonging in different ways as they "misfit" the different romances on offer and whose bodies resist our "normal" as well as our "new normal."

For those of us who have experienced the failure of their families of origins, church communities, and political systems to support, welcome, and embrace us, "belonging may not be the sign of Christian community that we imagine it to be," argues disability theologian Erin Raffety. Belonging, we are acutely aware, "demands much more" of some bodies than of others, "to fit and conform to a norm and standard" even as we might identify those standards with what we hold to be good or holy—the family, the nation, the church.[15] Experiences of unbelonging and the violence they engender might also reveal, among other things, the ongoing "redemptive fix/ation[s]" of our society and our religious communities.[16] As disability theorists have taught us, as affect theorists continue to emphasize, pain is not an "argument against existence" or a form of materialized lack or guilt that must be isolated and excised; instead, pain is what "puts us on notice" in our inter-corporeal reality of interdependence and shared but unequally distributed vulnerability.

[13]Garland-Thomson, "Misfits," 597.

[14]Petra Kuppers, "Toward a Rhizomatic Model of Disability: Poetry, Performance, and Touch," *Journal of Literary & Cultural Disability Studies* 3 (December 1, 2009): 221–40.

[15]Erin Raffety, *From Inclusion to Justice: Disability, Ministry, and Congregational Leadership* (Waco, TX: Baylor University Press, 2022), 118.

[16]Sharon V. Betcher, "Crip/Tography: Disability Theology in the Ruins of God," *JCRT* 15, no. 2 (2016): 102.

The unbelonging, who have been with us all along despite the most brutal attempts to include or excise them, know what for those living in privileged fragility is unthinkable: that there is a wide landscape of possibility in that space between the two horizons of collapse. The unbelonging, then, might have much to teach us about the ambiguities of embodiment and homemaking, but also about keeping faith with "damaged life" and about inhabiting a world in which the "wholeness" that marks any of our romances with the home is at best a temporary and fleeting experience.

What if our pursuit of belonging was less guided by our own warm and fuzzy feelings, and also not simply by our feelings of being threatened? What if instead it were guided more by the experience of those being disafforded access to such visions? What can their "bad feelings" tell us about the reality we inhabit, their architectural, social, cultural, political, religious, and yes, theological features and affordances, as well as the shape of the bodies and souls they accommodate or fail to accommodate?

Rather than following our intuition away from unbelonging and toward belonging, we might do well to attend to the more ambiguous, more complicated, but also more promising feelings of "not-quite." The orientation to the "not-quite-at-home" stays in the here and now without imbuing the everyday with a halo, and it lingers on unbelonging but without projecting it into the future or beyond. Instead, it radically reorients us to the material (architectural, social, cultural, political) conditions of feeling unhoused and challenges them. Theologically, such an orientation invokes a different eschatological imaginary, neither heaven on earth nor happiness in the beyond; instead, it exercises the crucial eschatological function of "judgment." It cultivates prophetic imagination in attending to what happens at the margin; the negotiation that takes place at the boundary, sets into relief what happens there, what is not right, what surely *must* be otherwise in a different world.

For those who have been harmed, judgment has long been a category of promise and comfort rather than fear and dread. Rather than becoming utopian or dystopic, an eschatological focus on judgment will seek to articulate what it might mean to be "slightly more at home" in concrete material and social negotiations for concrete constituencies. Belonging remains an aspirational category, but it is neither one of utopian longing nor dystopian terror. Rather, it becomes a pragmatic quest for "eu-topias," i.e., neither ideal no-where-places nor places of terror but places of realistic, material, pragmatic negotiation about the conditions of possibility of "slightly more accommodating" dwelling in the here and now, which recognize the ever only partial nature of belonging. These limited eu-topias will always remain porous and fragmentary. They *will* materialize, but they will also ever remain subject to critique as we continue to ask how to make this space one that allows for dwelling as much as for escape, for shelter as much as for visitability.

Seek and Distrust

Riffing on A. N. Whitehead, we might conclude, "Seek belonging and distrust it." We should distrust our longing for belonging, precisely because it speaks to human, all-too-human human needs and affective dispositions. And we should distrust the wholesome vision of religion as a space of belonging, insofar as it tends to fall into one or the other romance of community.

How do we make space for the unbelonging? How do we make physical, material, social, and political space, and *epistemological* space—for those who do not belong, who will never belong, for whatever reason: because they don't fit in, because we'd rather not have them that close, because their bodies, needs, and souls are not supported by our designs, because they do not belong to us and refuse our grasp or evade it, or because—like God—they will never be ultimately accommodated by any space, institution, or community we create and design?

We have learned to ask the question "*cui bono?*" to the defenders of orthodoxy. We have learned to ask the defenders of Christian practice, "Who was left out"? To those investing in projects of what I have called *orthosocy*, then, we must learn to ask, "Who misfits" our visions of belonging, and what might such misfitting tell us about the way things are built?

Emmanuel Falque and the Sacramental Mediation of Animality

Trevor Williams

The French philosopher Emmanuel Falque presents a phenomenology of the Eucharist and posits the concept of "spread body" (*le corps épandu*) as neither reducible to objective body (*Körper*) nor the subjective flesh (*Leib*) of lived experience. For Falque, human beings are constituted by an animality that, Christina M. Gschwandtner suggests, includes "our fully embodied experience of the chemical and organic substructures of the body, the psychological 'chaos' of passions, impulses, and emotions, and our biological physicality, especially in its breakdown of illness, aging, and death."[1] Falque's arguments in *The Wedding Feast of the Lamb* (2011) build on this vision of human animality and its interpenetration of lived and objective body.[2] Humanity's mode of access to the world has long been a question in phenomenology and continental thought, with Falque being only one member among his generation to consider it. He grounds this account of access in a conception of embodiment that is more visceral than language, stressing that animality is the more fundamental point of mediation. Falque's book chapter for *Carnal Hermeneutics* puts it this way, saying that animality "provides a 'mode of access' to

[1]Christina M. Gschwandtner, "Mystery Manifested: Toward a Phenomenology of the Eucharist in Its Liturgical Context," *Religions* 10, no. 5 (2019): 315.

[2]Emmanuel Falque, *The Wedding Feast of the Lamb*, trans. George Hughes (New York: Fordham University Press, 2016).

our corporeality."[3] This "mode" of access is as active for human beings as it is for God. Indeed, Falque attests to the sacramental mediation of our animality because, in the incarnation, the Son assumes everything human.[4] The interpenetration of *Leib* and *Körper* in the "spread body" similarly clarifies the salvific stakes of mediation for the sacraments.

Falque's concept of "spread body" deliberately invokes the image of Christ's crucified body. The arms spread out on the cross signify a body that retains its dignity even as its lived-ness is in flux, which is a claim that complicates any hard boundaries between subject-object relationships.[5] Falque's argument offers theologians a portrait of animality that is applicable to the human stricken with illness, the victim traumatized by violence, or the encounter with "the other" more generally. He has written about the ethical application of his thought to limit situations and challenges of palliative care, but much more can be said about sacramental experience.[6] This essay argues that the incarnate Son *chooses* the mediation of animality as God's mode of access to human corporeality, bringing our finitude (including the darkest depths of suffering and the anxiety of death) into the life of the Trinity. By consuming the Eucharist, Christians participate in this mystery as Christ meets us in the bread broken for the world. Falque makes his anthropological commitments vital to sacramental mediation because both God and humanity find their access to corporeality through the structures shared by the animal world. His philosophy can augment current discussions in Christian anthropology and the relationship between liturgy and ethics in sacramental-liturgical theology. His writings attest

[3]Emmanuel Falque, "This Is My Body: Contribution to a Philosophy of the Eucharist," in *Carnal Hermeneutics*, ed. Richard Kearney and Brian Treanor (New York: Fordham University Press, 2015), 283.

[4]Falque follows the Patristic principle that whatever is not assumed is not saved.

[5]Falque also applies the concept of spread body to the nuptial mystery, which is a major part of his argument in *The Wedding Feast of the Lamb*. This potentially controversial aspect of Falque's thought cannot be fully addressed in this essay because of the spatial limitations.

[6]Cf. Emmanuel Falque, "Toward an Ethics of the Spread Body," in *Somatic Desire: Recovering Corporeality in Contemporary Thought*, ed. Sarah Horton, Stephen Mendelsohn, Christine Rojcewicz, and Richard Kearney (Lanham, MD: Lexington Books, 2019).

to a form of mediation that outstrips private thought worlds and scandalously grasps the visceral structures of finitude. This essay begins by examining the "access" question in phenomenology and then transitions to Falque's arguments about animality.

The Corporeal Access to the World

Humanity's "access to the world" is a prevalent topic in French and German phenomenology. Edmund Husserl (1859–1938) and Martin Heidegger (1889–1976), for example, contributed to the foundations of this inquiry: Husserl's *Urdoxa* points to what is "originary" about human experience, while Heidegger stressed our "thrownness" and formation in being-toward-death. In his book *Event and Time* (1999), Claude Romano comments on the role of mediation in phenomenology, writing that "there is no immediacy of a *givenness* from which one might expect all the light to come: every access to phenomena is irremediably mediated. We should renounce the myth of a 'pure given,' bound up with that myth (Cartesian and Husserlian) of a total absence of presuppositions of which description could avail itself."[7] The philosophy of Maurice Merleau-Ponty (1908–1961) provides another stream of thought around the question of access. Falque claims Merleau-Ponty as a decisive influence in his thought, which is evident in his approach to mediation, its peculiar focus on animality, and his use of terms such as "perceptive" or "animal" faith. His book *Crossing the Rubicon* (2013) posits that before the theological belief in God comes our perceptive (or perceptual) belief in the world. His emphasis arises from his background in French phenomenology and ongoing commitment to the "book of nature" in Franciscan thought.[8]

"Perceptive faith" designates the mediation of perception because it foregrounds the organic structures of our animality and the *senses* we share with the animal world. Falque's "Catholic

---

[7]Claude Romano, *Event and Time*, trans. Stephen E. Lewis (New York: Fordham University Press, 2014), 2.

[8]Emmanuel Falque, *Crossing the Rubicon: The Borderlands of Philosophy and Theology*, trans. Reuben Shank (New York: Fordham University Press, 2016). See also *Le libre de l'expérience: D'Anselme de Cantorbéry à Bernard de Clairvaux* (Paris: Les Éditions du Cerf, 2017).

hermeneutic" of body and voice relies on this same logic when he specifies that mediation has its foundation in our corporeality, not merely in language or the written text. This claim is firmly rooted in Falque's philosophy, but it is also non-competitively inspired by the structure of the Mass: liturgy of the Word and liturgy of the Eucharist. The Word proclaimed in Scripture points to the body that is offered. Falque's hermeneutic contends that speech is not received by way of a mind-to-mind transferal but a body-to-body act, for a voice always signifies a body.[9] Differently put, when a person speaks, she uses her vocal cords, mouth, and tongue to generate a sound that is interpreted by the organs of auditory perception in the other. Falque refuses to exclude this corporeal mediation, even applying it to the priestly words of consecration "this is my body" (*hoc est enim corpus meum*). For him, these words directly apply to the sensory organs that Christ assumes in the incarnation.[10] Merleau-Ponty addresses perceptual faith in *The Visible and the Invisible* (1964), writing that it is by "returning to the perceptual faith to rectify the Cartesian analysis that we will put an end to the crisis situation in which our knowledge finds itself when it thinks it is founded upon a philosophy that its own advances undermine."[11] Animal faith places our access to the world in our bodies.

Similar claims are made in Merleau-Ponty's other works, with *The Phenomenology of Perception* (1945) specifying that "sensation is, literally, a communion" and *Signs* (1960) adding a further phenomenological point that "the intentionality that ties together the stages of my exploration, the aspects of the thing, and the two series to each other is . . . the transition that as carnal subject I effect from one phase of movement to another, a transition which as a matter of principle is always possible for me because I am that animal of perception and movements called a body."[12] The body is what makes the world possible for us, and provides the basis for every encounter in the horizonal structure of experience.

[9]Falque, *Crossing the Rubicon*, 55–75.

[10]Falque, *The Wedding Feast of the Lamb*, xiii, 15.

[11]Maurice Merleau-Ponty, *The Visible and the Invisible*, trans. Alphonso Lingis (Evanston, IL: Northwestern University Press, 1968), 26.

[12]Maurice Merleau-Ponty, *The Phenomenology of Perception*, trans. Donald A. Landes (London: Routledge, 2012), 256; and *Signs*, trans. Richard C. McCleary (Evanston, IL: Northwestern University Press, 1964), 167.

Merleau-Ponty's claims here are also used to complicate subject-object distinctions, which is a move that Falque complements with his turn to animality. Merleau-Ponty's book *Signs* includes the "I touch myself touching" reflection that stretches the "perceiving thing" as "subject-object."[13] He comments that "in learning that my body is a 'perceiving thing,' that it is able to be stimulated (*reizbar*)—it, and not just my 'consciousness'—I prepared myself for understanding that there are other *animalia* and possibly other men."[14] This analogy ensures that the recognition of consciousness is not a mere cognitive act but one based in our animal bodies. He adds that,

> The reason why I have evidence of the other man's being-there when I shake his hand is that his hand is substituted for my left hand, and my body annexes the body of another person in that "sort of reflection" it is paradoxically the seat of. My two hands "coexist" or are "compresent" because they are one single body's hands. The other person appears through an extension of that compresence; he and I are like organs of one single intercorporeality.[15]

The intercorporeality established in Merleau-Ponty's analogy of hands is an extension of subjectivity to what one might initially perceive to be a mere object.

Merleau-Ponty uses the common object of a mannequin to clarify the difference here. He writes that

> I can construct . . . a presence to self modeled on my own; but it is still my self that I put in it, and it is then that there really is an "introjection." On the other hand, I know unquestionably that that man over there *sees*, that my sensible world is also his, because *I am present at his seeing*, it *is visible* in his eyes' grasp of the scene.[16]

Emmanuel Alloa argues that, for Merleau-Ponty, "All appearance . . . appears *through* something else, by virtue of which it

[13]Merleau-Ponty, *Signs*, 166.
[14]Merleau-Ponty, *Signs*, 168.
[15]Merleau-Ponty, *Signs*, 168.
[16]Merleau-Ponty, *Signs*, 169.

receives its meaning."[17] In *The Phenomenology of Perception*, Merleau-Ponty contends that each of us is a "sensing being" and that

> in this exchange between the subject of sensation and the sensible, it cannot be said that one acts while the other suffers the action, nor that one gives sense to the other. . . . The sensible gives back to me what I had lent to it, but I received it from the sensible in the first place.[18]

One of Merleau-Ponty's most important observations concerns the degree to which human consciousness is embroiled in the world, implicated in it, and given access to it *through* the sensible. Alloa concludes that "both animals and humans are at once *situated in* a milieu and *open to* it, though human beings potentiate that openness by creating their own worlds."[19] This fixation on the creation of a world portends Falque's "spread body" as a way of thinking about the sensible experience of animality.

For Falque, animal or perceptive faith is part of a "common" belief that is shared by all regardless of confessional perspective. He advances this point in *Crossing the Rubicon*, stating that "confessing belief in God draws first and always upon an 'ordinary' belief in others or in the world. Forgetting this, we would run the risk of failing to see the human per se in whom we take a stand before all else."[20] He adds—perhaps controversially for Augustinian thinkers—that "philosophical belief in the world precedes the theological belief in God and supports it through and through."[21] No matter what, then, if one is human, then one is "always believing" and never lacking in all belief.[22] This common faith is not primarily based on our intellectual faculties, the coherence of language, or states of consciousness; rather, it acknowledges how each of these things are preceded by our bodily life. Falque's arguments about eucharistic eros in *The Wedding Feast of the*

[17]Emmanuel Alloa, *Resistance of the Sensible World: An Introduction to Merleau-Ponty*, trans. Jane Marie Todd (New York: Fordham University, 2017), 14.

[18]Merleau-Ponty, *The Phenomenology of Perception*, 258–59.

[19]Alloa, *Resistance of the Sensible World*, 26.

[20]Falque, *Crossing the Rubicon*, 77.

[21]Falque, *Crossing the Rubicon*, 78.

[22]Falque, *Crossing the Rubicon*, 89.

Lamb rely on this anthropological conviction, not to secularize the body as some might suspect, but to provide a tangible, phenomenological connection between the world of Christians and the world of the unbeliever.[23] The eucharistic sacrament, for Falque, participates in the visceral structures of animality and so warrants further discussion.

The Sacramental Mediation of Animality

With the above background in mind, the intended meaning of the sacramental mediation of animality comes to greater clarity. Both Falque and Merleau-Ponty stress that our bodies give us the world. However, Falque's book *The Wedding Feast of the Lamb* marks a decisive turn to animality in his thought, which draws inspiration from the work of Jakob von Uexküll (1864–1944) and Jacques Derrida (1930–2004).[24] He makes the distinct contribution of identifying the manducation of the Eucharist—the physical act of eating—with our animality. *The Wedding Feast of the Lamb* forms this connection in the preface and reflects on the lamb from the Ghent Altarpiece (St. Bavo's Cathedral, Belgium). Falque explains this by citing Scripture, saying that there gathered "a great multitude that no one could count. . . . They cried out in a loud voice 'Salvation belongs to our God who is seated *in the throne*, and *to the Lamb*'" (Revelation 7:9–10).[25] For Falque, that Christ appears in the form of an animal is indicative of the incarnate Son's incorporation of finitude and its integral role in salvation. Falque's affirmation of finitude is not premised in the mere conceptual fact that we are not infinite but recalls the definition of animality posited at the beginning of this essay. As

[23]Falque's approach here raises the post-conciliar distinction between Karl Rahner, SJ, and Joseph Ratzinger, with the former approaching dialogue with what is in common and the latter approaching the world with explicit reference to Christ. Falque shares many similarities with Rahner on this score, but he cannot be reduced to this theological binary as he engages in Christocentric and theocentric modes of discourse.

[24]Jakob von Uexküll, *A Foray into the Worlds of Animals and Humans*, trans. Joseph D. O'Neil (Minneapolis: University of Minnesota Press, 2010); and Jacques Derrida, *The Animal That Therefore I Am*, trans. David Wills (New York: Fordham University Press, 2008).

[25]Quoted from Falque's translation of the Bible.

noted above, Gschwandtner suggested that this includes "our fully embodied experience of the chemical and organic substructures of the body, the psychological 'chaos' of passions, impulses, and emotions, and our biological physicality, especially in its breakdown of illness, aging, and death."[26] The sacramental mediation of animality indicates that God and humanity meet through these organic substructures.

Falque advances his thesis on eucharistic eros with his argument that the Lamb "takes on the shape of an animal, sign of a total assumption of the cosmos, just as Christ takes on the shape of a man substantially and totally united with the divine."[27] Indeed, he adds that "the mystic life becomes curiously zoological—not, of course, in that God becomes (the) animal, but in that God also takes on *our* part of animality, by espousing humanity. The viaticum of the eucharist gives Life to our life solely insofar as it carries, almost maternally, *all* our humanity and is metamorphosed."[28] Falque integrates the presence of the Lamb with this greater framework of sacramental meaning. For him, "the animal gaze is there in place of a monstrance, showing us the body of Christ in the ceremony of adoration of the Blessed Sacrament."[29] Those familiar with the ways that French phenomenology employs the Eucharist will be tempted to connect Falque's emphasis on Adoration with the givenness proposed by Jean-Luc Marion.[30] However, Falque's inclusion of the animal points in a different direction, for animality does not signify the excess of the given or the saturated phenomenon. Instead, finitude and the organic structures with which we experience the world are tied more immediately to the chaos explicated in the abyss or, biblically, the *tohu wa-bohu* from the Book of Genesis.

This identification should not be confused with problematic binaries that associate animality with chaos and humanity with

[26]Gschwandtner, "Mystery Manifested," 315.

[27]Falque, *The Wedding Feast of the Lamb*, xviii.

[28]Falque, *The Wedding Feast of the Lamb*, xix.

[29]Falque, *The Wedding Feast of the Lamb*, xix.

[30]Cf. Christina M. Gschwandtner, "Marion's Spirituality of Adoration and Its Implications for a Phenomenology of Religion," in *Breached Horizons: The Philosophy of Jean-Luc Marion*, ed. Rachel Bath, Antonio Calcagno, Kathryn Lawson, and Steve G. Lofts (London: Rowman & Littlefield, 2018).

order. Rather, in Falque's authorship, chaos can signify humanity, finitude, bodying life, or philosophy. To understand this multivalence, it helps to think back to the above discussion about our "common" humanity and animal faith. Falque conceives of divine revelation (theology) as transforming our humanity (and its finitude), not displacing it. Claude Dagens draws a helpful insight about Falque's work in a comparison with Pope Francis. He says that Falque and Francis begin with the "essential," that is, the revelation of God in Jesus Christ and the belief that salvation is about transformation, the assumption of all that is human. Dagens concludes that "evangelization for Pope Francis, like salvation for E. Falque, includes this radical assumption . . . which passes through the roots of human existence, from birth to death, through our body, our flesh, our passions and our drives."[31] This insight owes to the incarnational basis of Falque's thought. In *The Wedding Feast of the Lamb*, then, Falque asserts that "in coming to be incarnate in our humanity . . . the Word takes on—through us and no doubt for us—that part of animality that is undoubtedly in us."[32] Christ's assumption of human flesh proceeds through paths of perception that *necessarily* include animality; it is only through the organic structures that humans share with animals that the world gives itself to us.

To speak of the sacramental mediation of animality is thus to assert that our embodiment is a divine-human access point. Remember, Falque argues that animality "provides a 'mode of access' to our corporeality," but he goes on to say that "what matters is this chaos of passions and impulses that God came to assume, in a Eucharistic body-to-body [*corps-à-corps*], waiting to convert everything, including the 'realm of which one can no longer say anything' (Heidegger about Nietzsche), the 'mix of sensations,' absolutely resistant to any subsumption (Kant)."[33] The assumption of animality precedes and makes possible the mediation of language, which is not to denigrate speech or deny its capacity to communicate divine revelation. As was mentioned above, Falque

[31]Claude Dagens, "Passages du Rubicon et présence chrétienne au monde," in *Une analytique du passage: Rencontres et confrontations avec Emmanuel Falque*, ed. Claude Brunier-Coulin (Paris: Éditions Franciscaine, 2016), 25. Translation mine.

[32]Falque, *The Wedding Feast of the Lamb*, xx.

[33]Falque, "This Is My Body," 283.

holds to a "Catholic hermeneutic" of body and voice, for there is no speech without the consent of vocal cords and there is no voice without the flow of air from our lungs. In this sense, the very words of salvation are always taking part in the organicity of the body. Perhaps nowhere is this concept more evident than in the priestly words of consecration: "This is my body." In *The Wedding Feast of the Lamb*, Falque asserts that these words take on "exactly a mode of non-signifying of organic embodiedness—something that simply the lived experience of the flesh of the Resurrection could not express or even envisage."[34] Falque wishes to articulate something that lies "beneath" signification, and his turn to animality helps him do that.

His efforts are not in conflict with Merleau-Ponty's views, for in his transition to the residue of the body, Falque cites the toucher-touched notion, adding that "embodiedness is, if not extended [*étendue*], at least spread out [*épandue*]. It cannot be reduced to subjectivity nor declared purely objective. . . . It is that of the organic matter to deal with or operate on, which is not totally objective because it cannot be reduced to a geometric form" (i.e., a Cartesian space).[35] This trajectory is confirmed with the concept of "spread body," which Falque applies to the context of palliative care. Falque does not simply affirm finitude as a positive good without also incorporating the travails of our existence and the breakdown of our bodies. He specifies that

> there is a biological aspect to myself that is not quantifiable (not extended in geometric fashion in the body) but that nonetheless cannot simply be reduced to subjective qualities (how the ego copes with the flesh). The body spread out—on the operating table, certainly, but also dozing on a bed or even crucified on a cross—is more than the simple extension of matter (the objectivity of the body) and more than pure selfhood of the flesh (subjectivity of the flesh).[36]

Falque proposes the spread body as a conceptual description of what lies between subjective and objective flesh and body. The embodiedness of human life retains animality or else it risks

[34]Falque, *The Wedding Feast of the Lamb*, 12.
[35]Falque, *The Wedding Feast of the Lamb*, 12, 13.
[36]Falque, *The Wedding Feast of the Lamb*, 14.

forgetting the biological structures on which we depend for our access to the world. For Falque, this embodiedness marks our "living body—embodied in an organic flesh made up of nerves, muscles, digestion, secretion, respiration, . . . things that can, like so much of *this is my body*, remain foreign to me if I am not fully able to make them my own."[37] God does not forgo these biological structures in the incarnation. Instead, both humanity and animality are assumed by God with the words "this is my body," which is not only said of the eucharistic consecration, for Falque, but of humanity's incorporation into the divine life of the Trinity.

Conclusion

Falque's formulation of "spread body" is a response to his philosophical milieu as much as it is directed toward the substance of salvation. His work, in this light, can best be summarized with one word: Emmanuel ("God is with us"). Falque often asks about how the reality of God is incarnate in our lives and relates this to a Christian type of being in the world. Falque's turn to animality in *The Wedding Feast of the Lamb* builds on his continued efforts to address the true depths of this divine-human solidarity. Indeed, to speak of the sacramental mediation of animality is to stress that it is the mode, the path, where the Holy Trinity comes to meet human beings: God's mode of access to the world is also ours. That our point of access to the world is shared by God in the person of Jesus Christ foists on us a sacramental understanding of the world that is necessarily visceral. We cannot define the divine-human relationship as only active insofar as it takes part in our minds. Rather, as embodied human beings, our activity is recognizable in the body *spread* on the cross and on the operating table. The sacramental mediation of animality retains the "Lamb" in Falque's analysis when it partakes in what is shared by the animal world and recognizes it as such.

[37] Falque, *The Wedding Feast of the Lamb*, 113.

The Uses of Mystical Eros as Power in Feminist Theologies

Issues of Mediation, Consciousness, and Transformation

Amy Maxey

Feminist Theology, Mystical Eros, and Mediation

Many contemporary feminist retrievals of Christian mysticism, from theologians as diverse as Dorothee Soelle, Sarah Coakley, and Catherine Keller, leverage the power of mystical eros to ground liberating mystical-political visions.[1] Such feminist reformulations reverse the gendered hierarchy of Christian Neoplatonism, which associates the masculine with the "higher" elements of the rational and intellectual and the feminine with the "lower" elements of the bodily and affective. Reclaiming these "lower" elements amplifies the voices of women mystics and suggests a transgressive theological idiom that might be marshaled, along with a robust apophaticism, to destabilize masculinist theological paradigms. No longer is mystical eros a vehicle by which the soul

[1]See especially Dorothee Soelle, *The Silent Cry: Mysticism and Resistance*, trans. Barbara Rumscheidt and Martin Rumscheidt (Minneapolis: Fortress Press, 2001); Sarah Coakley, *God, Sexuality, and the Self: An Essay "On the Trinity"* (Cambridge: Cambridge University Press, 2013); Catherine Keller, *The Cloud of the Impossible: Negative Theology and Planetary Entanglement* (New York: Columbia University Press, 2015).

escapes the body beset by changeable passions; rather, it engenders a relational knowing that can energize efforts to transform oppressive social structures.

Our annual conference theme occasions questions regarding the epistemic dynamics involved in this new mediating economy of eros. For implicit in this contemporary feminist paradigm is a peculiar notion of mystical eros, one not simply lifted from history, but one that emerges by creatively reading "eros" against its tradition. In a bid to overcome overly restrictive modes of rationality, this rehabilitated eros implies an affective, intuitive, and unconscious manner of mystical knowing which collapses various dialectics of absence and presence. Yet as I argue in this essay, privileging the unconscious as the site of this erotic gnosis forecloses possibilities for feminist mystical-political endeavors. As an alternative, I propose conceiving of the power of erotic knowing as engendering a transformation of the subject to greater self-consciousness. My argument unfolds through analyses of two paradigms for an eroticized economy of noetic mediation.

I begin by probing an origin of this novel mystical eros, whose echoes can be discerned throughout many feminist rehabilitations of eros, for example, Luce Irigaray's early essay "*La Mystérique*."[2] Through an examination of the constellation of characteristics that Irigaray associates with the jouissance of *mystérique* (her analogue for mystical eros as transposed into a psychoanalytic discourse), I excavate the ambiguous way eros functions in an epistemological economy located at the site of the unconscious. Although Irigaray's formulation of this economy suggests a transgressive power, I contend that these epistemic ambiguities, particularly her privileging of the unconscious, problematize the potential for mystical eros in an Irigarayan mode to serve as a font for mystical-political energies. If the power of the erotic erupts from a jouissance unconsciously extracted or enjoyed through the intuition of the unknown, it is difficult to discern how the power of this mystical eros could be harnessed, except in a deconstructive mode.

As an alternative, I gesture toward the work of womanist Audre Lorde to offer a different epistemic of eros which holds promise

[2]Luce Irigaray, *Speculum of the Other Woman*, trans. Gillian C. Gill (Ithaca, NY: Cornell University Press, 1985), 191–202.

for a revitalized understanding of mystical eros. In "Uses of the Erotic: The Erotic as Power,"[3] Lorde proposes that the erotic awakens the subject to self-consciousness and so to responsibility, both to oneself and to others. This economy of eros mediates knowledge in a manner that involves the self-appropriation of a concretely embodied and conscious subject. Conceiving of eros in this manner grounds a notion of mystical erotic power that is not merely deconstructive but transformative, orienting subjects to new horizons of value which promote human flourishing.

Luce Irigaray's Eros: *Mystérique*, Jouissance, and the Unconscious

Irigaray distinguishes "*mystérique*" as "how one might refer to what, within a still theological onto-logical perspective is called mystic language or discourse."[4] The titular neologism alludes to mysticism, hysteria, mystery, and the "femaleness" that undergirds all three, indicating that Irigaray is not speaking about "mysticism" per se.[5] Instead, the discourse labeled "mysticism" serves as an occasion for exploring questions of women's subjectivity. Irigaray creates a syncretic mystical voice through a mimetic appropriation of language and themes from the Christian mystical tradition, eliding apophasis with postmodern deconstruction to suggest an imaginary and a symbolic for women's subjectivity alternative to the phallogocentric economy, where "woman" is, in the words of Françoise Meltzer, "inscribed in a gridwork of signifiers that are masculine and by which she is . . . a metaphor standing for incomprehensibility, lack, and an eternally synecdochical economy."[6] Although the essay is ostensibly about a mode of discourse, the consequential stakes are epistemological. In Margaret Whitford's evocative phrasing, "Irigaray is investigating the *passional foundations of reason*," which have been

[3]Audre Lorde, *Sister Outsider* (Berkeley, CA: Crossing Press, 2007), 53–59.

[4]Irigaray, *Speculum of the Other Woman*, 191.

[5]See the translator's note on this title in *Speculum of the Other Woman*, 191.

[6]François Meltzer, "Transfeminisms," in *Transfigurations: Theology and the French Feminists*, ed. C. W. Maggie Kim, Susan M. St. Ville, and Susan Simonaitis (Eugene, OR: Wipf and Stock, 1993), 22.

disavowed because they are feminine but which subconsciously continue to inflect presumedly rational discourses.[7] Irigaray rejects the masculinist economy in which objectivity is conceived of in terms of a penetrating gaze from a Cartesian, self-conscious subject whose mindful rationalizations legitimate conceptual knowledge. Instead, she exploits long-standing associations of women with affectivity, corporeality, and the unconscious to develop a "feminine" discourse that reflects the lack of subjectivity foisted upon women. Adapting mystical discourse enables her to reconceive a feminine subject and the epistemic economy, which gives rise to her as a kind of subject who "un/knows" through desire rather than through a dispassionate rationality. Mystical discourse is a remainder of a non-objective knowledge, and working backward from it, so to speak, discloses an unconscious subject whose un/knowing emerges through an economy with a different morphological basis and sensual mediation: one that is somatically feminine, in which a Lacanian jouissance facilitates the subject's passionate intuition of the other through a "touch" that blurs the boundaries of self and not-self.

Throughout *Speculum* Irigaray deconstructs the identification of "woman" as the mirror for the constitution of masculine subjectivity (responding to both Freudian and Lacanian permutations) and the resulting "specularization" of knowledge, where an idealized masculine reason gazes upon the world but does not acknowledge the complex system of femininized symbolic and imaginary refractions at its base.[8] In the words of Amy Hollywood, "The mirror image . . . is both central to masculine discourse and a source of its subversion."[9] Here, Irigaray draws on mystical traditions of conceiving the soul as the mirror of God and exploiting the slippage in the premodern Christian tradition between the metaphysical soul, the mind, and the subject. This

---

[7]Margaret Whitford, *Luce Irigaray: Philosophy in the Feminine* (London: Routledge, 1991), 10.

[8]This term is stylized as "specul(ariz)ation," in the English translation of *Speculum*. For a succinct discussion, see the glossary entry for "Specular" in Elizabeth Grosz, *Sexual Subversions: Three French Feminists* (Sydney: Allen and Unwin, 1989), xxi–xxii.

[9]Amy Hollywood, *Sensible Ecstasy: Mysticism, Sexual Difference, and the Demands of History* (Chicago: University of Chicago Press, 2002), 195.

allows a fluidity among the woman-mirror as ground for the specularizing subject and his mind, the feminine "non-subject," and the feminine mystical mirror-soul whose "nature" is to reflect the infinitely abyssal divine subject. This plurivocity is at play when Irigaray speculates on the base of subjectivity where, perhaps, "even in the depths of the abyss of the 'soul' a mirror await[s] her reflection and her light," which facilitates a union between the soul and the divine where "I [the 'soul'] have become your image in this nothingness that I am, and you gaze upon mine in your absence of being."[10] Through the exchange of reflections, objectivity dissolves into a mutually determining subjectivity: "A living mirror, thus, am I (to) your resemblance as you are mine . . . provided that nothing tarnishes the mirrors that fuse in the purity of their exchange."[11] By imaging the soul and God as an infinite regress of reverberating mirror images reflecting other-as-self and self-as-other, Irigaray's rhetoric performatively shatters the economy of specularized knowledge.

These quasi-spatial distortions prompt Irigaray to embrace the woman-identified unconscious as the atopical site for the mediating economy of *mystérique*. Because it is opaque to the gaze of masculinist consciousness, the unconscious is correlated with the hiddenness and void that Irigaray typically associates with female morphology. As such, the economy of *mystérique* renders a feminine, intuitive mode of un/knowing that does not function according to "the cold reasonableness of optics."[12] Instead, within a darkness in which "the higher mental faculties are in a deep slumber," there is a noetic occurrence of the unconscious which "takes place in such secrecy and deep oblivion that no intelligence, no common sense, can have precise knowledge of it."[13] This economy of un/knowing is ateleological, eschewing the purpose-driven economy of specularized knowledge and revealing a subject that is totally passive (yet another feminine and mystical marker) to the intuitive touch of the other. Elliptically developing the site of *mystérique*, Irigaray disrupts distinctions between inner and outer—a distinction instrumentalized by a masculinist,

---

[10]Irigaray, *Speculum of the Other Woman*, 197.
[11]Irigaray, *Speculum of the Other Woman*, 197.
[12]Irigaray, *Speculum of the Other Woman*, 194.
[13]Irigaray, *Speculum of the Other Woman*, 194.

self-enclosed concept of the subject—thereby rendering a fluid subjectivity realized through the interminable play of self and other which resists conceptual distinction(s).

To highlight the immediacy of this unconscious un-self-knowledge, in which "finding the self imposes a *proximity* that knows no aspect, mode, or figures," Irigaray equates this apophatic gnosis to a momentary poesis of jouissance.[14] Adapting mystical tropes, Irigaray describes the jouissance of *mystérique* as a beam of light, a luminous shadow, a wound, and a divine touch that penetrates the hidden soul/self, violently creating a slit in its boundary and constituting a way "through" the void of the unconscious. This touch bespeaks a noetic immediacy, an intuition, which eludes conceptual mediation. The traditional mystical trope of "dazzling darkness" is now reimagined under Irigaray's pen as an erotically charged, unconsciously experienced intuition, "an illumination so unbounded that un-knowledge thereby becomes desire."[15] As narrated by Irigaray's ventriloquist mystic: "*A lightning flash has lit up the sleeping understanding within me*. Resisting all knowledge that would not find its/my sense in this abyss. Now I know it/myself and by knowing, I love it/myself and by loving, I desire it/myself."[16] The ecstatic, violent depletion of the subject unveils an economy of knowledge whereby "*everything is relentlessly immediate* in this marriage of the unknowable," as the intuition of mystical knowledge and the jouissance which marks its acquisition resists any attempt to encode it discursively.[17]

Only the wounded body, whose boundaries have been rendered permeable by jouissance and its topology of inner and outer confused, seems able to mediate in this economy, albeit in an ambiguous manner. To explore these possibilities, Irigaray turns to the Body of Christ and its symbolic inscriptions. In the matrix of specularization, the wounded body of "that most female of men" is a revelation of passionate abandonment,[18] yet in the matrices of *mystérique* and in imitation of medieval women mystics, Christ's body is the remainder of the "ecstasy . . . in that

---

[14]Irigaray, *Speculum of the Other Woman*, 195.
[15]Irigaray, *Speculum of the Other Woman*, 194–95.
[16]Irigaray, *Speculum of the Other Woman*, 200.
[17]Irigaray, *Speculum of the Other Woman*, 196.
[18]Irigaray, *Speculum of the Other Woman*, 199.

glorious slit" of his pierced side, although "what she discovers in this divine passion, she neither can nor will translate."[19] This passionate knowledge is experienced solely by the parties of the mystically mirroring relationship, as "any other instrument, any hint, even, of theory, pulls me away from myself by pulling open—and sewing up—unnaturally the lips of that slit where I recognize myself, by touching myself there (almost) directly."[20]

Irigaray's displacement of the ocular by the somatic raises questions regarding the mediating function of the morphologically feminine body wounded by jouissance. Amy Hollywood argues that although the "slide from language to the body risks reasserting the logic of specularity precisely where Irigaray is most at pains to subvert it," Irigaray's recourse to touch suggests that "God's inscription occurs not *on* but *in* the mystic's body."[21] Although Hollywood may be correct that the inscription of jouissance occurs at a hidden site morphologically in the void-like concavity of an idealized body, there is nonetheless a transposition between inside and outside effected in the essay, especially in Irigaray's climactic account of Teresa of Avila's transverberation, in which the dart that pierces the mystic's body simultaneously tears out her entrails,[22] which implies that Hollywood's distinction between "in" and "on" the body is ultimately supervened. If a major thrust of Irigaray's proposal in *Speculum* is that morphology (male or female) effects subjectivity in ways that disrupt the specular economy's easy replacement of the "penis" for the "phallus," then Irigaray's explicit recourse to a female morphology stands in contrast to (or reflection of) the phallic economy which (unconvincingly) disavows its grounding morphology.

What matters is not the body, per se, but the possibilities for the body to mediate in an epistemic economy. By supplanting the ocular with the tactile, Irigaray attempts to position the body marked by the wounding of desire as the trace of a knowledge that can only be mediated intuitively through experience. In one sense, the body is a site of specular mediation through the transgressive marks of jouissance, but, in another, it resists the

[19]Irigaray, *Speculum of the Other Woman*, 200.
[20]Irigaray, *Speculum of the Other Woman*, 200.
[21]Hollywood, *Sensible Ecstasy*, 198.
[22]Irigaray, *Speculum of the Other Woman*, 201.

specular economy inasmuch as it conceals the hidden works of jouissance from the gaze. As such, "the body" remains an ever-ambiguous site of (im)mediation within this essay. Moreover, the jouissance of *mystérique*, which drives this economy, functions ambivalently, leaving the subject "Stretched out, once again, (on) the ground. In the dark. Always without consciousness."[23] Its immediacy functions noetically as an intuition for the unconscious which renders the absent proximate, yet it is also the trace for that which is unsignifiable and absolutely absent, which must remain unpresentable to maintain the economy. Irigaray posits an eroticized and unconscious mediating economy of intuitive touch that displaces the power of the rational in a phallogocentric economy. This disruptive power, which has fueled hopes that a rehabilitated mystical eros conceived along lines congenial to Irigaray's bricolage of *mystérique* could be enlisted for feminist mystical-political projects, can now be critically examined.

There is debate regarding whether Irigaray's thought terminates in an ahistorical gender essentialism which undercuts her feminist commitments to women's liberation, but regardless of her position,[24] I am not convinced that Irigaray's politics are associated with whatever power *mystérique* entails.[25] I distinguish my objections from the critique of Morny Joy, who suggests that despite her attempt to gesture toward the constructive capabilities of a feminine imaginary in this essay, Irigaray limits "the potentialities of women to mystic interludes," which offer "no recourse to remedial measures to restructure society."[26] This critique seems more aligned with pejorative associations with mysticism than with Irigaray's strategy in "*La Mystérique*."[27] I maintain that the

---

[23]Irigaray, *Speculum of the Other Woman*, 199.

[24]For a helpful discussion on this charge, see Whitford, *Luce Irigaray*, 9–25.

[25]While the later Irigaray does grant an ethical valence to the "amorous exchange," she does not do so in this essay. See Whitford, *Luce Irigaray*, 165–68.

[26]Morny Joy, *Divine Love: Luce Irigaray, Women, Gender and Religion*, Manchester Studies in Religion, Culture and Gender (Manchester: Manchester University Press, 2006), 18–19.

[27]Incidentally, this characterization is closer to Simone de Beauvoir's assessment of women mystics than Irigaray's. Simone de Beauvoir, *The Second Sex*, trans. Constance Borde and Shelia Malovany-Chevallier (New York: Vintage, 2011), 709–17.

crux of the problem lies with the forfeiture of consciousness in the intuitive epistemic of un/knowing, which ultimately forecloses possibilities for relating eros to the social. It is unclear how an unconscious subject could remember an experience of *mystérique*, a question Irigaray herself equivocates on,[28] and be transformed in such a way to appropriate a vision of just social life. If mystical eros exploits the hidden passivity within the soul/self, it is difficult to envision how it could be leveraged for the soul/self's active exercise of power in the world. Moreover, the troubling recourse to the body wounded by eros offers few possibilities for grounding resistance to oppressive regimes that capitalize on the wounded bodies of "others." I recall again the ambiguities of the erotic mediation of the subject to herself, through which the subject becomes both present to and absent from herself. Although the jouissance of *mystérique* involves alterity, the vacillating elusiveness of the subject-as-self and subject-as-other does not motivate compassion for the other but rather generates a passionate excess interminably spiraling in the wayless void of the unconscious. Feminist characterizations of mystical eros which are indebted, explicitly or implicitly, to the Irigarayan paradigm inherit these problems, which troubles the possibilities for developing an erotic mystical-political vision on this infrastructure.

Audre Lorde's Eros: Self-Consciousness, Power, and Responsibility

I suggest that an alternative to Irigaray's erotic economy is offered by Audre Lorde in "Uses of the Erotic: The Erotic as Power." Although she does not characterize eros in explicitly "mystical" terms, she witnesses to what Andrew Prevot has referred to as the "mysticism of ordinary life," which emerges from "the graced lives of Black women," and attending to this typically neglected testimony expands the imaginative horizons of the mystical to encompass the quotidian and the bodily.[29] Lorde describes eros

[28]"But how to remember all this if the fire was so fierce, the current so strong as to remove all traces? . . . Unless this 'center' has also always been of glass/ice too." Irigaray, *Speculum of the Other Woman*, 196.

[29]Andrew Prevot, *The Mysticism of Ordinary Life: Theology, Philosophy, and Feminism* (Oxford: Oxford University Press, 2023), 265. For a

as "a resource within each of us that lies in a deeply female and spiritual plane, firmly rooted in the power of our unexpressed or unrecognized feeling."[30] As the "the nurturer or nursemaid of all our deepest knowledge,"[31] the erotic mediates "information within our lives."[32] Patriarchal society, which fears the power of the erotic, has a vested interest in teaching women to denigrate this resource by eliding the erotic with the pornographic, which "emphasizes sensation without feeling" and reduces it to "plasticized sensation."[33] But when erotic feeling is embraced and reclaimed, the "deepest and nonrational knowledge" it mediates gives rise to a power that can resist oppressive structures.[34]

Like Irigaray's intuition of *mystérique*, Lorde's emphasis on the affective dimensions of this knowledge intimates a certain resistance to conceptual mediation; however, the significant point of departure is Lorde's insistence on the self-conscious self-appropriation of eros as power, where these terms denote one's self-awareness and self-affirmation as conscious knower, lover, and actor in the world.[35] Eros mediates a knowledge and satisfaction with oneself that sets a horizon for one's becoming that is charged with ethical importance, "for having experienced the fullness of this depth of feeling and recognizing its power, in honor and self-respect we can require no less of ourselves."[36] The power of the erotic is derived from the self-conscious recognition of one's erotic feeling(s), and as Lorde insists, "To refuse to be conscious of what we are feeling at any time, however comfortable that might seem, is to deny a large part of the experience, and to

---

brief discussion of Lorde's essay, see p. 257.

[30]Lorde, *Sister Outsider*, 53.

[31]Lorde, *Sister Outsider*, 56.

[32]Lorde, *Sister Outsider*, 53.

[33]Lorde, *Sister Outsider*, 54.

[34]Lorde, *Sister Outsider*, 53.

[35]By "self-appropriation" I intend the sense in which Bernard Lonergan speaks of the "self-affirmation of the knower," albeit in a less technical epistemological register. Self-appropriation entails the affirmation of the consciousness of one's conscious activities, which collectively function to render one self-conscious and conscious of the world. Bernard Lonergan, *Insight: A Study of Human Understanding*, ed. Frederick E. Crowe and Robert M. Doran, 5th ed., Collected Works of Bernard Lonergan 3 (Toronto: University of Toronto Press, 1992), 343.

[36]Lorde, *Sister Outsider*, 54.

allow ourselves to be reduced to the pornographic, the abused, and the absurd."[37] As such, in no way can this eroticized knowledge be configured as unconscious or ateleological. On the contrary, eros renders the subject more present to herself; it facilitates a heightening of consciousness not to what is absent or other but to what is present and under-noticed. Rather than attempt to harness an unconscious un/knowing, Lorde's configuration of eros invites the human person to claim herself as a transformed subject in freedom and power in a mode reminiscent of what M. Shawn Copeland has termed "critical cognitive praxis."[38]

In an oppressive social world that encourages mediocrity, where it is all too easy to be unintentional in living one's life, Lorde maintains that being responsive to the eros of one's self is to be active in directing one's destiny.[39] Lest this be seen as an entirely active endeavor, Lorde refuses the bifurcation of the spiritual and political, positioning the erotic as that which relates the two: "Within the celebration of the erotic in all our endeavors, my work becomes a conscious decision—a longed-for bed which I enter gratefully and from which I rise up empowered."[40] Thus, the power of eros is principally transformative of values and one's self-appropriated modes of being-in-the-world, or in other words, how self-conscious the subject is, how well she joins her self-empathy with empathy for the world, and "how acutely and fully [she] can feel in the doing."[41] By enabling the subject to consciously claim herself as a subject, eros frees the subject from coercive self-narratives imposed from without. Ultimately, this liberation opens upon new horizons of freedom for conscious self-determination that correlate with greater degrees of responsibility to others. In Lorde's words,

> When we begin to live from within outward, in touch with the power of the erotic within ourselves, and allowing that

[37]Lorde, *Sister Outsider*, 59.

[38]M. Shawn Copeland, "A Thinking Margin: The Womanist Movement as Critical Cognitive Praxis," in *Deeper Shades of Purple: Womanism in Religion and Society*, ed. Stacy Floyd-Thomas (New York: New York University Press, 2006), 226–35.

[39]Lorde, *Sister Outsider*, 54.

[40]Lorde, *Sister Outsider*, 55.

[41]Lorde, *Sister Outsider*, 54.

> power to inform and illuminate our actions upon the world around us, then we begin to be responsible to ourselves in the deepest sense. For . . . we begin to give up, of necessity, being satisfied with suffering and self-negation, and with the numbness which so often seems like their only alternative in our society. Our acts against oppression become integral with self, motivated and empowered from within.[42]

Significantly, this ethical responsibility emerges from the subject's conscious self-appropriation of eros, which enables the subject to realize a self-presence that prompts self-transcendence. In contrast to Irigaray's essay, Lorde's articulation of an erotic economy of self-knowledge connects the subject to broader social worlds and celebrates bodily integrity in resistance of a world where violence to non-white women's bodies remains common. Eros awakens the human person to the power of being a conscious agent who has the responsibility to live in such a way so that this eroticized satisfaction with one's living may be realized over and against a world that seeks to suppress it.[43] This eros, when transposed into a feminist mystical-political key, suggests that the transformations wrought by mystical eros are oriented toward values of the transcendental Good and open the possibility for the human person to live in right relations with herself, the divine, her communities, and all of creation.

A Mystical-Political Conclusion: Eros Transformed, Eros Transforming

In many of the rehabilitations of eros that have been deployed for feminist mystical-political ambitions, the epistemic dimensions of a new mediating economy have remained subterranean. I have argued that feminist theologians endeavoring to leverage mystical eros for mystical-political energies must critically examine these erotic infrastructures and disentangle themselves from an Irigarayan heritage that posits the unconscious as a site of intuitive mystical mediation. As an alternative, I have gestured toward Lorde's affirmation that eros, as a consciously appropri-

[42]Lorde, *Sister Outsider*, 58.
[43]Lorde, *Sister Outsider*, 57.

ated agent of transformation, awakens the subject to her own self-consciousness in freedom and engenders responsibilities to self and others. Resisting the emotional and psychical numbness foisted upon women means refusing the role of a somnambulist: it means being awakened to the erotic power within and consciously integrating it into the habitual textures of living in order to resist oppressive social structures and promote human flourishing in all its material and spiritual dimensions.

Brick by Brick

Using Feminist Citational Practices and Visual Culture to Render the Absent(ed) Present in Theological Discourse and Praxis

Laura Taylor

With his life-size clay sculpture, *Baltimore Pietà*, Black Catholic artist Wayman Scott IV offers a powerful reimagining of Michelangelo's famous *Pietà* enshrined in St. Peter's Basilica. Whereas Michelangelo's Renaissance sculpture depicts a youthful, serene image of Mary sorrowfully cradling her dead son, with her left palm turned upward toward the heavens in prayerful resignation, Scott's twenty-first-century sculpture (re)presents Mary as an African American woman clutching her son's lifeless body, her fist clenched and her brow furrowed in a gesture of righteous and holy indignation. Scott also portrays Jesus as a young contemporary African American man. Wearing locs, jeans, and Nike sneakers, his muscular frame lies unresponsive across his mother's lap.

Scott's *Baltimore Pietà* is both a provocative image and a prophetic call to action. At the same time that it exposes the scourge of fatal shootings of unarmed Black folks, it also makes visible the inherent value and presence of God in Black lives.[1] Additionally, Scott's pietà centers the grief, heartbreak, and trauma of

[1]Christopher Parker, "Black Catholic Artist's 'Baltimore Pietà' Reimagines Michelangelo's Masterpiece through the Lens of Police Brutality," *America Magazine* online, January 28, 2023.

Black mothers who must carry on after their children's lives were brutally and unnecessarily extinguished. As womanist theologian Courtney Hall Lee points out, Black mothers who have lost their children to state-sanctioned violence rarely receive the reverence and adoration given to Mary, the mother of Jesus. Instead, they are regularly met with blame and vilification for the death of their children, who are killed with impunity.[2] To cite the words M. Shawn Copeland uses to describe the Black Lives Matter movement in a 2017 editorial, Scott's sculpture exemplifies "a fierce political and spiritual cry: a cry of presence from a position of invisibility, a cry of justice from within a site of injustice, a cry for freedom in a condition of absurdity."[3]

In this essay, I explore the subversive potential of feminist visual culture, such as Wayman Scott's *Baltimore Pietà,* Kelly Latimore's *The Trinity,* Renee Cox's photograph, *Yo Mama's Last Supper*, and Esther Hernandez's digital print, *La Virgen de Las Calles*, to break open our theological imaginations and render the absent(ed) present in theological discourse and praxis. Drawing on queer, feminist scholar Sara Ahmed's notion of citational practice, alongside the rich theologies and everyday lived experiences of women of color, I seek to demonstrate the ways in which these visual images not only reveal the faithful act of challenging racism and sexism in mediating the divine, but also call us into the spiritual practice of building a more just world so that all may have life, and have it abundantly (John 10:10).

In her blog post, "Making Feminist Points," feminist scholar Sara Ahmed describes academic citation as a "successful reproductive technology" or "screening technique" that reproduces a world (or a discipline) around certain voices and bodies. Here, Ahmed calls attention to the ways in which standard citational practices and traditional disciplinary canons overtly center white men, while screening out all "others" so that their very existence becomes imperceptible.[4]

---

[2]Courtney Hall Lee, *The Black Madonna: A Womanist Look at Mary of Nazareth* (Eugene, OR: Pickwick, 2017), 80.

[3]M. Shawn Copeland, "Memory, #BlackLivesMatter, and Theologians," *Political Theology* 17, no. 1 (March 17, 2016), 2.

[4]Sara Ahmed, "Making Feminist Points," *Feminist Killjoys* (blog), September 11, 2013.

Ahmed's discussion of citational practice calls attention to the ways in which the universal norms found in disciplinary canons not only "universalize" particular bodies but also invite those same bodies to be accommodated, protected, and safe.[5] To question who appears and who does not appear in these spaces, Ahmed argues, is to register as an imposition, a source of discomfort, or even as a threat to those who see themselves as having been there first. Thus, she writes, "It is almost as if we have a duty not to notice who turns up and who doesn't."[6]

Recent works from feminist theologians of color, such as Grace Ji-Sun Kim's *Invisible: Theology and the Experience of Asian American Women*, Angela Parker's *If God Still Breathes, Why Can't I: Black Lives Matter and Biblical Authority*, and Kat Armas's *Abuelita Faith: What Women on the Margins Teach Us about Wisdom, Persistence, and Strength*, clearly demonstrate the ways in which the Western theological imagination has and continues to perpetuate this standard citational reproduction by canonizing white, Euro-American, heteromasculine voices as authoritative and objective universal truth-tellers.[7]

This conflation of whiteness and heteromasculinity with notions of objectivity and universality has foreclosed on race, gender, sexuality, socioeconomic status, and other social identities as legitimate sites of theological inquiry. It also highlights the ways in which racism and sexism have permeated our academic, ecclesial, and social contexts. In her chapter, "To Think Better than We Have Been Trained: Thirty Years Later," womanist biblical scholar Renita Weems notes that "academies have not been able to shake their missional past, which has been to assimilate students around a (white male) universal norm."[8]

---

[5]Sara Ahmed, *Living a Feminist Life* (Durham, NC: Duke University Press, 2017), 111.

[6]Ahmed, "Making Feminist Points."

[7]See Grace Ji-Sun Kim, *Invisible: Theology and the Experience of Asian American Women* (Minneapolis: Fortress Press, 2021); Angela Parker, *If God Still Breathes, Why Can't I: Black Lives Matter and Biblical Authority* (Grand Rapids, MI: Wm. B. Eerdmans, 2021); Kat Armas, *Abuelita Faith: What Women on the Margins Teach Us about Wisdom, Persistence, and Strength* (Grand Rapids, MI: Brazos Press, 2021).

[8]Renita Weems, "To Think Better than We Have Been Trained: Thirty Years Later," in *Bitter the Chastening Rod: Africana Biblical Interpretation after Stony the Road We Trod in the Age of BLM, SayHerName, and Me*

Moreover, the dominant categories of whiteness and heteromasculinity have been used historically and still practically to justify and legitimate deadly structures of violence and oppression, including white supremacy, enslavement, colonialism, genocide, xenophobia, and heterosexism. In her editorial "Memory, #BlackLivesMatter, and Theologians," M. Shawn Copeland demonstrates the ways in which these dominant norms and structures imply that some lives matter and should be defended at any cost, while other lives are understood as precarious, and disposable.

Linking the history of enslavement and segregation in the United States with contemporary systems that disproportionally target persons of color, Copeland reveals the historical amnesia of US Christian theologians who fail to call out the fatal police shootings of unarmed Black people, the prison system, the criminalization of poverty, as well as the unjust treatment of the migrant, the refugee, the mentally ill, the differently abled, and the unhoused. Copeland asks, "Have we Christian theologians 'reasoned away' those Black bodies 'piling up' throughout our nation . . . ? Have we *forgotten* the racialized, shattered, and lynched body that lies at the heart of our religious belief and practice?" Copeland answers her question by stating, "We repress and erase; we edit and delete."[9]

As a white, US-born, able-bodied, cisgender woman, who is a well-educated, housed, tenured theologian, and who lives and works on the ancestral homelands of the Dakhóta and Anishinaabe peoples, I recognize that I benefit from a multitude of unearned, visible, and invisible cultural privileges. In the wake of the murders of unarmed Black folks, such as Ahmaud Aubrey, Breonna Taylor, George Floyd, and Ralph Yarl, along with the increasing violence against women and LGBTQ2S+, white cisgender Christian theologians (such as myself) must heed the call of Copeland and other theologians of color by taking on the difficult process of self-examination and the articulation of our complicity in the devastating, ongoing legacies of white supremacy and heteromasculine privilege in scholarship and praxis.

How might we begin to render the absent and absented present in theological discourse? How can we de-center whiteness and

Too, ed. Mitzi J. Smith, Angela N. Parker, and Ericka S. Dunbar Hill (Lanham, MD: Lexington Books/Fortress Academic, 2022), 272.

[9]Copeland, "Memory, #BlackLivesMatter, and Theologians," 1.

make visible the voices, subjectivities, experiences, bodies, and spiritual histories that have been repressed and erased from the Christian theological tradition? I believe that Ahmed's notion of feminist citational practice, particularly when applied to visual culture, offers us a powerful way forward.

In her book *Living a Feminist Life*, Sara Ahmed adopts a strict feminist citational policy in which she does not cite any white men, which she refers to as both an institution and the method of reproducing the institutional structures.[10] Ahmed notes that feminism does not mean adopting a certain set of ideals or strict norms of conduct. Instead, she suggests that feminism entails the following:

> Asking ethical questions of how to live better in an unjust and unequal world (in a not-feminist and antifeminist world); how to create relationships with others that are more equal; how to find ways to support those who are not supported or are less supported by social systems; how to keep coming up against histories that have become concrete, histories that have become as solid as walls.[11]

Thus, Ahmed chooses to cite only those persons whom she identifies as contributing to the

> "intellectual genealogy of feminism and antiracism," and who forge new paths or "desire lines" beyond those typically defined by a discipline.[12] She writes, "We need feminists and anti-racist critiques because we need to understand how it is that the world takes shape by restricting the forms in which we gather. . . . We need this critique now, if we are to learn how not to reproduce what we inherit."[13]

For Ahmed, feminism is world making, and feminist citations are the bricks from which we can create feminist dwellings. Brick by brick and citation by citation, Ahmed pays tribute to feminists

[10] Ahmed, *Living a Feminist Life,* 15.
[11] Ahmed, *Living a Feminist Life,* 1.
[12] Ahmed, *Living a Feminist Life,* 15.
[13] Ahmed, "Making Feminist Points."

of color on whose shoulders she stands, forming new intellectual genealogies. As such, Ahmed seeks to dismantle the institutions of patriarchal whiteness and build feminist worlds or shelters that create room for others to simply be, regardless. [14]

If Christian theologies are to become similarly transformative and expansive, we must work to dismantle the hegemonic white male paradigms, including those found in white feminist theological frameworks. As Puerto Rican *evangélica* theologian Loida Martell states, "We must 'hear against the grain,' which entails listening to the silences, to sense the crevices and liminal spaces that remain hidden in what is espoused, and being attentive to what or who is absent from this conversation."[15]

Likewise, I argue that applying the method of feminist citational practice to visual culture can help us to "see against the grain." As Eric Copage suggests in his *New York Times* article, "Searching for a Jesus Who Looks More Like Me," representation matters.[16] Visual culture has the unique power to evoke and express emotion and manifest stories of the divine. Moreover, through the spiritual practice of visio-divina (or sacred seeing), it can also offer us a space to experience the divine and make present that which God is calling us to do.

In her recently completed series titled *A Women's Lectionary for the Whole Church*, womanist theologian Wilda C. Gafney centers women's biblical stories in the context of feminist and womanist commitments. In an interview with Grace Ji-Sun Kim published in the *Christian Century* on this lectionary, Gafney draws attention to the various ways in which European male theologians and biblical scholars have bequeathed us with over two thousand years of masculine language and imagery for God. Consequently, Gafney observes, when people use gender-neutral or inclusive language for God, they are not necessarily able to shift the hold of this dominant paradigm. To illustrate her point, Gafney uses as an example those persons who inevitably envi-

[14]Ahmed, "Making Feminist Points,"15.

[15]Loida I. Martell, "Reading against the Grain: Scripture and Constructive Evangélica Theology," in *Latino/a Theology and the Bible: Ethnic-Racial Reflections on Interpretation*, ed. Francisco Lozada Jr. and Fernando F. Segovia (Lanham, MD: Lexington Books/Fortress Academic, 2021), 107.

[16]Eric V. Copage, "Searching for a Jesus Who Looks Like Me," *New York Times* online, April 10, 2020.

sion God as an old white man with a beard. Here, Gafney notes that even if the words "Creator," "Redeemer," or "Sustainer" are stated, these persons unsurprisingly hear "Father." However, Gafney argues, that when one uses more gendered language for God, such as "Mother," the listener is ultimately forced to reckon with or readjust their previous male-dominated image of God.[17]

The long-standing hold of masculine imagery for the divine can be further disrupted, I suggest, when one *sees* divinity (re)presented in the image and likeness of women.[18] The subversive, yet powerful feminist imagery can help break open new spaces to encounter the divine and reveal divine action and presence in our world. Moreover, it can create new opportunities for us to relate to God, to ourselves, and to others.

Take, for example, Kelly Latimore's modern-day painting *The Trinity*, which is based on the famous fifteenth-century Russian icon by Andrei Rublev. In his painting, Kelly (re)presents the traditional three angels as women of color. The three women sit at the table, holding hands. The image of God, clad in red robes, is seated on the left with her right hand pointing out toward the viewer, acknowledging their existence. In the center is the Christ figure, who wears her hair in locs, and on the right is the image of the Holy Spirit. Dressed in green robes, the Holy Spirit holds out her hand as an invitation for the viewer to join the women at the Eucharist table, creating a space for all to be.

The table, which sits in front of the women, is covered with a rainbow cloth and topped with a bowl of grapes and a chaff of wheat. According to Latimore, these adornments not only symbolize that all are welcome at the Eucharist table, but also that there is still so much more work we need do.[19]

The African American artist Renee Cox's controversial photograph, *Yo Mama's Last Supper,* also steps outside the white patriarchal frame by featuring a (re)presentation of Jesus in the image and likeness of a woman of color. Cox's photograph, which

---

[17]Grace Ji-Sun Kim, "A New Lectionary that Centers Women: An Interview with Wil Gafney," *Christian Century* online, February 23, 2022.

[18]I use Sara Ahmed's definition of women as "all those who travel under the sign *women,*" including trans women. Ahmed, *Living a Feminist Life*, 14.

[19]Kelly Latimore Icons, "It's Trinity Sunday," Facebook, June 7, 2020.

is set in the style of Leonardo da Vinci's *Last Supper*, consists of five panels. The female figure of Jesus (a nude self-portrait of Cox holding a shroud behind her body) occupies the central panel. Standing behind a table set with bowls of fruit and a chalice, the Christ figure's arms are outstretched, and her palms are turned up toward the heavens in a cruciform pose. The two panels to the left and to the right feature the twelve disciples—six on each side—seated around the table. All of the disciples are all depicted as African American men, with the exception of Judas, who is portrayed as a white man holding the piece of bread given to him by Jesus.

When Cox's work debuted at the Brooklyn Museum of Art in 2001 as part of an exhibition called *Committed to the Image: Contemporary Black Photographers*, Mayor Rudy Giuliani labeled the photograph as offensive, indecent, heretical, and anti-Catholic, and he called for the creation of a panel to create decency standards for artwork displayed at publicly funded museums in the city.[20] The controversy surrounding this photograph clearly demonstrates how much resistance can be faced in rendering the absented present. It also drives home the point that the theological task is never singular, static, or neutral.

Finally, Chicanix visual artist Esther Hernandez's digital print, *The Virgin de Las Calles*, offers a provocative (re)presentation of the venerated image of Our Lady of Guadalupe. Dressed in jeans, black Nike sneakers, and a red sweatshirt with the letters USA emblazoned across the front, Hernandez's print features a Latina woman standing in front of a bucket of red and white roses imprinted with a colorful logo that says, "Futura." The woman also wears a green shawl with red stripes and the forty-seven stars associated with the Guadalupe image. According to Esther Hernandez's artist statement, the print "pays tribute to the dignity, strength, and perseverance of immigrant women as they strive for a better life for themselves and their families."[21]

Together these images offer a form of sacred seeing that centers

---

[20]Elisabeth Bumiller, "Affronted by Nude 'Last Supper,' Giuliani Calls for Decency Panel," *New York Times* online, February 16, 2001.

[21]"La Virgen de Las Calles," Esther Hernandez Artista Visual, accessed June 30, 2023, https://esterhernandez.com/digital-prints/la-virgen-de-las-calles.

the lived realities of marginalized people who are crying out for justice and liberation. As Nancy Pineda-Madrid states:

> Poor women of color belong at the center of our theologizing, not as a form of identity politics, but because our world's social forces render these women disproportionately vulnerable to systemic suffering. Placing the most vulnerable to systemic suffering at the center of our theologizing holds us accountable and helps our theology to remain prophetic and honest.[22]

Moreover, this feminist methodology helps conceptualize theology as a constructive, imaginative, "worldmaking" praxis in the context of the divine promise that all may have life and have it abundantly. Brick by brick, we can render the absented present in our theological discourse and praxis, bringing into being a world that is less oppressive, less harmful, more just, and ultimately more life-giving.

---

[22]Nancy Pineda-Madrid, "In Light of the People: Theologize in Our Time," in *Latino/a Theology and the Bible: Ethnic-Racial Reflections on Interpretation*, ed. Francisco Lozada Jr. and Fernando F. Segovia (Lanham, MD: Lexington Books/Fortress Academic, 2021), 18.

Both Catholic and Trans

Commensurate Sources for a Theology of the Trans Body

Matthew Gummess

> *"Beauty" unmasks ideology—a beauty that is as much ethical as aesthetic. A radiance of beauty issues where we least expect it. . . . To perceive it is to be changed. To share it with another, to reach it together, is to love; to love in this way is "no longer to belong to this world."*
> *. . . Beauty awakens a man* [sic] *from the stupor of cynicism, conferring insight that no human life can be contained by an abstraction.*[1]

Where to begin? The starting point for the official Catholic response to the present-day debate over gender therapy[2] *is* an

---

I use "trans" here as an umbrella term to include all people who identify as gender-diverse, whether they identify as transsexual, transgender, gender non-binary, or otherwise. Alternatives include "trans*" and the acronym TGD (transgender and gender-diverse). See Talia Mae Bettcher, "Feminist Perspectives on Trans Issues," in *The Stanford Encyclopedia of Philosophy*, ed. Edward N. Zalta, Fall 2020 (Metaphysics Research Lab, Stanford University, 2020), sec. 1, plato.stanford.edu, for a discussion of this terminology.

[1]Erik Varden, *The Shattering of Loneliness: On Christian Remembrance* (London: Bloomsbury Continuum, 2018), 107, NOOK. Emphasis added.

[2]Emily Bazelon, "The Battle over Gender Therapy," *New York Times*, June 15, 2022, sec. Magazine, www.nytimes.com. I use the term "gender therapy" to refer to a range of medical interventions ranging from hormone treatment to gender-affirming surgery.

abstraction—we prescind or abstract from the real, concrete lives of trans persons and assume the invalidity of trans speech and experience.[3] Instead, we begin with a "theology of the body" that derives in large part from John Paul II's teaching of the same.[4] We hold that bodies mediate a truth we can read off them objectively: the "spousal character of the body," expressed through binary gender difference (DN 5; cf. TOB 13:1, 103:4–6). In marriage, according to this viewpoint, bodies mediate or speak a prophetic message of total self-gift, which points to God's total self-gift to creation, including God's gift of the body itself—the *imago Dei* (DN 7; TOB 13:2, 16:1, 104:1–4). But trans bodies have no entry in the official vocabulary to this "language of the body" (TOB 103:4). "A soul can never be in another body, much less be in the wrong body," says the US Bishops' Committee on Doctrine (DN 4). Without considering other possible interpretations of trans experience beyond the "wrong-body model," the committee then assumes the impossibility of such an experience.[5] It reads the trans body as the incarnation of (Cartesian) dualism, which it takes to contradict the truth of the unity of body and soul (DN 4).[6] From this perspective, the body could not possibly mediate a trans word.

But what if we were to begin differently, by assuming the *validity* of trans speech and experience as our starting point? "Instead

---

[3]See, e.g., Committee on Doctrine, United States Conference of Catholic Bishops, *Doctrinal Note on the Moral Limits to Technological Manipulation of the Human Body* (United States Conference of Catholic Bishops, 2023), nos. 5–6, www.usccb.org. Hereafter abbreviated DN. For a response to this document, see Dan Horan, "US Bishops' Document against Transgender Health Care Is a Disaster," *National Catholic Reporter*, March 23, 2023, www.ncronline.org.

[4]John Paul II, *Man and Woman He Created Them: A Theology of the Body*, trans. Michael Waldstein (Boston: Pauline, 2006). Hereafter abbreviated TOB. For an explanation of the standard system of reference to TOB, see John Paul II, 731–35. Space does not allow for a rigorous comparison of contemporary magisterial statements with TOB, but I have tried to indicate parallels where I can.

[5]See below for a definition and critique of the wrong-body model from Transgender Studies scholar Talia Mae Bettcher. Trained in analytic philosophy, Bettcher describes herself as a "trans philosopher." She is former chair of the Philosophy Department at California State University, Los Angeles. For an autobiographical essay, see Talia Mae Bettcher, "How I Became a Trans Philosopher," *Journal of World Philosophies* 7, no. 1 (July 18, 2022): 145–56.

[6]Cf. John Paul II, *Letter to Families*, 1994, no. 19.

of trying to justify trans self-identity claims," says Transgender Studies scholar Talia Mae Bettcher, "such claims ought to be accepted as presumptively valid as a starting point for trans theory and politics."[7] We should assume their validity a priori. In this essay, I follow Bettcher's suggestion, taking the presumptive validity of trans self-identity claims as the starting point for a Catholic theology of the trans body. I am not concerned, then, with validating trans identity from a Catholic perspective. Rather, I would like to see what happens to our theology when we assume that people are who they say they are. Doing so yields a surprising result: a gender-diverse theology of the body, commensurate with body-sex-gender holism, which better captures the belonging of gender to the *imago Dei* than a binary view does.

I proceed in three parts. First, I explain Bettcher's argument for "presumptive validity" as a first principle, which includes her argument against the "wrong-body" model of sex-gender[8] as an interpretation of trans experience. Second, I survey a number of alternative models of sex-gender, both within and beyond the West, in order to illustrate Bettcher's argument and set standard theology of the body within a broader historical and cultural context. Finally, I turn to a constructive critique of theology of the body. I retain its emphasis on the body and on difference as central to Catholic theological anthropology, but leave its binary view of gender aside, in favor of a gender-diverse view ultimately rooted in the Thomistic understanding of God's commensuration of body and soul. Sometimes, I suggest, God commensurates the soul, not to the *wrong* body, but to a trans body. I conclude with a preliminary evaluation of my proposal.[9]

---

[7]Bettcher, "Feminist Perspectives on Trans Issues," sec. 10.3; for further details, see Talia Mae Bettcher, "Trans Women and the Meaning of 'Woman,'" in *The Philosophy of Sex: Contemporary Readings*, ed. Nicholas Power, Raja Halwani, and Alan Soble, 6th ed. (Lanham, MD: Rowman & Littlefield, 2013), 245–56.

[8]See Edward Stein, *The Mismeasure of Desire: The Science, Theory, and Ethics of Sexual Orientation*, illustrated edition (Oxford: Oxford University Press USA, 1999), 33–38. I borrow the term "sex-gender" from Stein, who uses it as an umbrella term to sidestep the various conceptual difficulties that arise in the precise determination of the meaning of the terms "sex" and "gender."

[9]For another approach, see Craig A. Ford Jr., "Transgender Bodies, Catholic Schools, and a Queer Natural Law Theology of Exploration," *Journal of Moral Theology* 7, no. 1 (January 1, 2018): 70–98.

Talia Mae Bettcher: For Presumptive Validity, against "Reality Enforcement"

Bettcher's first principle is mine: the "presumptive validity [of trans self-identity claims] as a starting point of trans theory and politics."[10] This move runs parallel to the move the gay community made in the 1950s.[11] Just as gay men and women challenged psychiatry's assumption of *sickness* then, Bettcher challenges society's assumption of *incongruence* in trans lives today—that is, the assumption that there is "a misalignment between gender identity and sexed body" for people who are trans.[12] For Bettcher, there is no such misalignment. She understands trans people to be *exactly* who they say they are.

The assumption of "incongruence" is highly problematic, for Bettcher, because it is constitutive of what she calls "reality enforcement," which she identifies as the basic form of transphobia.[13] The paradigm of reality enforcement is the unique kind of sexual abuse that threatens all trans people: forced "genital verification" to establish the "truth" of a person's gender, as the interrogator sees it. What Bettcher recognizes is that an "appearance-reality contrast" is a necessary condition of possibility for reality enforcement.[14] Take away the contrast between reality and appearance, and reality enforcement becomes inconceivable. When a penis-bodied individual says that she is a woman, she is paradigmatically so, for Bettcher: there is no question of incongruence.

Bettcher is particularly concerned to uphold as presumptively valid the self-identity claims of trans persons who opt not to have surgery or to take hormones.[15] How does the "wrong-body" model of trans identity fare on this account? Bettcher defines this

[10]Bettcher, "Feminist Perspectives on Trans Issues," sec. 10.3; see Bettcher, "Trans Women and the Meaning of 'Woman,' " 245–46.

[11]See Katie Batza, "Sickness and Wellness," in *The Routledge History of Queer America*, ed. Don Romesburg (New York: Routledge, 2018), 287–99.

[12]Bettcher, "Trans Women and the Meaning of 'Woman,' " 233–34.

[13]Talia Mae Bettcher, "Trapped in the Wrong Theory: Rethinking Trans Oppression and Resistance," *Signs: Journal of Women in Culture and Society* 39, no. 2 (2014): 392.

[14]Bettcher, "Trapped in the Wrong Theory," 392.

[15]Bettcher, "Trapped in the Wrong Theory," 402.

model as the dramatic reversal of reality enforcement: according to this model, gender identity determines real sex, so that one might say, for example, "that's really a man, disguised by a misleading body."[16] Bettcher credits the wrong-body narrative's political effectiveness in securing access to gender-affirming medical care and other rights, but she ultimately rejects it, because it still leaves unchallenged the basic contrastive element that is constitutive of reality enforcement. In this way, it too depends on the presumption of misalignment between body and gender. "It needs to leave the original appearance-reality contrast in place in order for the resistant appearance-reality contrast to reverse it."[17] Thereby it fails to protect or even to make sense of trans persons who may choose not to have surgery or to take hormones, for whatever reason.[18]

To be clear, Bettcher is not arguing *against* gender-affirming care, nor am I. In the same essay, Bettcher also warns against a kind of transphobia that views "the surgically constructed genitalia of trans people . . . as at odds with the genitalia that nature intended."[19] This view also presumes incongruence, and fails the principle of presumptive validity. We might, in fact, expand the principle of presumptive validity so that it covers not just trans identity claims but also "how that needs to look," as trans scholar and activist Dean Spade puts it.[20]

The key problem with the wrong-body model, then, is not gender-affirming care, but rather, the model's dependence on the appearance-reality contrast. For Bettcher, it locates resistance in the wrong place: within a trans-oppressive "world." It depends on an opposition that only makes sense within that world, and thus,

[16]Bettcher, "Trapped in the Wrong Theory," 399.

[17]Bettcher, "Trapped in the Wrong Theory," 400.

[18]Bettcher, "Trapped in the Wrong Theory," 401–2.

[19]Bettcher, "Trapped in the Wrong Theory," 393.

[20]Dean Spade, "Mutilating Gender," in *The Transgender Studies Reader*, ed. Susan Stryker and Stephen Whittle (New York: Routledge, 2006), 327. A Catholic ethics of gender-affirming care deserves full treatment in its own right, which falls beyond the scope of this essay. I address the subject, albeit inadequately, here and at the end of this essay, by way of an initial reflection. For a more thorough treatment of the subject, see, e.g., Becket Gremmels, "Sex Reassignment Surgery and the Catholic Moral Tradition: Insight from Pope Pius XII on the Principle of Totality," *Health Care Ethics USA: A Resource for the Catholic Health Ministry* 24, no. 1 (2016): 6–10.

"can never quite free itself" from it.[21] What Bettcher calls for, in its stead, "is fuller opposition to the very basis of reality enforcement," to the reality-appearance contrast itself.[22] She finds the basis for this opposition in multiple worlds of gender-sense, which do not depend in any way on the dominant model: "worlds in which there exist *different*, resistant gender practices."[23] In these worlds, trans identities in no way depend on the presumption of incongruence.

Interlude: A (small-c) catholic Imagination

I want now to wonder: Is there a Catholic world that can answer to the demand that Talia Mae Bettcher sets, a world that takes the presumptive validity of trans identity claims as its starting point? A *Catholic* world, a world grounded in the Catholic tradition, and a *trans* world, a world in which trans people might find themselves, from the beginning, truly at home?

Catholics can find spurs to our imagination both within the history of the West and beyond the West. According to historian Thomas Laqueur, the Western twofold, complementary model of sex-gender (central to theology of the body) is a product of both the Enlightenment and the Industrial Revolution (to telescope a far more complicated story).[24] Before the Enlightenment, various, radically different understandings of sex-gender obtained in the West, such as the single-sex model in premodern medicine, which understood both men and women as fundamentally having "one flesh."[25] Laqueur calls this model the "one-sex body."[26] We see some evidence of it in St. Thomas Aquinas. According to his account of human generation, in which the man is the active agent in procreation, the *virtus formativa* (or formative power) in semen normally produces a male body. This process, however,

[21] Bettcher, "Trapped in the Wrong Theory," 402.

[22] Bettcher, "Trapped in the Wrong Theory," 403.

[23] Bettcher, "Trapped in the Wrong Theory," 403.

[24] Thomas Laqueur, *Making Sex: Body and Gender from the Greeks to Freud*, ACLS Humanities E-Book (Cambridge, MA: Harvard University Press, 1992), chaps. 5–6; cf. Helen King, *The One-Sex Body on Trial: The Classical and Early Modern Evidence*, History of Medicine in Context (New York: Routledge, 2013).

[25] Laqueur, *Making Sex*, chap. 3.

[26] Laqueur, *Making Sex*, 63.

depends on several factors, which may produce a *more or less* male body—factors such as the relative strength of the *virtus formativa* or even the relative humidity.[27] Bracketing a discussion of the overall merits, or lack thereof, to this account, note that "sex" can be interpreted as a graded notion here—given the mechanics of human generation, as St. Thomas understood them, we can imagine sexual differentiation upon a gradient or spectrum, according to this model. Laqueur rightly argues that this "one-sex" or "one-flesh" model differs in kind from the later, post-Enlightenment model of ontologically distinct, complementary sexes. It not only demonstrates the historicity of the complementary model, but also provides a resource for Westerners to think gender differently.

Thinking beyond the West, many cultures have had, for centuries, and still have today, a profoundly different understanding of sex-gender, such as the Bugis in Indonesia.[28] For the Bugis, sex-gender encompasses a fivefold space of possibility, according to anthropologist Sharyn Graham: man, woman, *calalai'*, *calabai'*, and *bissu*.[29] The latter categories correspond, very roughly, to transmasculine, transfeminine, and gender non-binary, but these categories do not have any analogue in the wrong-body model. To be *calalai'* is to just be a "female-bodied" person who is *calalai'*, not a woman.[30] Graham's summary interpretation is

---

[27]Antonia Fitzpatrick, "Thomas Aquinas (I): Individuality and the Individual Body," in *Thomas Aquinas on Bodily Identity* (Oxford: Oxford University Press, 2017), 115. See *Summa Theologiae* (*ST*) 1.92.1.ad1. Fitzpatrick paraphrases: "A female body is the result of a weakness in the *virtus formativa*, or of an 'indisposition' or some disordered state within the material provided by the mother, or of the involvement of an external climatic or atmospheric factor that somehow inhibits the progression of the embryo, such as a moist southerly wind."

[28]Sharyn Graham, "It's Like One of Those Puzzles: Conceptualising Gender among Bugis," *Journal of Gender Studies* 13, no. 2 (July 2004): 107–16; see also Paul L. Vasey and Nancy H. Bartlett, "What Can the Samoan 'Fa'afafine' Teach Us about the Western Concept of Gender Identity Disorder in Childhood?" *Perspectives in Biology and Medicine* 50, no. 4 (2007): 481–90.

[29]Graham, "It's Like One of Those Puzzles," 108.

[30]Graham, "It's Like One of Those Puzzles," 110. Graham uses the term "female-bodied." Her account of the relationship between body and gender in Buginese culture does still reflect some contrastive elements, but interestingly, each example she cites reflects some intersection between Buginese culture and the West, whether Western religion (Islam), Western medicine,

that the Buginese have something like a fivefold understanding of the *body* as well as of gender: "because the body is understood to be constituted by various combinations of male and female, multiple identities are possible," she says.[31] While a woman's body shares some anatomical features with the body of someone who is *calalai'*, they differ in other respects. Graham cites a local tribal leader's understanding: "*calalai'* have an x-factor (*faktor-x*). It's a physiology (*fisiologi*) thing. While their sex (*kelamin*) is female, inside they are not like other women. They are different. They have some male aspects."[32] Note where the contrast falls here: it lies, *not* between the body of someone who is *calalai'* and "hir [*sic*]" gender, but rather, between *calalai'* bodies and other, different kinds of bodies, including women's bodies. In this context, the "wrong-body" model becomes inconceivable because its core component, the notion of incongruence, loses all meaning.

These two examples demonstrate that the Cartesian reading of the trans body is far from necessary. And there are many other such cultural examples, both modern and historical, which show that gender diversity need not entail "dualism." The gender-diverse body can speak another word. While there is no direct translation from these other cultures' understandings and practices to our own, such examples illuminate the concrete possibilities that may lie at the end of Bettcher's call to imagine worlds in which there exist different gender practices: worlds in which the presumption of validity creates broad, cultural conditions of possibility for both the subjective and objective perception of congruence in embodied, trans lives.

Both Catholic and Trans

Here, I now argue, an expanded Catholic imagination may have a real contribution to make, despite official protestations of "gender ideology" in response to the lived, embodied experiences of trans people. These protestations are founded on an ironic form

---

or Western science. Understandings of the relationship between the body and gender in modern Buginese culture reflect these diverse cultural influences.

[31]Graham, "It's Like One of Those Puzzles," 110.

[32]Graham, "It's Like One of Those Puzzles," 110.

of gender essentialism that takes the Western gender binary to be eternal, when, in fact, it is sharply circumscribed in both space and time, as we have just seen. But it is worth unraveling the official protestation a bit to see what hidden possibilities it might contain.

What the magisterial church has called "gender ideology" is to be contrasted with a binary view of gender that prioritizes both the *body* and *difference* (DN 4–5). The binary difference between man and woman is grounded in the bodily difference between male and female, according to this view, which is valued as an incarnate mark of our likeness to the Triune God. I contend, however, that it is possible to separate the binary view from these underpinnings; and that the gender-diverse view I explain below is in fact more faithful to the traditional importance of the body and of difference in Catholic theology.

Bracketing the binary view then: the centrality of the body to the Catholic tradition cannot be overstressed.[33] At the heart of the Catholic faith is the incarnate form of Truth: Jesus Christ, who reveals, by his very incarnation, that God gives paramount value to the flesh. When Christians confess the "resurrection of the body" in the Creed, we confess the lasting value of this flesh of ours, which is a constituent part of our very being. According to the Catholic understanding, we *are* body-spirit beings; the body is not secondary nor disposable (DN 7). Popular renditions of heaven as the realm of separated souls, then, miss the mark. The kingdom of heaven that Jesus preached belongs not just to the spirit, but to resurrection-flesh: this is just what belief in the incarnation and in resurrection of the body mean.

So highly esteemed is the body in the Catholic tradition that it is taken to be a legible sign of Mystery Itself: the One-in-Three, the Divinity, the Triune God. The difference written into our very biology is a positive sign of its source and origin, of difference in the Trinity.[34] As Father and Son and Spirit differ, we too differ. As difference in the Trinity is compossible with communion,

---

[33]See Sarah Coakley, *God, Sexuality, and the Self: An Essay "on the Trinity"* (New York: Cambridge University Press, 2013), esp. 52–60. The views I express here are largely derivative of Coakley's, though written independently of her work. I have tried to indicate points of especially close contact here in the notes.

[34]Coakley, *God, Sexuality, and the Self*, 56.

difference makes true communion possible for us. "And God found it *very* good" (Gen. 1:31): this difference we bear in our flesh we *see* in the light of its likeness to Triune difference as fundamentally *good*.

The binary view and what I am calling the Catholic, gender-diverse view would so far be in perfect agreement on these points. But the binary view makes two mistakes: on the one hand, it holds us to be *too* similar to the Trinity, and, on the other hand, it does not hold us to be similar enough. On the first account, it forgets another *difference*, a difference which is fundamentally good as well, and as fundamental to the tradition: this, the difference between the Trinity and creation.[35] We are the image and likeness of God, but we are *not* God. This wonderful difference is the ground of our freedom and the condition of possibility for love—both being loved and loving.

The binary view of gender in the Catholic Church elides this difference by *essentializing* "man" and "woman." But our being is not like God's. Only God truly *is*. We can say that we too *are*, but only analogously. For we change and we die, and so too do our concepts: concepts too can change and perish, even concepts with a long history like "man" and "woman." They cannot be defined, now and for all eternity. They can do good and necessary work, but they can only ever be "fuzzy": there will always be a penumbra of real *difference* surrounding any human concept that radically stands in the way of any claim to the *essence* of the thing. "No human life can be contained by an abstraction," says Bishop Varden in the epigraph to this chapter.

For a human life is lived in free *relation* to others, and in this sense, the binary view also misses the mark, by failing to hold true the analogy between God's being and ours. The difference in the Trinity is a difference of *relation* only: the being of God is totally shared between Father, Son and Spirit.[36] The theology of the body developed by John Paul II actually holds the same for the difference between man and woman: it is primarily a difference of *relation*, to be discovered by each individual in relation

[35]Coakley, *God, Sexuality, and the Self*, 57.
[36]Coakley, *God, Sexuality, and the Self*, 57.

to other persons living and historical.[37] But theology of the body contradicts this Trinitarian likeness by subsequently "filling out" the concepts of man and woman with all kinds of "essential" abstraction, which ends up jeopardizing the very unity of the human race.[38]

What of the gender-diverse view? To gesture toward this view—which I must leave here very partial and incomplete—I would like to borrow a very traditional, Thomistic understanding of the moment at which God creates the individual person. According to the Jesuit theologian W. Norris Clarke,

> St Thomas speaks of each soul being "commensurated" or adapted actively by God to its own particular body. . . . Thus the soul itself becomes differentiated in itself from every other, not because it is a different kind of soul, but because it is joined with this particular body as its permanent instrument of self-expression.[39]

Against this view, Clarke critically contrasts a two-soul model, in which men and women have different kinds of souls:[40] "now we have broken the unity of the human species: men and women are no longer essentially equal complementary members of the same human species, bearing essentially the same human nature, but

---

[37]See, e.g., Prudence Allen, *The Concept of Woman* (Grand Rapids, MI: Eerdmans, 2016), 3:480–81.

[38]Allen, *The Concept of Woman*, 3:477–78, 501.

[39]W. Norris Clarke, *The One and the Many: A Contemporary Thomistic Metaphysics* (Notre Dame, IN: University of Notre Dame Pess, 2015), 103; quoted in Allen, *The Concept of Woman*, 3:421. For a more detailed account, see Fitzpatrick, "Thomas Aquinas (I)," esp. 91–92, 112–18. Clarke's account collapses two distinct concepts in Thomas, that of *commensuration* (*Summa Contra Gentiles* 2.80–1) and that of *ensoulment* (*ST* 1.90.3, 1.118.2–3); nevertheless, Thomas clearly identifies God as the immediate cause of every soul; likewise, he argues that soul and body are commensurate to each other, as form and matter. Thus, Clarke's assertion, that God commensurates the soul, is reasonable.

[40]See, e.g., John Finley, "The Metaphysics of Gender: A Thomistic Approach," *The Thomist* 79, no. 4 (2015): 585–614; cf. William Newton, "Why Aquinas's Metaphysics of Gender Is Fundamentally Correct: A Response to John Finley," *The Linacre Quarterly* 87, no. 2 (May 1, 2020): 198–205.

are qualitatively different kinds of being."[41] St. Thomas, however, preserves both the unity of the species *and* a holistic understanding of the commensurate relationship between body and soul, wherein the soul is the form of *this* body, and not just a generic soul, by tying the individual soul's difference to an individual, creative act of God. If neither matter nor spirit can constrain the free act of the Creator, then a more expansive view, a gender-diverse view is equally possible: that in some beautiful cases, God commensurates a human soul, not to the *wrong* body, but to a *trans* body: to a body with a penis that is, just so, a woman; or to a body with a vagina that is, just so, a man; or to a body that is, just so, *however*-so—however that needs to look—*bissu*; or *calalai'*; or *calabai'*—such that the trans body and the trans soul are fundamentally commensurate—congruent.

Why? The logic and metaphysics of commensuration are not so unintelligible as they might appear at first glance. We have here a particular instance of the more general Christian metaphysics of gracious *gift*, which holds that God is intimately involved in the existence of every aspect of creation, making everything that is fundamentally *gift*.[42]

"Blessed are those / who believe themselves unworthy of blessing / what inconceivable wonders you hold," writes trans poet Jay Hulme, in his beautiful poem, "Beatitudes for a Queerer Church."[43] *Wonder, gift, beauty*—if we need a reason for these, then perhaps it is Bishop Varden's—to perceive the radiance of beauty is to be changed. Perhaps God leaves radiant traces of the divine beauty in creation to remind us not to hold so fast to

---

[41] Clarke, *The One and the Many*, 104.

[42] See, e.g., John Milbank, *The Suspended Middle: Henri de Lubac and the Renewed Split in Modern Catholic Theology*, 2nd ed. (Grand Rapids, MI: Eerdmans, 2014), esp. chap. 8; Michael Hanby, *No God, No Science? Theology, Cosmology, Biology* (Malden, MA: Wiley-Blackwell, 2013), 83–90, esp. 86. This view, while not universally held among modern Thomists, reflects a reading of Thomistic metaphysics prominent among adherents to Milbank's school of Radical Orthodoxy. It distinguishes between Aristotelian and Thomistic metaphysics precisely in its account of difference as arising, not from matter, but from God's act of creation, which configures each existent thing, in its uniqueness from all other things, as a particular gift.

[43] Jay Hulme, *The Backwater Sermons* (London: Canterbury Press, 2021), 90.

our categories and to our concepts that we forget to *see* this real person in all their concrete glory, and to love them as they really *are*, and not as we think they ought to be.

To conclude with some brief, evaluative comments: this account, first of all, passes Bettcher's "congruence" test—trans identity upon this account depends, not on a mismatch between gender identity and a misleading body, but on a loving act of God, which commensurates the trans body and soul. It also remains open to the possibility of gender-affirming care, such as surgery or hormone replacement therapy, without necessitating either. Note that bodily alteration in no way changes the fundamental *congruence* between body and spirit that informs the Catholic, gender-diverse view.[44] This congruence does not depend on the body's history: it will remain equally the case that the body of a person who has received gender-affirming surgery is still, *just so*, the *commensurate* body for that person. For commensuration does not depend on what genitals a person may happen to have, but rather on the *this-ness* of the body, such that *this body* expresses the true depth of *this person* at all times, as made in the image and likeness of God (cf. DN 4).

Finally, this account also retains the central importance of the body as the integral expression of the soul in Catholic theology, and of sex-gender difference as a paradoxical sign of both our likeness to and our difference from the Triune God. To admit of more than two genders does not relativize the importance of gender difference as an incarnate mark of the godliness of difference; on the contrary, it magnifies it. But the gender-diverse view advocated here *does* remind us that our gender *concepts* are human, not divine, and thus fallible—even our oldest and most important concepts, such as the concept of "woman" and "man." More important, it calls into question the church's assumptions about gender, opening up surprising new territories for both orthodoxy and trans persons, who are fundamentally *whole*:

[44]Cf. Bettcher, "Trapped in the Wrong Theory," 393. I hope this account avoids the kind of transphobia, quoted above, which views "the surgically constructed genitalia of trans people . . . as at odds with the genitalia that nature intended."

"Blessed are the broken," says Jay Hulme,
for they are not broken. . . .
"Blessed are those who try;
those who transform, who transition. . . .
. . . What inconceivable wonders you hold."[45]

[45]Hulme, *The Backwater Sermons*, 90.

Communicating a Theology of Parenthood

Or, What Parenthood Is and Is Not

Jacob M. Kohlhaas

For a bit over a decade now, I have been writing on theology of parenthood and families. In this process, I have developed a well-informed sense of how I think parenthood and the family ought to be understood theologically from within the Catholic tradition. However, when I am asked by other parents what I can say to them about parenthood, I often find myself at a loss for words. In what follows, I reflect on why such conversations are so difficult, and why, if I can find something useful to say to actual, faithful parents, it may be in the key of sacramental theology under the guidance of the late Bruno Latour.[1]

The Moral Foundations of Parenthood

Let us begin at the beginning. What makes a parent a parent? Parenthood imposes widely recognized obligations, and so this question has important moral, theological, philosophical, social, and legal implications. If I am going to say something useful to parents, we should first understand who they are.

At present, the two leading contenders for answering this

[1]The personal tone adapted in portions of this essay, as well as the more formal tone adapted in other sections, is an intentional, though simplified, reference to Bruno Latour's own style.

question are the "causal" and the "voluntarist" approaches. These contenders base parenthood in deliberate reproductive acts or willful acceptance of parental obligations, respectively.[2] The causal approach is based in the natural law tradition and has been generally favored by modern Catholic accounts of parenthood.[3] This perspective tends to hold biological, social, and legal parenthood closely together. The causal approach traces back at least to Aristotle and was enshrined in Roman law via the *patria potestas*.[4] In its strongest form, the causal approach argues that anyone who voluntarily undertakes an action which may result in the birth of a child has a de facto obligation to parent that child.[5]

However, the causal approach offers limited explanation for *why* biological reproduction should necessarily be considered so compelling. Instead, it tends to rely on uncritical appeals to nature to defend this claim. In so doing, it can naïvely suggest that the capacity to reproduce and the capacity to parent necessarily co-emerge. This view is quite clearly contradicted by experience and is historically laden with significant sexist assumptions that have served to the detriment of women. Parenting requires having

---

[2]This dichotomy is a simplification as other approaches exist. For example, David Archard lists: gestational, genetic, causal, and intentional (i.e., voluntarist). The gestational approach favors mother's singular rights to parenthood by virtue of the gestational relationship. The genetic has been used to explain parenthood in response to new reproductive technologies. Both can be species of either the causal or voluntarist depending on how they are defended. David Benatar and David Archard, eds., *Procreation and Parenthood* (Oxford: Clarendon Press, 2011), 28.

[3]Bernard G. Prusak observes that conventional legal understanding tends to support the causal approach (e.g., child support), but decisions regarding new reproductive technologies have begun to rely more heavily on the voluntarist approach (e.g., anonymity for gamete donors). Bernard G. Prusak, *Parental Obligations and Bioethics: The Duties of a Creator* (New York: Routledge, 2013), 3–4.

[4]John Locke recognized the problem of mixing the status of children with that of property and attempted to differentiate a causal account of parental obligations distinct from standard property rights, though his attempt has been criticized. Benatar and Archard, *Procreation and Parenthood,* 109.

[5]See Margaret Somerville, "Children's Human Rights and Unlinking Child-Parent Biological Bonds with Adoption, Same-Sex Marriage and New Reproductive Technologies," *Journal of Family Studies* 13 no. 2 (November 2007): 179–201.

relational capacities and developing caregiving skills that cannot be replaced by naïve appeals to "natural feminine intuition." Though they are both present in many people, the capacity to reproduce and the capacities necessary for social parenthood are simply not the same thing.

In opposition to the strong causal approach, the strong voluntarist approach bases parental obligations on an informed act of consent. One advocate of this position, Jacqueline Stevens, has argued against "genetic privilege" within family law and objected to the causalist notion that genetic contribution somehow yields specific custody rights.[6] Stevens suggests mothers be given time after birth to decide to care for a child or make arrangements for adoption to others.[7] But the ease with which Stevens disregards the value of genetic kinship is concerning and also contradicts much lived experience. Moreover, she simply accepts current diversities in child-rearing, such as historically high rates of divorce and cohabitation, without contest, even when evidence suggests that stable families are among the most significant predictors of child well-being. Because the strong voluntarist approach centers individualistically on the free choices of adults, it tends to disparage natural conditions for child well-being and the lasting value of traditional social institutions.

In their strong versions, the narrow foundations of both the causal and the voluntarist approaches end up leaning into reductive anthropologies that fail to account for the complexity of actual experience. Consequently, several scholars have adopted views of the moral foundations of parenthood that stake out more moderate positions. For example, Elizabeth Brake argues that

---

[6]Jaqueline Stevens, "Methods of Adoption: Eliminating Genetic Privilege," in *Adoption Matters: Philosophical and Feminist Essays*, ed. Sally Haslanger and Charlotte Witt (Ithaca, NY: Cornell University Press, 2005), 69. To highlight the gap between genetic contribution and parenthood, Stevens compares awarding custody rights for conveying DNA to bestowing a Pulitzer Prize for delivering the newspaper.

[7]Stevens, "Methods of Adoption," 90. In practice, *prima facie* parental rights would belong to mothers on the basis of their voluntarist commitment to parenthood by having accepted gestational parenthood (e.g., by not having terminated the pregnancy). At birth, this previous decision would not bind the mother to further parental obligations but would put her alone in the position to arrange care for the child.

parental obligations must be grounded in informed acceptance of parental duties by adults who are capable of fulfilling these for specific children who are eligible to be parented by them.[8] Yet even her moderate voluntarist approach appears to mistake plurality for meaninglessness in historical and cultural understandings of parental obligations.[9]

From the moderate causalist camp, Bernard G. Prusak raises concern for how reproductive technologies could discourage unconditional love and encourage viewing children as products of consumer choice.[10] Prusak contends that procreators are causally bound to parental obligations as a *prima facie* duty that should only be abandoned for serious reasons. This relatively high valuation of biological continuity opens Prusak to criticism for failing to adequately explore how social conventions shape the meanings attached to biological kinship.

David Archard offers an even more restrictive version of the causal approach by arguing that procreators are only responsible for assuring a reasonably good upbringing and need not themselves assume the parental duties generated by their actions.[11] Although his position is much more truncated than others in this camp, Archard favors the causal approach because it clearly assigns obligations to parties who undertook inherently risky behavior, regardless of their intent, and thus assures that a resulting child will not be harmed.[12]

In response to all of this, I have argued that a weak causal account of *prima facie* parental obligations joined to a voluntarist account of parental responsibilities most clearly captures the Catholic theological position by acknowledging both the obligations that result from actions as well as the chosen nature of

[8]Elizabeth Brake, "Willing Parents: A Voluntarist Account of the Parental Role," in *Procreation and Parenthood*, ed. David Benatar and David Archard (Oxford: Clarendon Press, 2011), 152. This is how Brake distinguishes her view from the less precise voluntarist view advanced by Onora O'Neill.

[9]Brake, "Willing Parents," 164.

[10]Bernard G. Prusak, *Parental Obligations and Bioethics: The Duties of a Creator* (New York: Routledge, 2013), 4.

[11]Benatar and Archard, *Procreation and Parenthood*, 104.

[12]Benatar and Archard, *Procreation and Parenthood*,116.

parenthood.[13] From this starting point, parenthood can be understood theologically as founded on both an underlying relationship *and* willful acts of caregiving. Parenthood is labor inasmuch as it requires the exertion of effort for the sake of a larger goal, but parenthood is also uniquely specified by the asymmetrical, reciprocal, and unrepeatable relationship between caregiver and child that is contextualized within a kin relationship. Christian parenthood, in particular, is characterized by a depth of love that expresses itself in both specific relational commitments as well as its willingness to extend bonds of love in response to the needs of others. Through this joining of lives, a parental vocation is begun in which loving commitment to another and the relational reciprocity this initiates create the context for growth and self-discovery as a person and parent.

On Saying Something Useful

There we have it. Citing several sources along the way, I have offered you, in highly summarized form, an explanation of the moral theological foundations of parenthood. I hope you found it interesting. I find it interesting. But if you want to know what parenthood is, or more precisely, what the Catholic theological tradition offers to your understanding of your being a faithful Christian parent, have I actually communicated anything of real value? Have I even understood your concern? Or was this all just a bit of interesting but ultimately wasted time?

I confess, I have not found my research all that practically beneficial to my role as a parent. I cannot say I am a much better dad to my kids because I have undertaken an extensive academic study of parenthood from within my discipline. I think I have a good argument for what parenthood "is" from within my academic discipline, but at the same time I am not convinced I have really said much of lasting value about what parenthood "is" in relation to my actual experience of it.

Perhaps I need to look elsewhere for concerns such as these. After all, why should academic discourse have much to say to the

[13]Cf. Jacob Kohlhaas, *Beyond Biology: Rethinking Parenthood in the Catholic Tradition* (Washington, DC: Georgetown University Press, 2021), 196–202.

ordinary lives of regular people? For this, translation is required. Theological ideas need to be interpreted for practical use by those with the gifts to explain and simplify matters to the ideas that are both most basic and most meaningful. The work of practical theologians and catechists is surely much better equipped to transfer speculative theological ideas into meaningful, actionable concepts. Books like *A Catechism for Family Life*, edited by Sara Bartel and John S. Grabowski,[14] or the little preparatory book for the 2015 World Meeting of Families, *Love Is Our Mission*,[15] do just this.

Admittedly, I do not find these books particularly helpful for saying something meaningful to parents either. This is in large part because they participate in the same sorts of problematic rhetoric and ideological priorities I have criticized in Magisterial writing.[16] They exemplify the sort of abstractions and cultural reactionary posturing that I have spent a good bit of energy arguing needs reform and improvement through greater dialogue with actual parental experience. So I am left unhappy with what I have said and unhappy with what others have said—a dissatisfied curmudgeon who recognizes a need but gripes about the efforts to fill it.

In what remains of this essay, I want to explore one potential pathway out. My guide here is Bruno Latour, a French intellectual whose philosophical projects blurred disciplinary boundaries with theology, anthropology, and sociology. Before his death in 2022, Latour made a career out of critically observing many things that the modern world takes for granted, which was summed up most clearly in his 1991 monograph, later translated to English as *We Have Never Been Modern*.[17] Though his work is widely recognized as creative and engaging, his influence within philosophy and theology has been somewhat limited.

[14]Sarah Bartel and John S. Grabowski, *A Catechism for Family Life: Insights from Catholic Teaching on Love, Marriage, Sex, and Parenting* (Washington, DC: Catholic University of America Press, 2018).

[15]World Meeting of Families, *Love Is Our Mission* (Philadelphia: World Meeting of Families, 2014).

[16]Kohlhaas, *Beyond Biology*, 36–59. Cf. Jacob Kohlhaas, "Constructing Parenthood: Catholic Teaching 1880 to the Present," *Theological Studies* 79 no. 3 (2018): 610–33.

[17]Cf. Bruno Latour, *We Have Never Been Modern* (Cambridge, MA: Harvard University Press, 1993).

Latour's work suggests I ought to be suspicious of searching for a solution among the different available options and instead should critically question what defines the agreed-upon terrain in the first place. This insight suggests that my inability to speak meaningfully to actual parents about parenthood and my disappointment with available resources that also attempt to do so are likely two manifestations of the same problem. Communicating effectively with actual parents may not have much to do with simplifying and clarifying my research or with adding a more academically defensible approach to what others have attempted. Rather, the challenge may arise from the mode of communication that my field tends to appropriate being simply unfit for the purpose of reaching parents truthfully in their actual, daily realities. This is not to say that there is no value in any of it; it has value within its own proper realm. But it is valueless, and perhaps even mendacious, for the particular type of communication parents are seeking when they ask about the implications of my research.

Latour on Religious Speech

In Latour's essay, "Thou Shall Not Freeze-Frame" he warns of the dangers of separating information from the "regime of enunciation" for which it is fit and out of which it secures the "conditions of felicity" which give it meaning and ultimately make communication truthful.[18] Latour's concern is that, by misunderstanding how communicative modes differ, the contemporary world has profoundly confused itself about the nature of all manner of communication. In this essay, the difference between scientific and religious communication takes center stage.

In popular opinion, science is understood as the study of present, firm, and tangible realities whereas religion (here Latour is speaking explicitly of Christianity) communicates transcendent, mysterious, and otherworldly truths. According to Latour, through a great comedy of errors, we have gotten things nearly exactly backward. Drawing on his anthropological studies of laboratory scientists, undertaken as a Western scholar might study some re-

[18]Bruno Latour, " 'Thou Shall Not Freeze-Frame' or How Not to Misunderstand the Science and Religion Debate," *Science, Religion, and the Human Experience* (May 2005): 28.

mote Amazonian tribe, Latour describes the scientific enterprise as a highly specialized and orchestrated process of skilled translations.[19] These translations move from distant and inaccessible realities, such as the firing of a single neuron, through instrumentation and a good deal of subjective judgment, before reaching their very practical manifestation in the form of a scientific essay. Science, not religion, speaks truthfully when it faithfully translates the transcendent, mysterious, and otherworldly into meaningful and digestible communication in the here and now.[20]

Religious speech operates through an entirely different mode of communication. Importantly, Latour is not reasserting Gould's "Non-Overlapping Magisteria" thesis, where religion and science simply speak of separate realms of knowledge.[21] It is not as if science speaks about things in one realm and religion of things in another; rather they inhabit the same existence yet occupy "incommensurable ecological niches."[22] Unlike the dominant models of relating scientific and religious knowledge, typified for example in Haught's categorization as conflict, contrast, and convergence,[23] Latour suggests their differences have little to do with appropriately dividing out the subject matter's conceptual terrain and much to do with the quality of the communication necessary for succeeding in its inherent purpose.

Religious speech does not seek to translate information across vast distances while still arriving at the truthful communication of its message. Religious communication does not contain a message at all, not as defined in terms of information content anyway. Rather, religious communication is truthful when it is transformative and person-making. Religious forms of speech "are able to transfer *persons* not information, either because they produce in part personhood, or because new states . . . are generated in

[19]Cf. Bruno Latour and Steve Woolgar, *Laboratory Life: The Construction of Scientific Facts* (Princeton, NJ: Princeton University Press, 1986).

[20]Latour, "Thou Shall Not Freeze-Frame," 36.

[21]Stephen Jay Gould, "Nonoverlapping Magisteria," *Natural History* 106 (March 1997): 16–22.

[22]Bruno Latour, *Rejoicing: Or the Torments of Religious Speech*, trans. Julie Rose (Cambridge: Polity, 2013), 28.

[23]See John Haught, *Science and Faith: A New Introduction* (Mahwah, NJ: Paulist Press, 2013).

the persons thus addressed."[24] In contrast to the present volume's theme, religious speech does not "render the absent present," that better describes the mediation of information appropriate to the sciences. For Latour, religious speech brings nothing external along with it; it sets askew what is already here and now.[25]

What Latour finally gets comfortable admitting toward the end of *Rejoicing: Or the Torments of Religious Speech* is that religious communication in its native form is either sacramental or it is nothing at all.[26] The problem we religious hearers face in the contemporary world is that we have become deeply accustomed to accepting "nothing at all" speech as religious discourse. We have sought to create room for viable religious discourse within terms established by the modern world's preference for scientific discourse. This has alienated religious communication from its native mode and left the very sacramentality of religious communication to wither. Unfortunately, few are interested in rehabilitating this mode of communication because we have become so singularly convinced that only particular communicative regimes have value.[27]

Implications

Let me take a moment to admit that it is a profoundly odd move to look for a solution in my inability to communicate meaningfully to regular, faithful parents about my work in theology by turning to a recently deceased French intellectual known for his committed social constructionism in order to pull out his very peculiar indications toward a materialist sacramental theology.[28] Tellingly, however, Latour insists that he is not really explain-

[24]Latour, "Thou Shalt Not Freeze Frame," 30.

[25]Latour, *Rejoicing*, 89.

[26]Latour, *Rejoicing*, 149ff.

[27]Latour, *Rejoicing*, 191.

[28]Elsewhere, Latour's discussion of St. Paul's distinction between spirit and flesh helps elucidate his approach to sacramentality. In moving these terms out of their common metaphysical packaging, Latour writes "My formulation will be the following: there is no other spirit than the letter *slightly askew*." Bruno Latour, "'Thou Shalt Not Take the Lord's Name in Vain'—Being a Sort of Sermon on the Hesitations of Religious Speech," *Anthropology and Aesthetics* 39 (March 2001): 9.

ing anything beyond what Christians already ought to know.[29] Moreover, his primary experiential referent is almost shockingly simple. Throughout *Rejoicing*, he repeatedly returns to how the simple act of affirming love might be done truthfully and felicitously between two lovers. The space between this metaphor and, for example, Michael Himes's examples of a hug or a birthday party to experientially ground sacramental theology is not so terribly distant.[30]

What both have in common is an insistence on the immanent, the experiential, the transformative, not only *in* the here and now, but *of* the here and now. The larger trajectory of modernity has been to double down on abstraction as the key to meaningfully conveying religious truth in response to the growing place of science as the standard for knowledge. Latour would have us know that we are not bound to Neoplatonic flights into metaphysical fantasy for communicating religious meaning. But whatever these may have accomplished in their particular sociohistorical context that led to the re-creation of people through the word thus preached, *that* is the obligation we now have to take upon ourselves if we are to make this fragile word truthful again. We cannot re-create some now dead word through dogged reaffirmation of the idea that knowledge of some distance spiritual reality or some deeply hidden divine truth remains the core of religious communication in a world that finds atheism a comfortable common point of reference.[31]

This attempt to safeguard the value of religious communication against the dominance of scientific regimes of discourse through epistemological one-upmanship turns to Neoplatonic dualism to offer sacramental theologies that insist on external, transcendent reference as the key to spiritual value. In this view, sacraments "render the absent present" through otherworldly mediation. For example, unlike ordinary bread, the consecrated bread is substantially transformed into the sacramental presence

[29]Latour, *Rejoicing*, 84.

[30]Michael Himes, "Catholics: Why We Are a Sacramental People," *Church in the 21st Century, You Tube* (January 30, 2014), https://www.youtube.com/watch?v=F1_0iutCuV8. Cf. Michael Himes, *The Mystery of Faith* (Cincinnati, OH: Franciscan Media, 2004), 11–18.

[31]Latour, *Rejoicing*, 14.

of a distant, divinized Christ. Unlike ordinary forgiveness, the sacrament of reconciliation cleanses and wipes clean the spiritual substance of our ephemeral souls. Unlike ordinary confessions of commitment, the sacrament of marriage creates an unbreakable bond that exists supernaturally and external to the couple's lived devotion, or lack thereof. The metaphysical, supernatural, external, distant, transcendent, mysterious other is transported into the here and now through the sacramental act, transforming and elevating mundane reality in the wake of its influx. We owe reverence and awe, and if we do it correctly, we might just be conformed more closely to that spiritual otherness about which ordinary life, ordinarily, has little to say.

Latour's rejoinder is simple: "Words that do what they say are sacramental."[32] In sacramental communication, the present itself is rendered anew. Sacraments must either transform persons or they are nothing at all. Sacraments do not conform us to some spiritual other; they transform us in the here and now. In other words, the "Good News" brings along no content. It is incarnational pronouncement, person-making communication.[33]

To speak religiously, that is in a sacramental register, has to do with setting aside the transfer of information and seeking the transformation of persons. One can debate and reconstruct notions of the moral foundations of parenthood as thoroughly as one likes and even arrive at a defensible constructive position. But this pattern of communication cannot speak truthfully about the real sacramental realities of parenthood. For this, communication must involve persons in active transformation through representing, that is re-presenting, their reality in the here and now. Speaking meaningfully, sacramentally, of parenthood requires avoiding the double trap of believing that the conveyance of information is our primary task or that meaning can be found in making the here and now, person-making realities of parenthood, referential to something external for their validation and valuation. The trick that so much religious communication seems to miss is that it is no longer about connecting ordinary parental responsibilities to the extraordinary promises of God's grace. This is akin to confusing a liturgical rubric that assures conditions for sacramental validity

[32]Latour, *Rejoicing*, 149.
[33]Latour, *Rejoicing*, 139.

with the sacrament itself. One communicates information; the other transforms persons.

Gathering the wherewithal to attempt to speak religiously, truthfully, sacramentally in such a manner is no small task. The odds of getting it all wrong and saying something useless, or even idiotic, are very high. Not to transfer information, but to transform persons, this manner of communication appears daunting and far too fragile. Nonetheless it redirects attention to the here and now and the hard task of seeking transformation. Actual parenthood is not a set of conditions met in relation to a child; it is the process of being made someone with and for someone else. I am not "a parent" to "a child," I am "Dad" to Adeline and Claire, and a "Godfather" to Miriam. In other words, the sacraments do not lay out some framework for appreciating parenthood any better than philosophical or theological discourse that abstracts reality from the present; but the transformative experience of parenting may well disclose what it means to be sacramental.

MEDIATION

AND

PLACE

Numipunm Wéetespe (Nez Perce Earth)

The Land and the Mediation of Catholic Peoplehood on the Palouse

Joseph S. Flipper

Returning to Nimíipuu Country

In February of 2022, I flew into the Lewiston, Idaho, airport with a backpack and a few changes of clothes. My mother passed away a few months before, and I was returning to take care of her house. An old friend drove me to Sunday mass at All Saints Catholic Church, a new parish formed from recent parish mergers. It looked like an Idaho architect's idea of a Roman basilica, descending from heaven onto the prairie. Walking into the church, I did not see any connection to the church I knew from my youth. Nothing acknowledged the Jesuit-run parish that I grew up in, the laypeople who built the church over generations, or generations of Indigenous Catholics. My immediate impression was that it was a kind of architectural erasure, lacking visual markers of continuity or place. The parish history on the All Saints website confirmed my intuition. It reads, "All Saints Catholic Church is a deeply committed faith community that traces its roots back more than one hundred and fifty years."[1] It makes no mention

I am grateful to the people who have provided guidance for this research, including scholars at the North American Institute for Indigenous Theological Studies, Indigenous Catholic Research Council members, Philip Stevens

of the real people—Indigenous, missionary, and settler—who constituted the church community in this region. When I mentioned the website to a student at North American Institute for Indigenous Theological Studies, he described it as an instance of "settler audacity." The architecture and the parish history is a study in forgetfulness, especially when one considers the history of Indigenous Nimíipuu people (called Nez Perce by settlers).

"Settler audacity" is difficult to ignore when I return home. The house I grew up in stands seven miles from Lapwai, the administrative capital of the Nez Perce Reservation, on the land stolen from the Nimíipuu people. Some of my white friends grew up on farms on the reservation, acquired just a couple of generations ago through the allotment. It was a long time before I understood this history. And settler audacity is hard to ignore in my local church. The predominantly white parish now administers the church on the reservation, now described as a "station" of All Saints.

I am not Indigenous. My father was Black and non-practicing AME; my mother was of European descent and practicing Catholic. We moved to the ancestral homelands of the Nimíipuu when I was in grade school. It would not be unfair to label us *settlers*.[2] But *settler* fails to capture how we were welcomed into Indigenous life. My mother held the literal keys to Sacred Heart Catholic Church on the Nez Perce Reservation. She would often open the church before mass or begin eucharistic adoration when the caretaker of the church could not. I also knew the Nimíipuu people through my father, who was frequently on the Rez. I would accompany him to visit Allen Slickpoo, a Nimíipuu tribal archivist. Slickpoo had a small house with a back yard that slowly declined down to a creek. A dome-tent-sized sweat lodge constructed with heavy canvas tarps sat in his backyard, next to it a fire pit. My dad would go out and sweat. Allen Slickpoo was a revivalist of Seven Drums religion. His son, Allen Slickpoo Jr., confirmed to me that the

---

of the Warm Springs Apache people and University of Idaho, and Nimíipuu Catholics of Sacred Heart Church. Any inadequacies are mine alone.

[1]"Parish History," All Saints Catholic Church, accessed April 14, 2023, https://allsaintslewiston.org/parish-history/.

[2]Anthony Morgan prefers to refer to Black people as "displanted" rather than "settlers" to better portray the historical causes of Black presence on Indigenous land. Anthony Morgan, "Black People in Canada Are Not Settlers," *Ricochet* online, March 12, 2019.

sweat lodge was part of the family homestead. Slickpoo Jr., also a Seven Drums revivalist, comes from a Nez Perce Catholic family. In a 1995 interview, he discussed his sweat lodge saying, "This is sacred. This is my church. This is one of the oldest religions, right here." He spoke about his grandfather Samuel: "My grandfather and others used to practice their own religion, and on Sunday, they'd be Catholics."[3] Slickpoo Jr.'s comments might be taken as downplaying Catholic identity. However, the *very same people who transmitted Catholic faith in this region also preserved traditional Nimíipuu religion and culture.* I did not recognize it at the time, but the sweat lodge was a practice preserved by Nimíipuu Catholics at the Jesuit-run mission.

At this moment, I am attempting to reconcile my theology with the place that formed me as a Catholic. Vatican II asserts that the local church is fully the Church of Christ. I am committed to this teaching. But it also exposes some profound tensions. Despite my familial ties to the Nimíipuu, my church was and is a settler church. The church was not dropped on the Palouse from Rome but was woven into a fabric of human relationships that were distorted by dispossession, occupation, and settlement. These realities have mediated my belonging to a Catholic people. Recognition of the people whose land we occupy is long overdue in ecclesial spaces. Does this acknowledgment of land and people, however, not obligate me to revise my ecclesiology?

The Mediation of the Land

In her book *Virtual Communion*, Katherine Schmidt writes about the mediation of "ancillary spaces."[4] Ancillary spaces are, as she explains, the social spaces that radiate out from the Eucharistic assembly. They are the spaces through which individuals are brought into contact with Christian community, but also where Christian community lives. She explains, "These ancillary

---

[3]Richard Roesler, "Praying to a Different Beat: Group of Nez Perce Reviving Tribe's Native Beliefs; Not Everyone Is Pleased," *The Spokesman-Review*, July 31, 1995.

[4]Katherine G. Schmidt, *Virtual Communion: Theology of the Internet and the Catholic Sacramental Imagination* (Lanham, MD: Lexington/Fortress Academic, 2020), 131.

spaces constitute the broader social nature of the church without being the cause of it."[5] The church has—or should have—social density and porous borders through which we are drawn into the mysteries of salvation. As Henri de Lubac says, the sacraments effect union with Christ, thereby drawing us into Christian community; and by union with the community we are drawn to Christ. As Schmidt says, these are liminal spaces—"thresholds or doorways"—that enable the two-way movement between the Body of Christ and the community.[6] But also, they are not just in-between. They are a pattern of spatial relationships through which the Christian communion is realized visibly.

I want to think about the *land* in this mediating role, specifically in the mediation of a Catholic peoplehood. My Catholic belonging is mediated by *the local church*, a network of ecclesial relationships in all their particularity, density, culture, and geography. I was formed as a Catholic in Northern Idaho, in Nimíipuu territory, within the matrices of Indigenous life and settler presence. But it is easy to forget the land. Geography is often imagined as natural and unchanging (simply a container or extended space). This sense of geography erases the activity of its production, legitimating the way things are or helping us forget the violence that made it so. But geography is not static and neutral, but rather historically produced and ideological. In her book *Demonic Grounds* Katherine McKittrick explains, "Geography is not, however, secure and unwavering; we produce space, we produce its meanings, and we work very hard to make geography what it is."[7] Dominant geographies *place* bodies and peoples "'within an ideological order,' unevenly."[8] The ghetto, the redlined neighborhoods, the reservation.

In *The Christian Imagination*, Willie Jennings diagnoses the Christian entanglement in the production of these dominant geographies. Due to colonization and enslavement, people were grafted to the Body of Christ under conditions of geographical

[5]Schmidt, *Virtual Communion*, 131.

[6]Schmidt, *Virtual Communion*, 132.

[7]Katherine McKittrick, *Demonic Grounds: Black Women and the Cartographies of Struggle* (Minneapolis: University of Minnesota Press, 2006), x.

[8]McKittrick, *Demonic Grounds*, xv.

displacement. Jennings writes that the "discovery and conquest began a process of transformation of land and identity. . . . The deepest theological distortion taking place is that the earth, the ground, the spaces, and places are being removed as living organizers of identity and facilitators of identity."[9] Colonialism, he explains, was not only about control over territory but also a process of human displacement for planting and extraction. He adds, "The earth itself was barred from being a constant signifier of identity."[10] And as a result, skin rather than the earth became the key marker of who we are.

When I look to the Palouse, however, I find different conditions. Indigenous people in the Northwest were never a people who are simply removed from their relationship to land. *Settler colonialism sought their reconfiguration through land*. Early European Catholic and Protestant missionaries joined state processes of geographical transformation of land and people. And the preservation of Indigenous life required geographic struggle. To tell the story of the church I grew up in, I need to foreground the land.

I am going to highlight three moments where land has mediated peoplehood on the Palouse, that is, where land, spirituality, and identity were entwined and contested: first, the Indigenous prophetic resistance to settlement; second, the Euro-Christian missionary imposition of new agricultural practices and patterns of settled life; and third, amid these spiritual struggles over land, the founders of the church in my region, Nez Perce Catholics, preserved traditional relationships to land and to each other by inscribing the church within their geographies.

It is the story of the *Numipunm Wéetespe* (Nez Perce Earth) to which I must turn.

Nimipunm Wéetespe (Nimíipuu Earth)

The Palouse is the high grasslands region of the Columbia Plateau in Washington State, Idaho, and Oregon. Its prairies and rolling hills meet the west side of the Rocky Mountains and the Blue Mountains to the south. It is now an agricultural region

---

[9]Willie James Jennings, *The Christian Imagination: Theology and the Origins of Race* (New Haven, CT: Yale University Press, 2010), 39.

[10]Jennings, *The Christian Imagination*, 43.

that produces wheat and peas. The Palouse is the home of the Nimíipuu (or Nez Perce, as they were called by French traders), the Schitsu'umsh (Coeur d'Alene), the Salish, the Spokan, and other Indigenous peoples. The Palouse is a place of recent Indigenous displacement and dispossession, but Indigenous presence is ancient and continuous.[11] The elevations of traditional Nimíipuu territory range from 650 feet in the west to 9,000 feet in the Bitterroot Mountains in the East where late summer and autumn camps were located.[12] Traditional ways of life that continued relatively undisturbed until the 1860s were entwined in this diverse topography. The deep canyons carved by the rivers—where Nimíipuu made their winter settlements—remain temperate in the winter and hot in the summer. When spring came and migrating animals returned, the winter camp broke up and families from different bands and linguistic groups would end up in the same area, hunting or fishing together. With the return of the salmon, what Christopher Miller has described as "task villages" made up of people from different linguistic groups were formed at sites like The Dalles and Kettle Falls.[13] In late summer and autumn, groups would form for hunting or fishing at new locations, returning to rebuild their winter settlements in late autumn.

Different bands used distinctive traditional lands and the intensive exchange and cooperation among groups ensured survival. Because the Columbia Plateau is made up of many microclimates, a failure to find food in one place would not result in regional disaster.[14] Nimíipuu identity was built within these networks, exchanges, and movements. The relationship between Nez Perce earth and the individual is particular. During the vision quest,

[11]The Cooper's Ferry site in Nimíipuu territory has been occupied for at least 16,000 years. See Paulette F. C. Steeves, *The Indigenous Paleolithic of the Western Hemisphere* (Lincoln: University of Nebraska Press, 2021), 204.

[12]Alan G. Marshall and Samuel M. Watters, "Nimíipuu at the Edge of History," in *Rising from the Ashes: Survival, Sovereignty, and Native America*, ed. William Willard, Alan G. Marshall, and J. Diane Pearson (Lincoln: University of Nebraska Press, 2020), 6.

[13]Christopher L. Miller, *Prophetic Worlds: Indians and Whites on the Columbia Plateau* (New Brunswick, NJ: Rutgers University Press, 1985). See Larry Cebula, *Plateau Indians and the Quest for Spiritual Power, 1700–1850* (Lincoln: University of Nebraska Press, 2003), 23.

[14]Marshall and Watters, "Nimíipuu at the Edge of History," 6–13.

almost universal among Plateau peoples, young people would seek their guardian spirit on particular mountains. The spirit, or *wyakin* in Nimipuutímpt, appeared as an animal who would grant them spiritual power to serve their people. If the guardian spirit was the salmon, the individual might possess the charism of fishing. The *wyakin* would tie them to traditional locations for fishing and patterns of life. They would return to particular places to hunt, gather herbs and medicines, and to pray. *Numipunm Wéetespe* governed the social relations among the animals, plants, and spirits.

The interdependence on each other, on the land, and spirits was celebrated with winter dances. After building winter camps, different bands would begin to hold celebrations. Ending in one location, the dances sprang up in another camp, with neighbors visiting, and so on until the enthusiasm for these dances wore out. The winter dances occasioned travel, visiting relatives, and giving of gifts. The dances, however, were primarily spiritual. They celebrated relationship with the guardian spirits and the earth, and they involved singing, a medium of spiritual power.[15] The winter dances were the occasion of religious exchange. Indeed, Christianity spread first to the Nimíipuu people during the winter dances.[16]

Alan Marshall and Sam Watters explain that Nimíipuu Wéetespe, Nez Perce Earth, is a social reality. Every individual has specific knowledge and relationship with the land. They write, "No single person could embody all the knowledge, the motivation, or the full behavioral repertoire needed to produce all the artifacts necessary for Nimíipuu individual, social, and spiritual survival. . . . It was a community disciplined by the 'Nez Perce Land.'"[17] Land is certainly material, but it is not only territory or space. It is, as Yellowknives Dene scholar Glen Coulthard says, a "system of reciprocal relations and obligations."[18] To put it another way, land is the complex network of exchanges by which the human, the nonhuman peoples, and spirits are in harmony.

[15]Miller, *Prophetic Worlds*, 21.

[16]Cebula, *Plateau Indians and the Quest for Spiritual Power*, 82.

[17]Marshall and Watters, "Nimíipuu at the Edge of History," 8.

[18]Glen Coulthard, *Red Skin, White Masks: Rejecting the Colonial Politics of Recognition* (Minneapolis: University of Minnesota Press, 2014), 13.

The Indigenous struggle for land is not just about ownership or juridical control; it is about preserving these systems of relations and obligations. The land mediates peoplehood.

Prophetic Resistance to Settlement

Even before European missionaries and settlers arrived, Palouse Indigenous people's lives were being spatially transformed by the gun, the horse, and smallpox. These disruptions and the eruptive activity of Mount St. Helens or Mount Hood in the eighteenth century occasioned new prophetic activity. Some Palouse people were practicing forms of Christian practice received from other Indigenous people. They began to measure the week in seven days, keep the sabbath, hold religious services on the sabbath, with dancing following services, then gambling and horse racing. Christianity may have exercised an influence on Indigenous prophets, who foretold the coming of a new human being, the end of the world, and the resurrection of the dead. In the 1820s, a Nimíipuu prophet, Tawis Waikt, sang a song that was passed down through other Nimíipuu singers: "My spirit tells me that this earth is going to be turned over, and the *koq álx* (buffalo or cattle) is going to be all over this country, and there will be no more vacant land as there is today."[19] By singing this, Tawis Waikt foretold the "overturning" of an entire way of life.

If land mediated peoplehood, by changing the land, settler society threatened to sever the bonds of common life. Sometime between 1858 and 1860, Wanapum prophet *Shmoquala* (or Smohalla) died while mourning the death of his young daughter. The people gathered, prepared his body, and prayed throughout the night. In the morning, his body twitched, he opened his eyes, rose to his knees, but did not speak. Two days later he gathered people around to tell how he visited the "land in the sky" and *Nami Piap*, the Creator, gave him a sacred *washat* and religious songs. It was the second time he had returned from the dead. After the first time, he took the name Smohalla—meaning preacher, dreamer, or teacher—and began to foretell the destruction of the world

[19] In Loren Olsen and Sol Webb, *Nez Perce Songs of Historical Significance: As Sung by "Sol" Webb* (Nez Perce Indian Tribe of Idaho, in cooperation with the Music Department, Washington State University, 1972), 3.

and the restoration of the old ways of life. Smohalla preached peaceful resistance to the settler incursion and the preservation of traditional Indigenous life. But he also introduced novel elements inspired by Christian contact, erecting a churchlike structure and gathering his followers for a ritual meal. Instead of bread and wine, it was water and salmon. Adherents of *Washani* religion resisted being relegated to reservations. This was a religious perspective on the land.[20] Followers of Smohalla said that those who signed treaties would be punished by God. The key point of contention was the entire *settled* existence. Smohalla preached, "You ask me to plow the ground! Shall I take a knife and tear my mother's bosom? Then when I die she will not take me to her bosom to rest. You ask me to dig for stone! Shall I dig under her skin for her bones? You ask me to cut grass and make hay and sell it and be rich like white men! But how dare I cut off my mother's hair? It is a bad law and my people cannot obey it. I want my people to stay with me here. All the dead men will come to life again; their spirits will come to their bodies again. We must wait here, in the homes of our fathers, and be ready to meet them in the bosom of our mother."[21]

Indian Agents characterized *Washani* religion as an extremist cult that taught against agricultural cultivation and land improvement.[22] This was not simply Indigenous conservatism. It was a spiritual perspective on settling and cultivation of land that was a key contributor to the Nez Perce War in 1877. In 1863, the US government coerced some Nez Perce chiefs to sign a treaty, an abrogation of the 1855 treaty that established the geographical boundaries of the Nez Perce territory. The 1863 treaty—known

---

[20]See Chad S. Hamill, *Songs of Power and Prayer in the Columbia Plateau: The Jesuit, the Medicine Man, and the Indian Hymn Singer* (Corvallis: Oregon State University Press, 2012), 13–17; Clifford E. Trafzer and Margery Ann Beach, "Smohalla, the Washani, and Religion," *American Indian Quarterly* 9, no. 3 (Summer 1985), 309–24.

[21]Junius Wilson MacMurray, "The 'Dreamers' of the Columbia River Valley, in Washington Territory," in *Transactions of the Albany Institute* XI (Albany, NY: Weed, Parsons & Co., 1887), 248.

[22]See "Report of Civil and Military Commission to the Nez Percé Indians, Washington Territory and the Northwest," *Report of the Commissioner of Indian Affairs*, H.R. Exec. Doc. No. 1, 45th Cong., 2nd Sess. (1877), 607–10.

as the "Thief Treaty" or the "Steal Treaty"—additionally reduced the Nimíipuu lands by around 90 percent. Chiefs of bands whose traditional land was outside of the new reservation boundaries walked out of the treaty council. But over fifty chiefs who lived within the new reservation boundaries signed the agreement, which was enforced against all the Nez Perce.

At the Lapwai Council (1877), chiefs met with General Oliver O. Howard and Nez Perce Agent John Montieth, who ordered the non-treaty Nez Perces onto the reservation. Some bands already abandoned their traditional lands for the reservation. Others whose winter camps were on the ceded territory rebelled. Chief Toohoolhoolzote stated, "White people get together, measure the earth, and then divide it. . . . The earth is part of my body . . . and I never gave up the earth."[23] Chief Joseph, the Nez Perce uprising leader and follower of Smohalla, said, "The Creative Power, when he made the earth, made no marks, no lines of division or separation on it." Chief Joseph's father had told him, "This country holds your father's body. Never sell the bones of your father and your mother."[24] The root source of Indigenous resistance to settlement was their spiritual and moral perspective on the land.

Chief Joseph led several bands of Nimíipuu and Palouse people who refused the treaty toward Canada. The US Army pursued them for five months and 1,170 miles. The Indigenous rebels fought a series of skirmishes before being captured and exiled to Oklahoma. Following the end of the Nez Perce War and the surrender of Chief Joseph, the government forced or induced native people onto land. The Homestead Act of 1874 offered 160 acres to Indians filing for a homestead. The law required them to make improvements to the land in order to keep it. Strict Washani religionists resisted this. Eli L. Huggins, who visited Smohalla around 1890, reported that he said, "My young men shall never work. . . . Men who work cannot dream. And wisdom comes to us from dreams."[25] For Smohalla, land mediates spiritual power, and

[23]Cited in Trafzer and Margery Ann Beach, "Smohalla, the Washani, and Religion," 317. Original in Document 213B/70 McWhorter Collection, WSU.

[24]Young Joseph and William H. Hare, "An Indian's View of Indian Affairs," *North American Review* 128, no. 269 (1879): 419.

[25]Eli L. Huggins, "Smohalla, the Prophet of Priest Rapids," *Overland Monthly and Out West Magazine* 17, no. 98 (February 1891): 213.

peoplehood is tied to the land. Agricultural cultivation sought by the government and missionaries was incompatible with receiving the gifts of the earth and spiritual wisdom.

The Jesuits and the Conversion of the Land

In her book *Heathen*, Kathryn Gin Lum, dedicates a chapter to landscapes. She notes the association that Christian missionaries in the US made between conversion and land. In this imagination, the land itself is *heathen*: wild, untamed, uncultivated, and neglected.[26] Conversion would bring about transformation of both the soul and the land. Jesuit missionaries in the nineteenth-century Northwest shared this association. When Belgian-born Jesuit missionary Pierre-Jean De Smet (1801–1873) entered the interior Northwest in the 1840s, his vision was the establishment of a "kingdom" of Christian Indians in the Rocky Mountains. Fearing white settlers would bring a "system of extermination" westward, he wanted to establish control over land to impede this flow. De Smet was correct about the threat of white incursion.[27] But he was insistent that the semi-nomadic lifestyle of Indigenous people was an obstacle to conversion and to land claims.

In his chronicle of the mission, Fr. De Smet recounts arriving in 1840 in the camp of Tjolzhitsay, a Salish chief who greets the Blackrobes after sending a delegation for them in Saint Louis. Tjolzhitsay says the Great Spirit has heard their prayer to send Blackrobes to a "people, poor, plain, and submerged in the darkness of ignorance." Bracket De Smet's description of a people in darkness for a moment and listen to how he responded to Tjolzhitsay's greeting. He writes:

> I then spoke at length to these good people upon the subject of religion. I told them the object of my mission, and asked

[26]Kathryn Gin Lum, *Heathen: Religion, Race, and American History* (Cambridge, MA: Harvard University Press, 2022), 73–96.

[27]In 1838 De Smet founded the mission in Potawatomi territory for people who had been removed from Illinois. De Smet could have anticipated that adopting European-style agriculture and customs would not protect their claims to the land. He arrived in Salish country in what is now Wyoming in 1840, just two years after the Cherokee were forcibly removed in the Trail of Tears.

> them to give up their wandering life and settle in a fertile district. All declared themselves ready and willing to exchange the bow and arrow for the spade and the plow. . . . After a short instruction, night prayers were said. Before retiring they sang in admirable harmony three hymns in praise of the Great Spirit of their own composition. No words can express how deeply I was touched.[28]

This was a moment of encounter manifesting the Salish reception of the Jesuits, and Jesuit receptiveness to the song and prayer of the Salish people. But the Jesuits also insisted that the spade and the plow were just as essential to conversion as the rosary or the cross. A prominent element in the Rocky Mountain Mission narratives is the attempt of Jesuit missionaries to convince Indigenous people to adopt practices of permanent settlement and agricultural production.[29]

French Jesuit Nicholas Point was one of the men called to establish this stability. Point arrived with De Smet in September 1841 in the territory of the Bitterroot Salish and began to construct a wood-frame church in the Bitterroot Valley. He had trained as an architect and was also a self-taught artist who worked in pencil, pen, and watercolor. He drew images of missions built around European-style churches and an ordered agricultural life. He proceeded to erect a Salish village on a quadrangle: houses were fifty feet apart, each had a lawn of sixty square feet, and the church was at the center of one edge.[30] From a Salish perspective, the open layout of the village was impractical and could not be defended against enemies. And the Jesuits lacked awareness of the Salish religious and social understanding of the land. In *Wilderness Kingdom*, Point writes

[28]Eugene Laveille, *The Life of Father De Smet, SJ*, trans. Marian Lindsay (New York: P. J. Kenedy, 1915), 108–9.

[29]See Catherine O'Donnell, *Jesuits in the North American Colonies and the United States: Faith, Conflict, and Adaptation* (Leiden: Brill, 2020). See also Cornelius M. Buckley, *Nicholas Point, SJ: His Life and Northwest Indian Chronicles* (Chicago: Loyola University Press, 1989).

[30]Ellen Baumler, "A Cross in the Wilderness: St. Mary's Mission Celebrates 175 Years," *Montana: The Magazine of Western History* 66, no. 1 (Spring 2016): 25.

> It was our first concern to introduce them, little by little, to a much more sedentary existence. This could be one only by substituting the fruits of agriculture for those of the chase, the innocent pleasures of the fireside for those offered by the varied life of the hunter. Above all, religion had to assume an important position in their lives. Hence, the construction of a chapel first; then the cultivation of fields.[31]

The History of the Diocese of Boise captures this perfectly. "When spring came Father Point initiated his Indians into the mysteries of plowing and planting."[32]

When the Nez Perce War broke out, the Spokane Council of 1877 convened representatives of General Oliver Otis Howard and chiefs of the Spokane and Coeur d'Alene people. Howard was concerned that the Spokane and Coeur d'Alene people would join Chief Joseph's uprising. The Jesuits attended this meeting as well. Sicilian Jesuit Joseph Cataldo convinced US army representatives that his "Catholic Indians" were not going to join Chief Joseph's rebellion. The Report to the Secretary of War reads that on the second day of the council, "Father Cataldo, at the earnest solicitation of the inspector, then gave the Indians excellent instruction, especially in the direction of the cultivation of the soil, the sin of sloth, the necessity of giving the inspector a decided answer."[33] In Cataldo's attempt to dissociate the Jesuit mission from Chief Joseph's rebellion, he signaled that his "Catholic Indians" were pious, they were cultivating the soil, and they were settled.[34]

The Dawes Act of 1887 required the division of the reserva-

---

[31]Nicholas Point, *Wilderness Kingdom: Indian Life in the Rocky Mountains: 1840–1847: The Journals and Paintings of Nicholas Point*, trans. Joseph P. Donnelly (Chicago: Loyola Chicago Press, 1967), 43. Translated from Point's manuscript *Souvenirs des Montagnes Roucheuses*.

[32]Cyprian Bradley, *History of the Diocese of Boise, 1863–1952* (Boise, ID: Caxton, 1953), 75.

[33]*Report of the Secretary of War*, H.R. Exec. Doc. No. 1, 45th Cong., 2nd Sess. (1877), 645.

[34]Cataldo's assertion that his "Catholic Indians" refused to join the rebellion was inaccurate. See J. Diane Pearson, *The Nez Perces in the Indian Territory: Nimíipuu Survival* (Norman: University of Oklahoma Press, 2008), 244. Cataldo, however, sought to keep Catholic Nez Perce and Coeur d'Alene warriors neutral in the war the US Army waged on the Nez Perce bands led by Chief Joseph.

tion lands into individual plots awarded to individuals. Alice C. Fletcher, anthropologist and Indian agent of the United States government, proceeded to divide the jointly held Nez Perce Reservation land into small allotments.[35] In 1893, the Nimíipuu were forced to accept an agreement by which the unalloted land would be declared "surplus." Surplus land was sold to the United States for the purposes of homesteading. From an original homeland of over thirteen million acres, the Nimíipuu people were forced onto a small reservation subsequently subdivided into individual parcels. Moreover, the Nimíipuu had to demonstrate that they were appropriately and successfully cultivating the land. If not cultivated or insufficiently used, these parcels would be designated by the government as surplus and sold to settlers. The allotment functioned to reorder aboriginal economic life toward settled agricultural practices. Indian education supported by the US government and often carried out by religious groups aimed at supplanting Indigenous knowledge and practices with new ones.

For both Protestant and Catholic European missionaries in the Palouse during the late nineteenth century, land practices were entwined with Christian identity. For the Jesuit missionaries, cultivation of the land was a precondition of conversion or, at least, cultivation was so strongly associated with conversion that farming became one of the principal mission goals. More than a practical prerequisite for sustenance or for gathering people together for preaching, *land* became the principal marker of a Christian subjectivity. And the power to remake land a principal marker of Christian belonging. Fred Moten and Stefano Harney recognize the capacity for ownership of land is entwined with the power to improve land for monocultural production. "The ability to own," they explain, "—and that ability's first derivative, self-possession—is entwined with the ability to make more productive. In order to be improved, to be rendered more productive, land must be violently reduced to its productivity, which is the regulatory diminishment and management of earthly

[35]See Nicole Tonkovich, *The Allotment Plot: Alice C. Fletcher, E. Jane Gay, and Nez Perce Survivance* (Lincoln: University of Nebraska Press, 2012).

generativity."[36] Settlement and cultivation of land became sacraments of colonial Christian subjectivity. And at the moment when the Nez Perce were forced onto the reservation, land mediated Christian belonging.

Indigenous Catholic Geographies

My church was founded amid profound geographical dislocation and removal of the Nimíipuu people from traditional winter homes to the reservation. In the face of dispossession, allotments, and settlement, Indigenous Christians were not passive victims but frequently sought to preserve traditional relationships to land and their people.

In 1867, Fr. Joseph Cataldo was sent to Fort Lapwai to take over the government-established day school, but Presbyterian Nimíipuu opposed his presence. White Presbyterian missionaries, Presbyterian Nimíipuu, and Indian agents opposed a Catholic mission, forcing Cataldo to set up in Lewiston. Lapwai—close to the Presbyterian Spalding mission—was the center of tribal government, a US Army fort, and the site of government schools. And Nimíipuu Presbyterian leadership tended to enforce white cultural hegemony, imposing norms on dress, religion, language, culture, and alcohol use.

Cataldo began to minister to the Nimíipuu people who were already Catholic, though possibly unbaptized. From 1867 to 1870, Cataldo began living on the reservation by the invitation of Indigenous Catholics. Chief Stuptup invited him to stay on his land on the Clearwater River above the Spalding Mission and to learn the Nez Perce language. And with permission of the Indian Agent, and with help from white miners, Cataldo had a cabin built on Stuptup's land and lived there.[37] The first adult Nimíipuu man he baptized was Lakóskan in 1869, in a cabin near Arrow, Idaho.[38] Two chiefs, Slickpoo (Weeptes Sumpq'in [Feather Shirt]),

[36]Stefano Harney and Fred Moten, *All Incomplete* (New York: Minor Compositions, 2021), 29.

[37]Joseph Cataldo, "Father Cataldo's Missionary Career" (handwritten narrative in St. Joseph's Mission Baptismal Register), Nez Perce National Historical Park Archives, St. Joseph's Mission (hereafter, NEPE), 110–11

[38]"Mission Register, St. Joseph's Mission, Culdesac, Idaho," NEPE, 6.

also called T'simslikpuus, Anglicized as Slickpoo) and Wyaskasit, invited Cataldo onto their land to give catechetical instruction. The chiefs would not give consent for their children or their band to be baptized out of concern for what Cataldo relates as "strong opposition of the Protestant Indians."[39] Cataldo was reassigned to the Coeur d'Alene Mission. But Lakóskan traveled to the mission one hundred miles north to recall him. Cataldo writes what Lakóskan told him: "'Blackgown, you know that I am the only man you baptized among the Nez Perces; so the chiefs sent me to call you back. We did not listen to you; or rather to God; but now all are sorry. They want you back and promised to be baptized.'" Cataldo comments, "Joseph Lakoskan added much about opposition to his work by the personnel of the Indian agency and urged the priest to hurry back."[40] When Cataldo returned in 1872, Chief Slickpoo brought the children before him, and the children flawlessly recited the prayers taught to them previously. A surge of conversions and baptisms followed. Chief Webb was baptized with his small clan. In 1873, more than one hundred Nimíipuu were baptized. Many received their first communion at the camp of Simon Ky Way Puts (alteratively rendered Kaiwepaz, Kawipas) along Sweet Water Creek.[41]

Cataldo told the story of Wyaskasit (or Uyaskasit), a medicine man and chief who invited him to stay in a teepee and give instruction. Wyaskasit wanted the baptism of his entire band, but his own obstacle was that he had two wives. Wyaskasit made the heart-wrenching decision to let go of the younger wife but take care of her material needs. Though she was devastated by his decision, after praying the rosary, she was overcome by God's grace. The conversion narrative written by Cataldo reads: "With the baby in her arms she walked toward Father Cataldo. When she raised her head, all could see the tears, glistening in her eyes. Lifting up her child to the priest, she said, "Here is my little boy. Baptize him. Let me too receive this grace. I am converted. I join

[39]Joseph Cataldo, "Father Cataldo's Missionary Career," NEPE, 112.

[40]"Statement of Michael O'Malley, Representing the Catholic Mission at Slickpoo, Idaho," Hearings Before the Subcommittee on Public Lands of the Committee on Interior and Insular Affairs, S. Doc. 88th Cong., 2nd sess. (1964), 75.

[41]"Mission Register, St. Joseph's Mission, Culdesac, Idaho," NEPE, 11–12.

my sacrifice with that of Wyaskasit."[42] Cataldo's recollections of the early mission are sometimes saccharine and dramatic conversion narratives, but he provides a valuable understanding of the early Indigenous Catholic Church in my region.

The Jesuits were received onto the lands of Nimíipuu who are geographically on the margins of the sphere of influence of the tribal government, the US Army, and the Presbyterian leadership. Many were refugees resettled from lands seized in the 1863 treaty who organized themselves in a traditional manner as small bands composed of several extended families. Cataldo described several Catholic chiefs as being "in control, on the north bank of the Clearwater."[43] After a protracted struggle with the Indian Agent, Cataldo received permission to set up a mission church in 1874. And Chief Slickpoo invited him to set up on his land. This was such an interesting moment. Slickpoo belonged to the Siminekempu (Confluence) band of Nimíipuu whose traditional winter camps were at the confluence of the Snake and Clearwater rivers. The treaty of 1863 had already dispossessed his people of their land. Slickpoo resettled his people onto the reservation, about ten miles from the city of Lapwai, along a small creek now referred to as Mission Creek. But there was continued concern on the reservation about the incursion by whites. Slickpoo invited the Jesuits to establish their mission on his land, a place called Assinima (from Ahise, a medicinal plant found there). Why did he take the initiative to ensure that the church of what would be called St. Joseph's Mission would be built on the new land of his displaced people?

On my trip out to St. Joseph's Mission, I saw why. From Lapwai, you follow Lapwai Creek to Mission Creek, and then about five miles up a winding road through the tight valley. I noticed that even by car, it was a trek to get to the church. The old mission church was being rehabilitated. When the mission closed in 1958, the National Park Service took care of the church for a while, but now it is privately owned. The mission was remote from everything. The Jesuits, there at the invitation of the various Catholic chiefs, were not in the same situation as the Presbyterians. The Jesuits had little power over these spaces. The mission was being

---

[42]Joseph Cataldo, SJ, "The Story of Abraham Wyaskasit," NEPE.
[43]Cataldo, "Father Cataldo's Missionary Career," 115.

founded on *Numipunm Wéetespe*, the Nez Perce earth.

Photos from the early twentieth century show the church, a rectory, barns, and numerous small houses that stood on the other side of the road. Deward Walker's map of the Slickpoo Catholic Mission showed there were thirty-one houses, and between the houses and Mission Creek were two sweat baths, where Nimíipuu ceremonies took place. Cataldo's journal evidences how the mission land was used. The "Catholic Indians," as he called them, built cabins near Mission Creek. "They came with their families to spend a week, or a few days, at Christmas, at Easter, or at Corpus Christi to attend service in the church."[44] Anthony Morvillo, a Jesuit linguist, stated that on Sundays, entire bands would come to the church from up to twenty miles away and, on major feasts, Protestants and "infidels" as he called them, would come too. Nimíipuu would show up during Corpus Christi, with over a hundred participating in Catholic ceremonies.[45] A. D. Willebrand, SJ, concurred:

> On the feast of Corpus Christi, which is the big feast of the mission, and on Christmas and Easter we have Indians from all over the reservation, from Lapwai, Sweetwater, Culdesac, Webb, Spaulding, and from the surrounding neighbourhoods. There is an old Indian Catechist called Jim Doolittle who always leads the Corpus Christi procession. In old times the Indians came on horseback and in wagons and camped for several days. Now they come in cars.[46]

For many years, the cabins at the mission were not permanent residences but housing for major festivals.

The Catholic Nimíipuu elected a chief of the Catholic Nez Perces and selected a council of chiefs, a body independent from the Jesuits.[47] Unlike the Presbyterian-controlled council of chiefs that would later be recognized by the US government, this was not

---

[44]Cataldo, "Father Cataldo's Missionary Career," 118.

[45]"Corpus Christi," *The Teller* (May 31, 1894), 4.

[46]A. D. Willebrand, SJ, "Letter to John F. Hurley," n.d., NEPE.

[47]Deward Walker, *Conflict and Schism in Nez Perce Acculturation: A Study of Religion and Politics* (Moscow: University of Idaho Press, 1985), 63.

a tribal political body. Rather, it concerned itself with organizing the life of the small village around the church and enforcing a kind of order. Unlike the councils on the Presbyterian missions, the Catholics did not ban drinking, gambling, long hair, or native clothing. Instead, they led celebrations of major holy days, translated prayers, and created songs in their language.

Nez Perce Catholics preserved traditional Nimíipuu cultural and religious practices, and the Jesuit priests were more permissive of these than the Presbyterian missionaries on the reservation. Historically, Catholic Nimíipuu tended to maintain the traditions of shamanism and relationships with tutelary spirits. Traditional dances and gatherings were aligned with major liturgical feasts. Anthropologist Deward Walker notes that the Catholic Nimíipuu (along with practitioners of traditional Nimíipuu religion and backsliding Presbyterians) kept up the "Indian" celebrations, like tutelary spirit dances. Catholic Nimíipuu were numerous among those participating in traditional celebrations.[48] A Catholic Nimíipuu woman at Sacred Heart Catholic Church in Lapwai related to me that her Catholic grandmother participated in medicine dances at multiday church gatherings.

I do not want to paint an idealistic picture of the mission. It was founded only because of the massive displacement of Nimíipuu people and their concentration on the reservation.

However, I think that we can make some observations about Nimíipuu Catholic geographies in the late nineteenth century. First, the chapels on the land of Catholic Nimíipuu chiefs and, subsequently, St. Joseph's Mission were not primarily spaces of surveillance, discipline, and assimilation into the national space. The remoteness of sites for ecclesial gathering, as well as the presence of the Jesuits, provided distance from the overlapping hegemonic forces of the army, the tribal government, and the Presbyterian churches in Lapwai. Instead, these were spaces through which traditional relationships among people and land could be preserved in the face of the pressures of colonial assimilation. Second, the Jesuits were invited guests on the land, at least initially. Because of their dependence on the graciousness of the Catholic chiefs, they had to enter into a cultural and religious dialogue. The mission became a space of continuity with traditional Indigenous

[48]Walker, *Conflict and Schism*, 64.

social and land relations. Third, in gathering for the Eucharist and major feast days, the Nimíipuu were able to approximate the patterns of travel, celebration, and renewal of relationship traditional to the winter festivities and dances.[49] In the history of my church, land mediates peoplehood.

Following Michel de Certeau, one might say that the Nimíipuu employed the tactics or "*ways of using*" or "manipulation" of the hegemonic "organization of space."[50] But for Certeau the weak have only the option of transforming the spatial relations imposed upon them. Nimíipuu history suggests an already-existing geography. Nimíipuu ethnographer Nakia Williamson-Cloud speaks of "continuity" that the Nimíipuu have maintained with the land that is embodied in material culture.[51] Even if the Nimíipuu could not escape the geographies the state was imposing upon them, we still speak with Mark Rifkin of "countervailing political mappings," that is, the geographies that existed before and continued to exist in "defiance" of the settler colonial order.[52]

Conclusion: "Unforgetting" Nimipunm Wéetespe

On the Palouse, land mediates Nimíipuu and Catholic peoplehood. Amid enormous coercive pressures to settle—ostensibly legitimating their claims to land—Nimíipuu Catholics preserved

---

[49]Paul L. Gareau and Jeanine Leblanc make a similar observation. They argue that Catholic Mi'kma'ki and Métis practices of pilgrimage conserve traditional epistemology and relations to water, land, and people. They "are more than sites of institutional Catholic pilgrimage; they are movements in relational engagement through traditional territory and homelands to sacred places that affirm *pilgrimage as peoplehood*." "Pilgrimage as Peoplehood: Indigenous Relations and Self-Determination at Places of Catholic Pilgrimage in Mi'kma'ki and the Métis Homeland," *Material Religion* 18, no. 1 (2022): 32–45.

[50]Michel de Certeau, *The Practice of Everyday Life*, trans. Steven Rendall (Berkeley: University of California Press, 1988), xiii, 38.

[51]Nakia Williamson-Cloud, "On the Continuity of the Nez Perce People and Their Relationship to the Land," Audio recording, Plateau Peoples' Web Portal, Washington State University, accessed May 15, 2023, https://plateauportal.libraries.wsu.edu/digital-heritage/nakia-williamson-cloud-continuity-nez-perce-people-and-their-relationship-land.

[52]Mark Rifkin, *Manifesting America: The Imperial Construction of U.S. National Space* (Oxford: Oxford University Press, 2009), 28.

traditional relationships with humans, other-than-human peoples, and the land. Traditional song and dance, locations of spiritual power, ritual, and social relations were renewed within Catholic liturgy, feasts, and pilgrimage. Nimíipuu Catholics transmitted and preserved Indigenous practices of land and spiritualities of movement.

The local church that formed me contains many complexities, and I am certain that I have failed to captured them all here. But I want to begin to tell its story better. Alexis Shotwell says that "a central feature of white settler colonial subjectivity is forgetting," that is the active, continuous suppression of knowledge of our present and past. Its opposite, unforgetting, requires not only the "acknowledgment" of the past but "reckoning with the social organization of forgetting."[53] A professor at the North American Institute for Indigenous Theological Studies said to me, "What a simple act it would be to tell the parish history on the website." In the case of the church on the Palouse, unforgetting begins with the land, by seeing a Catholic people whose identities have been mediated by the land. Moreover, it requires the active preservation of traditional patterns of relationship among people, other-than-human peoples, and the earth that are mutual and reciprocal. First, we can tell the story about who we are and how we came to be here on this land: the removals, allotments, the land theft, and also the cooperative relationships, sharing of resources, and love. Second, we can seek the removal of the designation of "station" of Sacred Heart Church in Lapwai, a title that designates subordination and dependence on the white parish in Lewiston. Sacred Heart needs a new designation and a new kind of administration. Third, and most important, we can seek the recovery of the land relationships that were common among the Indigenous founders of the church in our region. The gathering of Catholic people for holidays, feasts, and pilgrimage must renew these "reciprocal relations and obligations," perhaps by gathering on the land of Nimíipuu elders and by convening distant relatives, to meet together, to camp together, dance, sweat, dig camas root, fish, and hunt.[54]

[53]Alexis Shotwell, "Unforgetting as a Collective Tactic," in *White Self-Criticality beyond Anti-Racism: How Does It Feel to Be a White Problem?* ed. George Yancy (Lanham, MD: Lexington Books, 2015), 58, 65.

[54]Coulthard, *Red Skin, White Masks,*13.

Patty Krawec says, "You may not be guilty of the act of dispossession, but it is a relationship that you have inherited."[55] And for the church there is an obligation to unforget the land that makes the people.

[55]Patty Krawec, *Becoming Kin: An Indigenous Call to Unforgetting the Past and Reimagining Our Future* (Minneapolis: Broadleaf, 2022), 39.

Do Culture, Place, and Local Church Matter?

A New Schema of the *Sensus Fidei* for a Synodal Church

Deepan Rajaratnam

At the heart of Pope Francis's synodal reception of Vatican II lies the council's articulation of the sense of the faithful. Examining Francis's pontificate, *peritus* for the universal Synod of Bishops Rafael Luciani argues that Pope Francis's synodal reforms are less about synodality itself as they are a way to create structures and implement processes for the whole church that reflect Vatican II's theology of the sense of faith.[1] Similarly, Amanda Osheim, a leading scholar on the sense of the faithful, views synodality as essentially a "*ressourcement* of the *sensus fidelium*," and in this sense it is a continuation of the conciliar project of ecclesial reform.[2] Indeed, for those attentive to Pope Francis's penchant for pneumatic metaphors like "the flock has its nose to find new paths" or "the smell of the sheep," Pope Francis's strong pneumatology and the centrality of the sense of the faithful to his synodal reforms have been clear from the outset.[3]

[1]Rafael Luciani, *Synodality: A New Way of Proceeding in the Church*, trans. Joseph Owens (Mahwah, NJ: Paulist Press, 2022), 101.

[2]Amanda C. Osheim, "Stepping toward a Synodal Church," *Theological Studies* 80, no. 2 (2019): 391.

[3]Francis, *Evangelii Gaudium* (2013), nos. 31, 24. I have relied on the Vatican website for translation of papal and conciliar documents checking them against the original language and modifying them at times.

As a central category for synodality, the sense of the faithful is a communal, infallible, and Spirit-produced instinct that enables the church to grasp, know, and witness to the truth. Building on its conciliar basis in *Lumen Gentium* no. 12, recent scholarship has used the term *sensus fidelium* to name this communal capacity, the term *sensus fidei fidelis* to designate its personal complement, and the term *sensus fidei* to describe jointly these personal and communal capacities.[4] Retrospectively, the *sensus fidei* enables believers to judge spontaneously whether a particular teaching or practice conforms with the Gospel and the apostolic faith.[5] Prospectively, the *sensus fidei* enables believers to sense, in new historical and cultural contexts, the most appropriate ways to give authentic witness to the truth of Jesus Christ.[6] In other words, the *sensus fidei* enables Christians individually and communally to intuit the truth amid ambiguity and to exercise ecclesial mission in its religious and social dimensions.

To make sense of the council's articulation of the *sensus fidelium* and its relationship to different ecclesial vocations in the church, Ormond Rush—one of the foremost scholars on the *sensus fidelium*—develops a tripartite schematization of the *sensus fidelium*. In doing so, Rush takes up the trichotomy of laity, theologian, and bishop heavily used by postconciliar theologians to make sense of the Spirit's ordering of the church and the Spirit's work through the entire people of God. Drawing on this widely used trichotomy, Rush creatively models the *sensus fidelium* as three distinct but universal categories that name the collective exercise of the sense of faith by the majority of the church (*sensus laicorum*), by the global community of theologians (*sensus theologorum*), and by the college of bishops (*sensus episcoporum*).[7] By foregrounding the Spirit's work through the variously ordered *fideles*, or faithful, Rush builds on the council's attempt to overcome a pyramidal understanding of the church, and for this reason, Rush's work influences a number of postconciliar scholars who draw on his

[4]International Theological Commission (ITC), Sensus Fidei *in the Life of the Church* (2014), no. 3.

[5]ITC, Sensus Fidei *in the Life of the Church*, no. 49.

[6]ITC, Sensus Fidei *in the Life of the Church*, nos. 65, 70.

[7]Ormond Rush, *The Eyes of Faith: The Sense of the Faithful and the Church's Reception of Revelation* (Washington, DC: Catholic University of America Press, 2009), 251.

work to further tease out the unique contribution of laypeople to the church's missionary life.

Problematically however, in the ordinary, everyday lives of the faithful, the *sensus fidei* is primarily exercised and experienced amid a web of local relationships that is significantly more diverse than this trichotomy reflects. In addition, culture and place both uniquely inform the actual exercise of the *sensus fidei* and concretely shape where in a locality the gospel is most needed. In this latter sense, culture and place intersect in different ways across localities to determine who inhabits the social and economic peripheries and what needs to be addressed by the social dimension of mission. For these reasons, a synodal church cannot neglect the impact that culture and place have on the *fideles* and their exercise of the *sensus fidei*.

As such, I argue that schematizing the *sensus fidelium* according to a universalized trichotomy does not reflect the lived reality of church. Instead, I contend that schematizing the *sensus fidelium* as mediated by the local church's sense of faith is a more appropriate framework for a synodal church. To develop this model, I rely on communion ecclesiology for its emphasis on the church as primarily constituted by relationships and its understanding of the local church. By schematizing the *sensus fidelium* as composed of and mediated by local communions, this model creates space to consider more inclusively the diverse ordering of the people of God, their unique relationships to the *sensus fidelium*, and the impact of culture and place on their *sensus fidei*. In doing so, this model promotes a deeper consideration of the social challenges facing the church today and promotes the project of synodal reform.

Advantages of a Schematization of the *Sensus Fidelium*

In Rush's schematization, the *sensus fidelium* is composed of three distinct, but universal categories—*sensus laicorum, sensus theologorum,* and *sensus episcoporum.*[8] With the term *sensus laicorum,* Rush names the collective exercise of the sense of faith by "the vast majority of individuals active in the Church's mission,"

[8]Rush, *Eyes of Faith*, 251.

whose lives synthesize the church's faith, doctrines, and traditions.[9] With the term *sensus theologorum,* Rush identifies the collective exercise of the sense of faith by the community of theologians. On the basis of her *sensus fidei fidelis,* a theologian offers her work to the broader theological community and through the open, dialogical process of scholarly exchange among the international community of theologians, a theologian's *sensus fidei fidelis* contributes to the *sensus theologorum.*[10] Finally, Rush describes the collective sense of faith of the bishops as the *sensus episcoporum* making sense of the collegial function of bishops in the discernment, formulation, and definition of doctrine.[11] While distinctly mediating and contributing to the *sensus fidelium* in their own way, the *sensus laicorum, sensus theologorum,* and the *sensus episcoporum* function interdependently as the laity, theologians, and bishops listen and learn from one another; only collectively do they constitute the universal church's *sensus fidelium.*

In terms of advancing the theology of the *sensus fidei,* Rush's threefold schema offers an implicit but indispensable insight. The *sensus fidelium* is mediated by smaller sets of ecclesial relationships and can be schematized accordingly. From this underlying insight, two advantages follow. First, a schematization of the *sensus fidelium* distinguishes the *sensus fidelium* from a facile equivocation with the popular opinion of the laity and blind submission to the magisterium—two crucial concerns for post-conciliar theologians.[12] As the council taught, all Christians are first and foremost *fideles* prior to any further ordering, and equating the *sensus fidelium* with either of these extremes diverges from this conciliar teaching.[13] Second, a schematization of the *sensus fidelium* resists a pyramidal, clerical understanding of the church that the council sought to overcome.[14] Instead, by highlighting the dialogical relationship specifically between bishops, theologians,

---

[9]Rush, *Eyes of Faith*, 252.

[10]Rush, *Eyes of Faith*, 261–62, 268.

[11]Rush, *Eyes of Faith*, 272.

[12]John Burkhard, "Sensus Fidei: Recent Theological Reflection (1990–2001), Part 2," *Heythrop Journal* 47, no. 1 (2006): 38–54.

[13]John W. O'Malley, *What Happened at Vatican II* (Cambridge, MA: Harvard University Press, 2010), 178; ITC, *Theology Today: Perspectives, Principles, and Criteria* (2011), no. 33.

[14]ITC, Sensus Fidei *in the Life of the Church*, no. 4.

and laypeople, this schema emphasizes the Spirit's work through the whole church and represents a genuine advance of the council's teaching on the *sensus fidei*.[15]

Limitations of a Universalizaed, Tripartite Approach to the *Sensus Fidelium*

Yet if the lived reality of church is taken seriously as it must be for a synodal church, the universalized categories of Rush's schema prove deficient. First, as ecclesiologist Anne Arabome argues, the postconciliar "trichotomy" provides an inappropriate entry point for thinking of the *sensus fidelium* because this schema insufficiently accounts for the significant role that culture and place play in shaping the lived faith of Christians.[16] Second, most of the faithful of these categories neither live their faith globally nor have sufficiently global relationships that warrant a cross-sectional division of the *sensus fidelium*. Third, this tripartite schema entirely neglects the reality of ecclesial and social ordering beyond lay discipleship, theological scholarship, and episcopal ministry.

To account for the lived reality of faith found among local churches, a synodal church requires a fuller schematization that recognizes the diverse array of social and ecclesial identities found among the people of God and their distinct mediation of the *sensus fidei*. This includes not only all of the ordained and the laity, but also those at the local peripheries. In relation to the ordained, a tripartite paradigm overlooks the ecclesial identities of priests and deacons who are particularly important to the life of the local church.[17] In the day-to-day of ecclesial life, priests and deacons are the ordained ecclesial ministers alongside whom the laity most frequently exercise their co-responsibility. In addition,

[15]Rush, *Eyes of Faith*, 271, 274.

[16]Anne Arabome, "How Are Theologians Challenged and Informed by Their Engagement with the Sense of the Faithful in the Local/Global Church?" in *Learning from All the Faithful: A Contemporary Theology of the Sensus Fidei*, ed. Brandford E. Hinze and Peter Phan (Eugene, OR: Wipf and Stock, 2016), 362.

[17]Anthony Epko, *The Breath of the Spirit in the Church: The "Sensus Fidelium" and Canon Law* (Strathfield, NSW: St Paul's Publications, 2014), 130–36, 140–47.

the local presbyterate also has a vital synodal role in the local church structured through the presbyteral council and the college of consultors where they facilitate the local bishop's relationship to the *sensus fidei* of his local church.[18] In relation to the laity, Rush's tripartite schema also overlooks ministerial ordering beyond ordained ecclesial ministry—a commonplace occurrence in local churches. In the US Catholic Church, lay ecclesial ministers serve as parish administrators, youth ministers, campus ministers, curial leaders, schoolteachers, and directors of religious education. While still lay, their ministerial ordering differentiates them in terms of relationship and function from lay missionary disciples and gives them unique insight into the *sensus fidei*.[19] In relation to the periphery, a tripartite schematization of the *sensus fidei* fails to structurally reflect and promote the preferential option for the poor and consequently, does not reckon with the various intersections of class, caste, and sex which marginalize differently across cultures and local churches.[20] For these reasons, a universalized, tripartite schematization of the *sensus fidelium* insufficiently accounts for the diversity of social and ecclesial ordering found in local churches.

A Path Forward through the Local Church?

To appreciate this diverse array of ecclesial positionality present in the lived reality of church, a more apt starting point is the local church understood through the lens of a communion ecclesiology.[21] Although theologians develop communion ecclesiology

---

[18]*Code of Canon Law* (1983), cc. 495 §1, 502 §1.

[19]Richard R. Gaillardetz, "The Ecclesiological Foundations of Ministry within an Ordered Communion," in *Ordering the Baptismal Priesthood: Theologies of Lay & Ordained Priesthood*, ed. Susan K. Wood (Collegeville, MN: Liturgical Press, 2003), 36, 44–47; Amanda C. Osheim, "The Lo cal Church in Dialogue: Toward an Orthopraxis of Reception," in *Visions of Hope: Emerging Theologians and the Future of the Church*, ed. Kevin J. Ahern (Maryknoll, NY: Orbis Books, 2013), 181–89.

[20]Natalia Imperatori-Lee, "Sin, Intimacy, and the Genuine Face of the Church: A Response to Ormond Rush," *Theological Studies* 74, no. 4 (2013): 805–6.

[21]For an overview of communion ecclesiology's critiques, see Richard Lennan, "Communion Ecclesiology: Foundations, Critiques, and Affirmations," *Pacifica: Australian Theological Studies* 20, no. 1 (February 2007):

in different ways with varying emphases, communion ecclesiologies generally eschew an understanding of the church as a pyramidal institution and instead approach the universal and local churches as webs of relationships composed of actual people.[22] An ecclesiology of communion with a strong pneumatological accent promotes the development of a number of critical themes necessary for a synodal reception of the council—the diversity of inculturated faith as a reflection of the Trinity, the catholicity of ecclesial communion as unity in diversity, the contribution of all the baptized as agents of mission, and the church itself as a communion of local communions. As Luciani notes, synodality requires more fully receiving "the model of Church as people of God walking in communion, a Church of churches."[23] According to the council, the local church is "in which and from which the one and only Catholic Church exists."[24] In other words, the local church is the universal church operative in a particular place and present among a particular people.[25] To recognize the local church's mediation of the universal church, the *sensus fidelium* is better schematized as made up of the sense of faith of local churches—a *sensus localium fidelium*.

Local Church and the Diversly Ordered People of God

This schema not only makes sense of the local church's mediation of the universal church and its *sensus fidelium*, but it also is well suited to represent the full array of ecclesial positionality found in local churches. Communion ecclesiology foregrounds the Spirit's animation of the local church communally and each person personally while simultaneously distinguishing between *fideles* in terms of relationship and function in a nuanced way. Indeed, communion ecclesiology already moves beyond a typical trichotomy and is used by a number of theologians to develop

---

24–39; Susan Bigelow Reynolds, "Beyond Unity in Diversity: Race, Culture, and Communion Ecclesiology in US Catholicism," *American Catholic Studies* 130, no. 4 (2019): 31–58.

[22]Dennis M. Doyle, *Communion Ecclesiology: Visions and Versions* (Maryknoll, NY: Orbis Books, 2000), 8.

[23]Luciani, *Synodality*, 41.

[24]Second Vatican Council, *Lumen Gentium*, no. 23.

[25]Second Vatican Council, *Christus Dominus* (1965), no. 30.

the co-responsible functions and collaborative relationships of priests and deacons to the local church.[26] Even more important, approaching the local church through communion ecclesiology makes sense of the experience of many laypeople whom the Spirit calls and equips to exercise lay ecclesial ministry. Ecclesial ordering in the church is broader than ordination and the Spirit's ordering of lay forms of ministry draws laypeople "into a new ecclesial relationship within the life of the Church."[27] In this way, communion ecclesiology provides a theological account of the lived reality of church and enables a consideration of the ways that different ordered ministries uniquely mediate and contribute to the *sensus localium fidelium*.

Local Church and Culture

Schematizing the *sensus fidelium* through the local church not only creates space to probe the distinct contributions of the diversely ordered faithful but also reckons with the significant impact of place and culture on the *sensus fidei* highlighted previously by Arabome. Cultures function both as a source of accumulated knowledge, value, and meaning for a people and as an interpretive lens through which this same people understand the world.[28] As Pope Francis puts it, "The concept of culture . . . has to do with the lifestyle of a given society, the specific way in which its members relate to one another, to other creatures and to God. Understood in this way, culture embraces the totality of a people's life."[29] Because the human person finds in her society and its culture, "a concrete way of relating to reality," persons involved in local churches in Sri Lanka relate to God, others, self, and creation in ways that differ from those in the local churches of South Africa, Finland, or Argentina.[30] As a result, the local church's exercise of

[26]Epko, *The Breath of the Spirit in the Church*, 130–36; Dennis Edwards, "Personal Symbol of Communion," in *The Spirituality of the Diocesan Priest*, ed. Donald Cozzens (Collegeville, MN: Liturgical Press, 1997), 73–84.

[27]Gaillardetz, "Ministry within an Ordered Communion," 36.

[28]Clifford Geertz, *The Interpretation of Cultures: Selected Essays* (New York: Basic Books, 2000), 89.

[29]Francis, *Evangelii Gaudium*, no. 115.

[30]Francis, *Evangelii Gaudium*, no. 115.

mission requires the integration of faith with the local cultures specific to that church. Driven by the *sensus fidei*, inculturation ultimately produces new ways of living the church's shared faith and singular mission that can be appreciated by the whole church.

For example, although monstrances differed in design during the early practice of Eucharistic adoration, the evangelization of the Americas dramatically impacted this design as Indigenous peoples found a strong connection between the Eucharist and their cultural emphasis on the sun. Just as the sun enables life to flourish and the sun's movement regulates the rhythms of human society, the God sacramentally present in the Eucharist is the font of life and orders creation. These connections identified through the *sensus fidei* of Indigenous Americans resonate with the broader church until the sunburst monstrance becomes ubiquitous.[31] Just as with the faith of Indigenous Americans, the *sensus fidei* operative in the culture of a particular people often mediates new forms of ecclesial life that enrich the church's shared faith and singular mission.

While the cultures of local churches offer new ways to live and express faith that positively enrich the entire people of God, cultures also inhibit the social dimension of mission because cultures themselves transmit and perpetuate forms of marginalization that render persons poor and violate their human dignity. As Pope Francis notes: "It is imperative to evangelize cultures . . . to inculturate the Gospel. . . . Each culture and social group needs purification and growth. . . . We can see deficiencies which need to be healed by the Gospel."[32] Yet the way these cultural deficiencies undermine the common good and render human persons disposable differ from one another because caste, class, and sex function and intersect differently within each culture. These differences place distinctive demands on the local church, and its preferential exercise of mission further distinguishes the *fideles* from one another locally.

If not directly addressed as a part of the church's missionary

---

[31]Jaime Lara, "The Sacramented Sun: Solar Eucharistic Worship in Colonial Latin America," in *EL Cuerpo de Christo: The Hispanic Presence in the US Catholic Church*, ed. Peter J. Casarella and Raúl Gómez (New York: Crossroad, 1998), 285–87.

[32]Francis, *Evangelii Gaudium*, no. 69.

activity, these cultural deficiencies can affect the relational web that constitutes the local church itself, as they did in the diocese of Alton.[33] In 1887, Alton held its first diocesan synod during which time it also boasted the nation's first Black Catholic priest—Augustus Tolton. Alton's bishop, James Ryan, called the synod for the local implementation of the plenary councils of Baltimore. Yet this synod failed to provide for the material and spiritual care of the formerly enslaved which the Second Plenary Council specifically entrusted to local churches.[34] The synod's final report simply notes Tolton's glaringly conspicuous presence in the otherwise all-white synod. The insignificance accorded to Tolton and his capacity to address racism contrasts with the First Black Catholic Congress in Washington, DC, where Tolton gave the keynote and Eucharistic benediction likely using a sunburst monstrance.[35] Indeed, Tolton's journey from enslavement to ordination and his pastorate in the only Black parish in Alton's Quincy deanery uniquely related him to the *sensus localium fidelium* easily confused at the time with the racism embedded in the dominant culture. Shaped by this culture, Bishop Ryan did not attend to Tolton's Spirit-filled insights and instead drove Tolton to leave the diocese. By not foregrounding the deficiencies of culture like the commitment to racial caste embedded in the dominant US culture, local churches can become ensnared in the social sins that the Spirit prompts them to rectify, and their synodal discernment of the *sensus fidei* can become impeded. For Alton, this led to the collapse of Quincy's Black Catholic population just months after the synod.[36]

Local Church and Place

In addition to purifying and integrating culture with faith, the local church can also uniquely respond to the impact of place. In

---

[33]Today, Alton is in the diocese of Springfield, Illinois.

[34]Cyprian Davis, *The History of Black Catholics in the United States* (New York: Crossroad, 1990), 120. Diocese of Alton, *Synodus Dioecesana, Altonensis Prima* (Saint Louis, 1889).

[35]Diocese of Alton, *Synodus Altonensis Prima*, x; Caroline Hemesath, *From Slave to Priest: A Biography of the Rev. Augustine Tolton (1854–1897), First Afro-American Priest of the United States* (Chicago: Franciscan Herald Press, 1973), 125.

[36]Hemesath, *Augustine Tolton*, 1–106, 127, 129.

recent years, US scholars have increasingly recognized place as a significant factor shaping people's everyday lives in markedly different ways.[37] Even as caste, class, and sex intersect differently across cultures, place itself compounds or moderates the way these various marginalizations intersect within a culture. Place determines the impact of climate change, the varieties in geography, the availability of resources, the presence of infrastructure, and the readiness of social supports to meet the inequities of people across cultural groups. Even where cultures are similar across place, the dissimilarities of place itself can cause differences in marginalization that are specific to locality. For example, public health scholars have found that despite the similar cultural and demographic makeup of Alabama and Mississippi, the disparity in life expectancy between Black and white women is greater in Mississippi than in Alabama.[38] Another study finds that even within a locality, place compounds the disparity of accessible work between white residents and residents of color.[39] When considered for their theological import, studies like these demonstrate that even though a shared faith and a singular mission unite the church, the unique but critical considerations of place set local churches apart from one another. Indeed, only by reckoning with the realities of place and culture and their variable impact on caste, class, and sex can a synodal church appropriately identify the peripheries, honestly respond to the *sensus fidei*, and boldly live the social dimension of mission. As such, a schematization of the *sensus fidelium* fitting for a synodal church must foreground the unique and significant impact of both culture and place on the *sensus fidei*.

---

[37]Jeanne Halgren Kilde, *The Oxford Handbook of Religious Space* (New York: Oxford University Press, 2022); Mary Jo Bane, "A House Divided," in *American Parishes: Remaking Local Catholicism*, ed. Gary J. Adler, Tricia Colleen Bruce, and Brian Starks, 1st ed., Catholic Practice in North America (New York: Fordham University Press, 2019), 152–70.

[38]Nazleen Bharmal et al., "State-Level Variations in Racial Disparities in Life Expectancy," *Health Services Research* 47, no. 1, pt 2 (February 2012): 544–55.

[39]John W. Frazier, Florence M. Margai, and Eugene Tettey-Fio, *Race and Place: Equity Issues in Urban America* (Boulder, CO: Westview Press, 2003), 229–51.

The Local Church's Mediation of the Universal Church's *Sensus Fidelium*

These examples from the Americas not only reveal the significance of culture and place for the *sensus fidei* but also demonstrate that schematization matters. As in the case of Alton, cultural deficiencies can impede the function of the *sensus fidei* and in these cases, the authentic *sensus fidei* may be mediated by people other than a bishop, theologian, or even the majority of laypeople. In contrast to a universal, tripartite schema that would overlook these mediations, a schematization of the *sensus fidelium* as mediated by each local church's sense of faith—its *sensus localium fidelium*—foregrounds the relationship of different local groups to the *sensus fidei*. Specifically, this schematization more comprehensively recognizes the diverse ordering of the *fideles* actually found among the people of God, which not only includes ordered ministries like priests, deacons, and lay ecclesial ministers but also those socially constrained to the peripheries by the variable intersections of caste, class, and sex. With this more expansive and inclusive approach, I consider more comprehensively how the diversely ordered people of God mediate and contribute to the *sensus fidelium*—the foundation and basis for synodality. In doing so, this model embodies the call of Isaiah embraced by the ongoing synod on synodality: "enlarge the space of your tent."[40]

[40]Synod of Bishops, *Enlarge the Space of Your Tent: Working Document for the Continental Stage* (2022), www.synod.va.

Theoretical Absence, Practical Mediation

From Eco-Theory to Sacrificial Praxis

Christopher Denny

"Lord, if you had been here, my brother would not have died" (John 11:21 NABRE). Martha's words to Jesus in the Gospel of John claim that Jesus's absence is what led to the death of Lazarus. In the subsequent narrative, Jesus's mediating presence makes the absent entombed Lazarus present again in a transformation from death back into life. Martha's monocausal link between Jesus's presence and Lazarus's life befits the Christocentrism of the Fourth Gospel: when Jesus is present, so are his disciples. As he prays to the Father on the night before his death: "I wish that where I am—they also may be with me" (John 17:24).

Human relationships require tangible connections between unique living beings in their irreducible singularity. Theoretical abstractions, however, are a different matter. Theories provide persons with a portable epistemology through an intellectual chain of human activity. What we experience in one context can provide us with intellectual constructions and hypotheses that can be applied in other contexts. When hypotheses and their accompanying expectations provide satisfactory explanations for succeeding experiences, the hypotheses increase in explanatory power, and after a time may eventually crystallize into theories outright. If we lose self-awareness that the theories we employ are in fact the result of deliberate abstractions applied in varying situations, theories can harden into inflexible dogmas that dictate our subsequent experiences and prevent us from appreciating the novel opportunity to experience other beings as the distinctive entities they are, thus making authentic relationships impossible. What could be an encounter with a genuine other in our experience becomes a mere datum to be plugged into our preconceived intellectual frames of reference.

This essay does not take a general stand on the comparative strength of various epistemologies. Instead, it provides an assessment of some pitfalls that a theoretical approach to ecotheology creates, and in turn lobbies for a resolutely empirical approach to ecological praxis that is sufficiently latitudinarian to allow not only for interreligious cooperation but also for collective environmental action between people with both religious and secular worldviews. Put more simply, I argue that ecological orthopraxis must be given priority over ecological theories, especially in a religiously pluralist world. It is unrealistic to expect that various religious traditions will reach agreement on metaphysical and theological accounts of the cosmos, and making such a desired agreement as a justification for coordinated ecological praxis is naïve. Prioritizing the theoretical over the empirical in ecology does the opposite of what Jesus of Nazareth does in the Gospel of John, namely, such prioritization makes our embodied relationship to the earth abstract, and in a sense absent to us, insofar as our perceived need to explain the cosmos and to try to convert others to our preferred metaphysics diverts our attention from the necessary priority of caring for our wounded material environment. This environment is one in which the rain falls upon the just and the unjust, and also upon the idealists, the materialists, the pragmatists, and the deep-ecology theorists.

The essay proceeds in three parts. First, I will note the shortcomings of a Romantic approach to ecotheology centered on fostering inspirational experiences of communion with the other-than-human world. Communion ecclesiologies have been faulted for smoothing over differences within the Christian church.[1] In a similar way what I call a "communion ecotheology" proffers a change in internal dispositions as the key to solving ecological

[1]See Joseph A. Komonchak, "Concepts of Communion: Past and Present," *Cristianesimo nella storia* 16 (1995): 334–40.

crises. Second, in the place of such romantic "communion eco-theologies," I commend a phenomenological ethics that privileges direct observation of the cosmos (not to be confused with naïve observation) over theoretical speculation. Finally, I advocate a pragmatic ethic of sacrificial restraint and limited consumption instead of promoting a theoretical metanarrative as a prerequisite to ecological action. Such eco-theological sacrifice privileges the mediation of our biological world and promotes socioeconomic resistance to the plague of overconsumption threatening our planetary home.

Ecology—More Than an Interiorized Disposition

At the start of his 1999 book *The Great Work: Our Way into the Future,* Thomas Berry states that the fundamental human responsibility in an Ecozoic era, an imagined future marked by a mutually beneficial relationship between humans and the rest of the earth, is to change our understanding. Specifically, Berry insists "that future can exist only when we understand the universe as composed of subjects to be communed with, not as objects to be exploited."[2] In Berry's exposition, overcoming such a utilitarian relationship to nature will enable intimacy to flourish. Berry is, of course, committed to praxes that will foster that intimacy, and his historical survey of classical and Indigenous civilizations demonstrates that he recognizes the diversity of human spiritualities. Nevertheless, his diagnosis of the *root* cause of current environmental degradation unabashedly centers on the intellectual. Berry writes, "The deepest cause of the present devastation is found in a mode of consciousness that has established a radical discontinuity between the human and other modes of being and the bestowal of all rights on the humans."[3] It is Berry's call for an appreciation of an ontological continuity that I here describe as a "communion ecotheology." Like communion ecclesiologies used to describe the Christian church, "communion ecotheology" encourages people to understand individual entities as part of a larger and

[2]Thomas Berry, *The Great Work: Our Way into the Future* (New York: Bell Tower, 1999), x.

[3]Berry, *The Great Work*, 4.

inescapable whole that supersedes both individual consciousness and voluntaristic preferences. Communion ecotheology does not simply advocate for the undeniable recognition of the organisms' biological interdependence, in the manner of the Gaia hypothesis formulated by James Lovelock and Lynn Margulis.[4] Communion ecotheology transcends biological formulation and advocates that people make metaphysical and spiritual commitments as well.

By comparison with other variants of communion ecology, the theological roots of Berry's Ecozoic are muted. For more overt theological representatives of the genre, one can cite Pierre Teilhard de Chardin, a major influence on Berry.[5] In *The Divine Milieu* Teilhard also emphasizes the continuity between the biotic and the abiotic with reference to humanity's relationship to God:

> Now how does the human world itself appear within the structure of the universe? . . . The more we think about it, the more we are struck by the obviousness and importance of the following conclusion: it appears as a zone of continuous spiritual transformation, where all inferior realities and forces without exception are sublimated into sensations, feelings, ideas, and the powers of knowledge and love. Around the earth, the center of our field of vision, our souls form, in some way, the incandescent surface of matter plunged in God. From the dynamic and biological point of view it is quite impossible to draw a line below it, as to draw a line between a plant and the environment that sustains it.[6]

Pope Francis's encyclical *Laudato Si'* provides an extensive argument for communion ecology with the pope's exposition of "integral ecology." Weaving environmental concerns with older strands of Catholic social teaching pertaining to just economic

---

[4]For a helpful overview of the Gaia hypothesis and the often-negative reaction to it among scientists, see Lawrence E. Joseph, *Gaia: The Growth of an Idea* (New York: St. Martin's Press, 1990).

[5]See Sean McDonagh, *On Care for Our Common Home: The Encyclical of Pope Francis on the Environment* Laudato Si' (Maryknoll, NY: Orbis Books, 2016), 137–42.

[6]Pierre Teilhard de Chardin, *The Divine Milieu,* trans. Siôn Cowell (Brighton, UK: Sussex Academic Press, 2004), 86–87.

structures, Francis notes that "an awareness of our common origin . . . would enable the development of new convictions, attitudes, and forms of life."[7]

Yet following upon Francis's own reminder in *Evangelii Gaudium* that "realities are more important than ideas," we might ask, what about the pragmatic role of technology in exacerbating humanity's alienation from nature?[8] After all, technology has enabled modern human beings to exploit the environment to an extent unimagined by our premodern ancestors. Will the ecological crisis be mitigated primarily by changing our thinking? Berry's prescription for healing environmental damage, like a number of similar prescriptions, is based on retrieval of premodern patterns of thinking and living. We must, Berry insists, reestablish the rapport that classic and Indigenous traditions had achieved in their respective cultural matrices. "Our great work," he writes, "has to do with a new understanding of the planet Earth."[9] Elsewhere Berry termed this new understanding the New Story, but this proffered new understanding is actually the retrieval of a much older understanding.[10]

Although Catholic priests such as Berry and theologians from groups such as the College Theology Society may be partial to a necessary recognition of a particular ecological cosmology, we should ask what stakeholders might be overlooked in Berry's imagined eco-spirituality. What about those individuals who do not share the prescriptive cosmology set forth by Berry? Those who are materialists and who do not hold with Berry that "the wisdom of the classical traditions is based on revelatory experiences of a spiritual realm," whom we might term the ecological-but-not-religious?[11] What about those who are committed to environmental stewardship but who still maintain privileging the anthropocentric over the rest of creation? What about those who

---

[7]Francis, *Laudato Si'* (May 24, 2015), no. 202.

[8]Francis, *Evangelii Gaudium* (November 24, 2013), no. 231.

[9]Francis, *Evangelii Gaudium*, no. 21.

[10]See Thomas Berry, *The Dream of the Earth* (San Francisco: Sierra Club Books, 1988); Thomas Berry and Thomas Swimme, *The Universe Story: From the Primordial Flaring Forth to the Ecozoic Era—A Celebration of the Unfolding of the Cosmos* (New York: HarperCollins, 1992).

[11]Berry, *The Great Work*, 185.

hold serious reservations about the ecological value of classic religious traditions?[12] Berry's ecological vision is at root a theoretical one, one predicated on a desired communion, a reconciliation, between human beings and the rest of the cosmos. It is well intentioned but exclusive to the extent that it centralizes right thinking as a prerequisite to ecological healing. Drawing on an analogy from the realm of political theology is helpful here. Since the Second Vatican Council, the vast majority of Catholic moral and political theologians have not insisted that a Catholic confessional state is a prerequisite for participation in social justice initiatives and action for the common good. At times enthusiastically and at other times more circumspectly, the current Catholic theological consensus differentiates between theology and action in learning to work with secular governments in pluralist societies. *Mutatis mutandis,* what can ecotheology learn from this development in seeking a pragmatic consensus that enables concerted efforts to offset environmental damage? To ask this question is not to claim that theological cosmologies or metanarrative are unimportant; nor does the question imply that any cosmological claim about the world is as true or false as any other. Rather, it is to acknowledge that prioritizing agreement on metaphysics or natural theology is a luxury requiring time that the ecosystem does not currently have. Is there another alternative?

One possibility is to forgo making a particular metaphysics or a particular spirituality a requirement for ecological action. In his recent book *In Our Own Image: Anthropomorphism, Apophaticism, and Ultimacy* philosophical theologian Wesley Wildman sets out a typology of approaches to engaging with the ideas of ultimacy and ultimate reality, ranging from those Wildman calls *mono-traditional investors* and *multi-traditional appreciators* to *responsible worriers* and *analytical ascetics.*[13] Broadly speaking, these approaches are arranged on a spectrum ranging from those such as the monotraditionalists who promote prescriptive theories

---

[12]The most famous attack on the mainstream Christian approach to ecology was launched over fifty years ago by Lynn White Jr. See "The Historical Roots of Our Ecological Crisis," *Science* 155 (1967): 1203–7.

[13]See Wesley J. Wildman, *In Our Own Image: Anthropomorphism, Apophaticism, and Ultimacy* (Oxford: Oxford University Press, 2017), 1–5.

about reality to those such as the analytic ascetics who eschew intellectual constructions when possible. Wildman describes himself as a comparing inquirer who supports a pluralistic philosophical project open to the possibility of constructive solutions, but finally chooses an apophatic approach for himself.

With the proper adjustments being made, what Wildman writes about the ultimate can be deftly applied to the ecological. Such a transposition may strike theologians from Abrahamic traditions as opening the door to worldviews they may find unacceptably materialist and violations of theism. One can respond that while the natural world may not be ultimate in the judgment of various religious practitioners, it is the one facet of human life that is most likely to qualify as inescapable or inevitable among the broadest swath of people living today. Where you go when you die, how you achieve liberation, the medium through which ultimate reality is made known to people—these are all matters on which there is no consensus across religious traditions. That people need clean air, clean water, adequate food, and are subject to the vagaries of changes in climate, however, is a matter admitting of far less dispute.

Even were one to grant Berry's declinist narrative, or that of Lynn White in his 1966 lecture "The Historical Roots of Our Ecological Crisis" blaming Judeo-Christian creation accounts for ecologically destructive anthropocentrism, critical issues remain outstanding. These philosophically idealist historiographies spend more time indicting humanity's degraded spiritual orientation to the environment than assessing what role material technological innovations such as the harvesting of petroleum, the ubiquitous use of the internal combustion engine, or the development of plastics have played in our current plight. The question remains, "What are we to do to change this situation?" More specifically, what are we to do in a secular world in which secularization in its most technologically developed regions is accelerating, and when the youngest generations display little inclination to turn back toward a more religious era? Waiting to get spiritual buy-in to undergird a program of ecological restoration is not advisable. Confessionalist ecotheologies or communion ecologies appealing to the ecological equivalent of a perennial philosophy are of limited efficacy in a world in which pollution, habitat loss, and climate change threaten human beings from all religious and secular traditions. We must turn to direct observation of nature itself to build appreciation and consensus.

Let's Get Empirical

In his book *Ecologies of Grace,* Willis Jenkins characterizes pragmatism in the context of ecology as follows:

> Pragmatists defuse pluralism's destabilizing threat by recognizing theoretical diversity as the reasonable outcome of a variety of thinkers addressing diverse and immaturely conceived practical problems. In order to appropriate the promise of that diversity, they say, environmental ethics needs to organize itself around practical civic engagement rather than endless debates for or against anthropocentrism.[14]

Jenkins is savvy enough to know that simply appealing to pragmatic methodology doesn't remove theoretical questions from the table, nor is such an appeal an a priori denial that theological constructions might not eventually have practical ecological consequences. Pragmatic ecology, however, orients ecotheology in the general direction of materiality and insists that ecotheology stay rooted in that domain, rather than, say, using an experience of embodiment only as a stepping-stone on the way to a blessed afterlife in heaven or liberation in nirvana, or identifying the natural world as a mere epiphenomenon of a transcendent unifying principle, be it the Plotinian One or the God of Israel or the Upanishadic Brahman. Properly speaking, such utilitarian appraisals of nature do not merit inclusion under the category of ecotheologies, as they display no abiding concern for the natural world on its own merits.

A plea to get empirical does not necessitate empiricism. A plea to turn to the material does not mandate materialism. It would be simplistic if this plea were no more than a recognition that all people already engage in sensory perception. A broader experience is entailed, and it is well described by philosophical theologian

[14]Willis Jenkins, *Ecologies of Grace: Environmental Ethics and Christian Theology* (New York: Oxford University Press, 2008), 34–35.

Robert Corrington in his book *Deep Pantheism: Toward a New Transcendentalism* (2016). Corrington's "new transcendentalism" builds on the original transcendentalism exemplified in Ralph Waldo Emerson's 1838 *Divinity School Address,* which Corrington characterizes as teaching us that "we are to find our religion in the bosom of nature" and that "revelation morphs into the sense of the sublime."[15] A naturalist can read Corrington's contrast between revelation and the sublime as a dichotomous either/or existential option, but a theist could just as well translate that relationship between revelation and the sublime as a both/and option. In either case the existential focus remains on the natural world. Corrington's update of Emerson's worldview removes Emerson's focus on connecting the experience of beauty to its backdrop against the whole of the cosmos, as he writes, "This new Transcendentalism is more inclined to de-emphasize this correlation of beauty with the whole and instead to see the beautiful order of relevance as standing on its own."[16] The new transcendentalism encounters a natural grace in which "natural grace is not dispensed by a supernatural or pan*en*theistic deity but comes from the heart of nature 'itself.' . . . It is unearned and not a product of 'downward' agape in the classical sense."[17]

Is Corrington's view simply an inverted version of Berry's appeal to a perennial premodern communion ecology? No, because of the explicitly apophatic character of Corrington's "It." It is easier for Corrington's new transcendentalism to overlap with alternative cosmologies, particularly secular cosmologies, than it is for classic communion ecology to be acceptable to many modern people. The new transcendentalism is more heuristically parsimonious, more analytically ascetic, to use Wildman's term, or more pragmatic, to use Jenkins's vocabulary. But what is specifically ecological about this new transcendentalism? Can scientific details be added to Corrington's philosophical framework to increase its explanatory efficacy and pragmatic scope?

Yes, and what is more, these details can integrate the attentiveness and respect for genuine biological diversity fostered by

---

[15]Robert Corrington, *Deep Pantheism: Toward a New Transcendentalism* (Lanham, MD: Lexington, 2016), 98.

[16]Corrington, *Deep Pantheism*, 101.

[17]Corrington, *Deep Pantheism*, 102. Emphasis in original.

phenomenology with evolutionary and emergent explanations of cosmic development. Adding a diachronic aspect to the new transcendentalism increases its pragmatic relevance in a world in which both biological and cultural matrices inevitably change, and in which confidence in a Romantic perennial communion ecology can appear static and ahistorical. Christian philosopher Philip Clayton is one representative of emergence theory, which seeks to provide a philosophical alternative to materialist and Cartesian dualist zero-sum accounts of the relationship of matter to mind. Emergence is a process, originating within the material world, by which higher-level entities and their accompanying properties emerge from lower-level entities and yet are irreducible to them. Clayton's succinct definition of emergence is "*the theory that cosmic evolution repeatedly includes unpredictable, irreducible, and novel appearances.*"[18] "Emergence," Clayton states in his book *Mind and Emergence: From Quantum to Consciousness*, "is interesting to scientifically minded thinkers only to the extent that it accepts the principle of parsimony, introducing no more metaphysical superstructure than is required by the data themselves."[19] Because of this very parsimoniousness, persons with conflicting philosophical commitments regarding ontology can nevertheless promote emergence theory, whether these persons adhere to a substance metaphysics or not. Here we have an evolutionary account of the world that is self-consciously pluralist, and that unlike the worldview of a theologian-scientist like Teilhard does not bundle this account with metaphysical and religious doctrines such as an evolutionary process tending toward a christic Omega Point and the like.[20] For those like Clayton who make the individual choice to invest emergence theory with personal religious commitments, the immanence of divine activity has been radicalized in a way that approaches Emerson's views, made from Emerson's very different transcendentalist starting point. Mediation of the divine presence to the world is still present for Clayton, but that

[18]Philip Clayton, *Mind and Emergence: From Quantum to Consciousness* (Oxford: Oxford University Press, 2004), 39. Emphasis in original.

[19]Clayton, *Mind and Emergence*, 15.

[20]See Pierre Teilhard de Chardin, *The Phenomenon of Man* (New York: Harper, 2008).

mediation emerges not from above the world but from within its processes of constant change.

Interreligious Sacrificial Praxis

Theoretical generosity is all well and good, but in keeping with this essay's stated goals at the outset here we move back to praxis to give it the ecological priority it deserves. Empirical observation of our world in the third decade of the twenty-first century demonstrates that the climate crisis caused by anthropogenic global warming is accelerating. This crisis is not a result of misplaced theorizing but is rather a result of human consumption—consumption of fossil fuels and the consumption of natural resources. Hopes that further technological development could allow humans to combine consumption with ecological well-being have not yielded viable strategies to slow, much less reverse, the deterioration of our planetary environment. Any honest appraisal of our ecological crisis must admit that there will be no mitigation or improvement without human beings engaging in broad-based practices of self-denial, collective asceticism, and "eco-sacrifice" on behalf of the earth. Eco-sacrifice is the ascetic practice of denying one's desire for excessive consumption in order to allow space for other organisms to flourish in the natural world. Anthropologist Mary Douglas once wrote, "Solidarity is only gesturing when it involves no sacrifice."[21] Yet since the period that Karl Jaspers called the "axial age" two millennia ago, world religions have moved toward spiritualized and individualized understandings of sacrifice intended to supersede earlier cultic practices.[22] Moreover, in recent decades sacrifice has come into conflict with psychologies and philosophies of self-affirmation and consumerism, which have willingly partnered with a late-modern economy based on consumption and the dissolution of social ties rooted in geographic proximity and family status.

Seen as a marker of psychological deviance and repression,

---

[21]Mary Douglas, *How Institutions Think* (Syracuse, NY: Syracuse University Press, 1986), 4.

[22]See Karl Jaspers, *The Origin and Goal of History,* trans. Michael Bullock (New York: Taylor and Francis, 2021), 3–90.

sacrifice is now due for a twenty-first-century comeback in an era in which the earth's finite resources will not be able to keep up with population growth and the continuing growth in inequality that characterizes liberal economies. Traditional privatized theologies of sacrifice, however, will not be convincing enough to people living in demythologized cultures. Fortunately for Christianity and in other religions there are resources available to help with the needed task of reinterpretation and, more important, ethical application. Christian resources would benefit from a constructive borrowing from other sacrificial and religious traditions that offer understandings of the self that challenge the ecologically destructive anthropology of modern capitalism. Additionally, since the problem of overconsumption is a problem for human beings from various spiritual traditions, a comparative theology of sacrifice has greater potential for impact around the world in our century.

The modern era has not been kind to classical understandings of religious sacrifice developed in the premodern era that Thomas Berry surveyed. Even in the classical age, a cross-cultural movement toward religious interiority arose in the Near East, in India, and in China.[23] Central to traditional propitiatory understandings of sacrifice is the claim that sacrifice's final efficacy is only realized in a cosmological plane of existence, absent from our current quotidian existence, beyond the normal experience of human beings. The sacrifices of ancient Greeks find their summation on Mount Olympus. The god of Noah appreciates the innovation of animal sacrifice from the place of his rainbow-clad heavenly abode. Classical priestly theologies of sacrifice require that participants have faith in a reality unseen; Christian sacramental theology claims that visible realities mediate invisible grace. In the twenty-first century, a theology of eco-sacrifice must be constructed upon the tangible and visible social benefits that sacrifice confers on people and the planet. Sallie McFague provides a model for an ecologically motivated interreligious praxis rooted in eco-sacrifice, when she writes

> I focus not on "belief in Jesus" or "belief in God" per se so much as the theme, common in most religions, that loving one's neighbor is tantamount to loving God. If the "neighbor"

[23]See Jaspers, *The Origin and Goal of History*, 3–90.

> is understood to include all living creatures, and indeed the planet itself, then what matters is not a discrete belief in a God (or "gods") so much as an understanding of the self . . . as radically inclusive love. The implication is that one should focus on what one sees (the visible neighbor) rather than on what one does not see (the invisible God).[24]

Rather than place our hopes in sacrifices that in theory will travel upward to placate divinities, McFague finds sacrifice modeled for us right before our too often unwitting sight. "Nature," she states, "is the grandest, most intricate, most complex system . . . of sacrifice (albeit unwilling sacrifice)."[25] These sacrifices that constitute nature do not depend on some working out of soteriological options or debt-satisfaction theories, as McFague insists that her view is not "wild, crazy idealism."[26] In the course of her books, McFague did argue for a radical shift in theological anthropology and Christian understandings of the God-world relationship.[27] Her articulation of the world as self has parallels in Vedic literature in the hymn known as the "Purusha-Sukta," a creation myth that describes the sacrifice of the cosmic giant, the god Purusha. The gods sacrifice Purusha, and from this sacrifice the whole cosmos is created—the Vedic gods Indra and Agni, the animal world, human beings, the sky, the sun and moon, the wind, and language.[28]

Readers may believe in this creation myth or not, just as readers can prefer Thomas Berry's cosmology to that of someone like Thomas Hobbes, but choices here do not conclusively forestall appreciation of the ecological applications of reinterpreted sacrificial practice, which has parallels in other traditions. These parallels include Augustine's call for Christians to "become what you receive" in the eucharistic ritual, the Tanakh's prophetic descriptions

---

[24]Sallie McFague, *Blessed Are the Consumers: Climate Change and the Practice of Restraint* (Minneapolis: Fortress, 2013), xiii–xiv.

[25]McFague, *Blessed Are the Consumers*, 20.

[26]McFague, *Blessed Are the Consumers*, 20.

[27]See Sallie McFague, *The Body of God: An Ecological Theology* (Minneapolis: Fortress, 1993).

[28]Rig Veda,10.90.6, 12–13, trans. Raimundo Panikkar, in *The Vedic Experience/Mantramañjarñ: An Anthology of the Vedas for Modern Man and Contemporary Celebration* (Delhi: Motilal Banarsidass, 1977), 75–76.

of how cultic sacrifice can be redefined as ethical behavior, and the Purusha-Sukta's insistence that human communities themselves are constituted by the very act of sacrifice.[29] Practices such as voluntary poverty and significant restraints on consumption qualify as kenotic sacrificial acts in McFague's estimation.[30]

Conclusion

Anglican priest Frederick Lewis Donaldson, in a 1925 sermon later promulgated by Gandhi, once identified religion without sacrifice as one of the seven social sins.[31] Yet in the early twenty-first century, few believe that the aroma of smoke and incense from religion's sacrificial altars travels up to heaven to be enjoyed by absent deities, and faith that ritual acts mediate between gods and humans has waned. Instead, the smoke produced by religious and secular humans alike becomes part of the incessant pollution wafted into the atmosphere by human economic activity, resulting in an ecological catastrophe that threatens the well-being of all living species on Earth. Political agreements to curb greenhouse emissions have been fraught with diplomatic tension, in large part because nations are reluctant to engage in eco-sacrifice on behalf of others. Given the simultaneity of religious resurgence in some parts of the globe and rampant secularization elsewhere, it makes sense to ask if there is a role religion can play in alleviating this crisis that is also respectful of spiritual and metaphysical pluralism. Far from enlisting religious commitment to a cause that might seem extraneous to its purview, an immanent redescription of eco-sacrifice accords with central claims in multiple religious traditions. Such sacrifice, however, should not be confined to traditional definitions of placating divinities, reenacting the passion of a savior understood to live only in heaven, or securing a blessed afterlife in a world currently invisible to human beings. Rather, attentive eco-theological sacrifice must honor the present world, the world that is visible to us, and promote socioeconomic resistance

---

[29]See John H. McKenna, *Become What You Receive: A Systematic Study of the Eucharist* (Chicago: Liturgy Training Publications, 2012).

[30]See McFague, *Blessed Are the Consumers,* 80–110.

[31]See Charles Hoffacker, "The Anglican Origin of the Seven Social Sins," *The Living Church* (December 1, 2022), at https://livingchurch.org.

to the plague of overconsumption threatening the well-being of our planetary home. For Christians, such restraint would model that of Jesus of Nazareth, who according to Philippians 2:5–11 did not remain separated from the world but became present to human beings by taking on the form of a visible servant. Imitating such a praxis, far more than achieving a state of interior belonging or pursuing a quest for eco-theoretical unanimity, provides the urgent praxis-centered mediation that our species desperately needs in the here and now.

The Pedagogy of the Campus Quad

Green Aesthetics and Ecological Conversion in Catholic Higher Education

Timothy Hanchin

I run the nature trail that encircles the campus of Haverford College, a Quaker liberal arts undergraduate college located on the "Main Line" in suburban Philadelphia. The campus is a picturesque 216-acre arboretum. As a professor at nearby Villanova University, I am struck by the difference in the two campus landscapes distanced by less than three miles on Lancaster Avenue. Haverford's well-worn nature trail is relatively wild and unkempt. The loop traces the boundaries of the main campus as it transitions from wooded passages to meadow views and expanses of the campus quad. The trail creates a porous border that invites the local community in for recreation in the green space. The horizontally oriented campus architecture defers to the glory of untamed green space. The green aesthetic of Haverford College offers a foil to the more domesticated landscape of Villanova, a Catholic university, which exhibits a common collegiate proclivity for heavily mulched shrubbery and highly manicured quads. The contrast in green aesthetics raises the question of the relationship between campus landscape and education. That significant economic resources are used to shape and maintain a university's green aesthetic suggests that it is not unimportant.

In the encyclical *Laudato Si'*, Pope Francis summons a pedagogy of ecological conversion.[1] He remarks: "Environmental education should facilitate making the leap towards the transcendent which gives ecological ethics its deepest meaning. It needs educators capable of developing an ethics of ecology, and helping people, through effective pedagogy, to grow in solidarity, responsibility, and compassionate care" (no. 210). Francis adds: "Our efforts at education will be inadequate and ineffectual unless we strive to promote a new way of thinking about human beings, life, society and our relationship with nature. Otherwise, the paradigm of consumerism will continue to advance, with the help of the media and the highly effective workings of the market" (no. 215). What are the implications for Catholic higher education amid the climate crisis? More specifically, how does university green space mediate divine encounter at a Catholic university?

In the following, I consider *Laudato Si'*s clarion call for a pedagogy that recognizes "the relationship between a good aesthetic education and the maintenance of a healthy environment" (no. 215). In particular, I examine campus landscape as a neglected pedagogical element in educating for ecological conversion in Catholic higher education. To this end, I first present campus landscape as a hidden curriculum that reifies the technocratic paradigm. In *Laudato Si'*, Pope Francis identifies the technocratic paradigm as one of the human roots of the climate crisis. Second, I outline the educational vision for ecological conversion put forth in *Laudato Si'*. Third, I reimagine the university's green aesthetic in a way that honors landscape ecology as a vital participant in the university's identity formation. Campus landscape that reflects ecological conversion mediates God's relationality through a way of perceiving the world that is attentive to fundamental interconnectedness.

Campus Landscape and the Technocratic Paradigm

Education environmentalist David Orr describes campus architecture as pedagogy. "Campus architecture is crystallized pedagogy that often reinforces passivity, monologue, domination,

[1]Pope Francis, *Laudato Si'*, May 24, 2015.

and artificiality. My point is simply that students are being taught in various and subtle ways beyond the overt content of sources."[2] Orr adds that "buildings have their own hidden curriculum that teaches as effectively as any course taught in them. What lessons are taught by the way we design, build, and operate academic buildings?"[3] First, campus building design often tacitly teaches the academic community that locality is unimportant. Building design regularly favors a generic collegiate aesthetic over explicit connections to the local setting. Second, buildings that waste energy communicate that those resources are infinite without concern for the immediate impact on the biotic family and future generations. Third, the university community often remains ignorant about the ecological costs of building materials and construction. This information includes the ecological impact of sourcing construction materials and the discarding of by-products. Regardless of the content of the curriculum, buildings immerse learning in a context that teaches the disconnection to the larger web of life.[4]

Higher education has become more conscious of the relationship between building architecture and a mission-inspired commitment to confront the climate crisis. For example, Villanova University recently completed the construction of The Commons, a living and learning community that houses 1,135 students. The design includes dark sky–compliant light fixtures; underground cisterns that reuse stormwater to cool the buildings; energy-efficient sensor light fixtures; and low-flow plumbing fixtures to reduce energy costs.[5] Yale Divinity School will soon begin construction on The Living Village. It will be the world's largest green-building residential complex by producing zero waste, using only the water that falls on the site, and capturing all the energy it needs from the sun. Yale Divinity proposes The Living Village to reflect a theological commitment and serve as a model for higher education.[6]

---

[2]David Orr, *Earth in Mind: On Education, Environment, and the Human Prospect* (Washington, DC: Island Press, 2004), 114.

[3]Orr, *Earth in Mind*, 113.

[4]David Orr, *The Nature of Design: Ecology, Culture, and Human Intention* (New York: Oxford University Press, 2002), 128.

[5]"The Commons: Fast Facts," Villanova University, accessed June 30, 2023, https://www1.villanova.edu.

[6]"Living Village Project," Yale University, accessed June 30, 2023, https://divinity.yale.edu.

Landscape architecture, however, has not evolved with the same growing ecological concern in imagining campus green spaces in higher education. This is problematic for Catholic universities beholden to Catholic social teaching, which includes *Laudato Si*'s insistence on education for ecological conversion. Landscape and building architecture are complementary but distinct. In general, landscape remains a subordinate concern that largely frames campus buildings. Campus landscape often displays a green aesthetic informed by the suburban war on crabgrass and beauty attuned to the country club fairway. This green aesthetic uncritically celebrates the Anthropocene as groundskeepers exercise exacting, dominating control over the local ecology in pursuit of the highly manicured quad that punctuates the pedagogical imagination of American higher education. The green aesthetic of Catholic higher education echoes the American ideal of the lush and tidy lawn. Andrew Jackson Downing, one of America's first landscape-philosophers, said, "When smiling lawns and tasteful cottages begin to embellish a country, we know that order and culture are established."[7] The American lawn symbolizes civic virtue. Megan Garber remarks, "Lawns became aesthetic extensions of Manifest Destiny, symbols of American entitlement and triumph, of the soft and verdant rewards that result when man's ongoing battles against nature are finally won."[8]

Just as Orr described campus buildings as "crystallized pedagogy," landscape educates the campus community about human membership in the biotic family. As faculty, students, and staff crisscross campus quads over the course of a day, the green aesthetic reifies the "technocratic paradigm," which *Laudato Si'* identifies as part of the human roots of the ecological crisis.[9] Although not reducible to technology, the technocratic paradigm includes modern technology that distorts the relationship between

[7]A. J. Downing, *The Architecture of County Houses* (New York: D. Appleton, 1859), v.

[8]Megan Garber, "The Life and Death of the American Lawn," *The Atlantic* online, August 28, 2015.

[9]On the technocratic paradigm in relation to higher education, see Vincent Miller, "Higher Education and the Ecological Crisis: Integral Ecology as Catalyst for Critical and Creative Transdisciplinary Engagement," in *Catholic Higher Education and Catholic Social Thought*, ed. Bernard Prusak and Jennifer Reed-Bouley (New York: Paulist Press, 2023), 128–29.

humans and the larger created order. The technocratic paradigm "exalts the concept of a subject, who, using logical and rational procedures, progressively approaches and gains control over an external object." It contrasts earlier interventions in nature which were "a matter of receiving what nature itself allowed, as if from its own hand" (no. 106). The technocratic paradigm emerges from an "inadequate presentation of Christian anthropology" that "gave rise to a wrong understanding of the relationship between human beings and the world." The paradigm reflects a faulty interpretation of the biblical notion of dominion fueled by a "Promethean vision of mastery" rather than an expression of human responsibility and mutual exchange (no. 116). Biologist E. O. Wilson has argued that humans experience and express a kind of love and affinity for other life-forms impressed into human biology and consciousness, which he calls *biophilia*.[10] The technocratic paradigm, in contrast, manifests a human propensity to practice a kind of "apartheid at the species level," in which *anthropophilia* (love and concern for humans) overrides an innate human exigence toward *biophilia*.[11]

Particularly relevant to education is how the technocratic paradigm functions as an "epistemological paradigm" that reduces human moral and cultural problems as adequately understood by the methods of the natural sciences and best addressed through technological solutions. This science fundamentalism rules out love and the bonds of affection in human knowing. Academic hyper-specialization and the fragmentation of knowledge "often leads to a loss of appreciation for the whole, for the relationships between things, and for the broader horizon, which then becomes irrelevant" (no. 110). In contrast to a technocratic epistemology with its protocols aimed at mastery, possession, and control, *Laudato Si'* appeals to sacred wondering and mystery. "Rather than a problem to be solved, the world is a joyful mystery to be contemplated with gladness and praise" (no. 12).

Pope Francis's account of the technocratic paradigm intersects with Willie James Jennings's lament of the disconnection of Christian identity with land. Jennings remarks: "I want Chris-

---

[10]Edward O. Wilson, *Biophilia* (Cambridge, MA: Harvard University Press, 1984), 85.

[11]Larry Rasmussen, *Earth-Honoring Faith: Religious Ethics in a New Key* (New York: Oxford University Press, 2012), 22.

tians to recognize the grotesque nature of a social performance of Christianity that imagines Christian identity floating above land, landscape, animals, place, and space, leaving such realities to the machinations of capitalist calculations and the commodity chains of private property."[12] Jennings provides a corrective to the ahistorical silence of *Laudato Si'* on the colonial roots of the technocratic objectification of creation. Jennings links the loss of land-based Christian identity with the church's profoundly complicit role in European colonialism. He comments, "Rather than a way of life that illumines the God of Israel as the reality between land and peoples, colonialism established ways of life that drove an abiding wedge between the land and peoples."[13] Jennings describes the racial-spatial dynamics at play in the formation of social existence. "Geography matters for race as well as for identity, vision, and the hope of how one might live life. It is this deep connection between place and identity that will be difficult for many to grasp because people have been formed in a world in which such connections are only imagined, only fictions enabled solely by volition and market desire, the parents of private property."[14] Jennings augments Francis's description of technocratic fragmentation through the racial and colonial analysis of our spatial identity. The mission of Catholic higher education obligates it to offer a counter vision to the technocratic paradigm.

An Educational Vision of Ecological Conversion

In *Laudato Si'*, Pope Francis develops a vision of ecological conversion by illuminating its ecstatic quality. The witness of St. Francis of Assisi illustrates that ecological conversion entails *ekstasis*, the going-beyond of the self and the human community in the Anthropocene. Pope Francis remarks:

> Just as happens when we fall in love with someone, whenever [St. Francis] would gaze at the sun, the moon or the smallest of animals, he burst into song, drawing all other creatures into

[12]Willie James Jennings, *The Christian Imagination: Theology and the Origins of Race* (New Haven, CT: Yale University Press, 2010), 293.

[13]Jennings, *The Christian Imagination*, 292.

[14]Jennings, *The Christian Imagination*, 289.

> this praise. He communed with all creation. . . . His response to the world around him was so much more than intellectual appreciation or economic calculus, for to him each and every creature was a sister united to him by bonds of affection. That is why he felt called to care for all that exists. (no. 11)

The model of St. Francis overturns an educational vision that relegates the moral, affective, and religious dimensions of human existence as secondary to intellectual development.

Chapter 6 of *Laudato Si'*, titled "Ecological Education and Spirituality," offers a substantial treatment of ecological conversion as central to confronting the great cultural, spiritual, and educational challenge of climate crisis. Conversion, *metanoia*, is a turning around toward God and new life. As ecological conversion, *metanoia* means turning away from complicity in ecological devastation and turning toward life swelling with ecological awareness and hope. Ecological conversion "entails a loving awareness that we are not disconnected from the rest of creatures, but joined in a splendid universal communion" (no. 220).

Pope Francis outlines fundamental dispositions and commitments, informed by Christian spirituality, that constitute ecological conversion. As with genuine worship, ecological conversion emerges from contrition. Pope Francis remarks, "In calling to mind the figure of Saint Francis of Assisi, we come to realize that a healthy relationship with creation is one dimension of overall personal conversion, which entails the recognition of our errors, sins, faults and failures, and leads to heartfelt repentance and desire to change" (no. 218). Personal conversion entails an inherent communal dimension. Individualism remains morally impotent in the face of unethical consumerism untethered from social and ecological concerns. Therefore, lasting transformation requires "community conversion" (no. 219). Ecological conversion entails interlocking social networks that counteract the reign of self-referential individualism. In addition to repentance and community, Pope Francis highlights gratitude as a wellspring of ecological conversion. The recognition of the world as gift shifts the human relationship with creation from a standpoint of dominion to stewardship and even friendship.

Pope Francis concludes his description of ecological conversion by specifying the transformed human relationship with nonhuman members of the biotic family in terms of friendship. "May the power and the light of the grace we have received also be evident in our relationship to other creatures and to the world around us. In this way, we will help nurture that sublime fraternity with all creation which Saint Francis of Assisi so radiantly embodied" (no. 221). The divine-human friendship made available in the Incarnation and the gift of the Holy Spirit is manifest in the quality of human relationships with all of creation. Ecological conversion restores divine-human relationships.

Reimagining Catholic Higher Education's Green Aesthetic

In *Laudato Si'*, Pope Francis's appeal for a good aesthetic education draws from Pope John Paul II's message for the celebration of the World Day of Peace in January of 1990.

> Finally, the aesthetic value of creation cannot be overlooked. Our very contact with nature has a deep restorative power; contemplation of its magnificence imparts peace and serenity. The Bible speaks again and again of the goodness and beauty of creation, which is called to glorify God (cf. Gen 1:4ff.; Ps 8:2; 104:1ff.; Wis 13:3–5; Sir 39:16, 33; 43:1, 9). More difficult perhaps, but no less profound, is the contemplation of the works of human ingenuity. Even cities can have a beauty all their own, one that ought to motivate people to care for their surroundings. Good urban planning is an important part of environmental protection, and respect for the natural contours of the land is an indispensable prerequisite for ecologically sound development. The relationship between a good aesthetic education and the maintenance of a healthy environment cannot be overlooked.[15]

Catholic higher education can reimagine its green aesthetic to better educate the university community for ecological conversion.

Catholic higher education can rewild the campus quad. Instead of campus green spaces that resemble PGA fairways, universities can sustain tall grassy meadows punctuated by untamed wildflowers. A Catholic green aesthetic can disregard the American

---

[15]Pope John Paul II, "Peace with God the Creator, Peace with All of Creation," January 1, 1990.

expectation of maintaining a "smiling lawn." Michael Pollan observes, "Lawns, I am convinced, are a symptom of, and a metaphor for, our skewed relationship to the land. They teach us that, with the help of petrochemicals and technology, we can bend nature to our will."[16] The seeds that mostly carpet the campus quads in the United States (Kentucky blues, originally from Europe and northern Asia, Bermudas originally from Africa, Zoysias originally from East Asia) are generally not natives. These grasses can survive but require more water and fertilizers to plump up the local nutrient content and alter the viability of the soil to achieve the "American Dream Perma-Green."[17] In addition, turfgrass lacks diversity and does not perform needed ecosystem services to wildlife.

Daniel Jeff Wilder, director of applied ecology at Norcross Wildlife Foundation in Wales, Massachusetts, suggests lawn alternatives.[18] Instead of unceasing growing and mowing, campus green space can replace neatly shorn grasses with low-growing wild strawberry (*Fragaria virginiana*), which can withstand foot traffic, while the plants produce small, edible fruit for human and wildlife enjoyment. Its white flowers also provide an ecosystem benefit to pollinators. The leaves turn fiery tones in the fall. Villanova University could employ Pennsylvania sedge (*Carex pensylvanica*), a grass look-alike that can be mowed, which is a perennial native that supports dozens of native caterpillars. Wilder advises, "Embrace some of what people call weeds. The lawn-care industry convinced us that having clover is a bad thing in a lawn. But it's a legume that naturally fixes nitrogen in the soil, reducing our need for fertilizer—so how is that bad?"[19]

Catholic higher education can begin by considering, "What is here? What will nature permit us to do here? What will nature help us to do here?"[20] Catholic universities can transform campus quads into butterfly highways that aim to restore native pol-

---

[16]Michael Pollan, "Why Mow? The Case against Lawns," *New York Times*, May 28, 1989.

[17]Garber, "The Life and Death of the American Lawn."

[18]Margaret Roach, "Yes, You Can Do Better Than the Great American Lawn," *New York Times*, June 15, 2022.

[19]Roach, "Yes, You Can Do Better."

[20]Wendell Berry, *Home Economics* (San Francisco: North Point Press, 1987), 146.

linator habitats to areas affected by urbanization, land use, and agriculture. Butterfly highways participate in a network of native flowering plants to support butterflies, bees, birds, and other pollen- and nectar-dependent wildlife. Campus walkways could be lined with apple trees, blackberry bushes, or other local edibles that offer students snacking alternatives to thc highly processed shrink-wrapped goodies sold at the campus coffee bar.[21]

Reimagining the green aesthetic of the campus quad invites students, faculty, and staff to enter mutual self-mediating relationships with nonhuman members of the local ecosystem. In Bernard Lonergan's essay "The Mediation of Christ in Prayer," he distinguishes between four kinds of mediation: simple mediation, self-mediation, mutual mediation, and mutual self-mediation.[22] Lonergan refers to communities under self-mediation. The "community mediates itself in history."[23] In contrast, mutual self-mediation includes more than the individual or community as self-constituting but also includes the influence of one upon the other. Robert Doran explains: "Mutual self-mediation occurs between two human beings when one reveals one's own self-discovery and commitment to another and receives the self-revelation of the other; one opens oneself to be influenced at the depth of one's being, and others open themselves to be influenced by us."[24] Genuine conversation—and friendship—exemplify mutual self-mediation. A green aesthetic that reflects ecological conversion enjoys mutual self-mediation between human and nonhuman members of the campus landscape ecosystem.

The mutual self-mediation of the learning community with the university's green spaces enriches intellectual, moral, and religious development. Education research indicates the cogni-

---

[21]The cost of transforming campus landscape raises important economic justice issues heightened in the age of institutional precarity for a growing number of Catholic colleges and universities. Data on campus landscape expenditures in Catholic higher education is not readily available.

[22]Bernard Lonergan, "The Mediation of Christ in Prayer," in *Philosophical and Theological Papers, 1958–1964*, vol. 6 in the Collected Works of Bernard Lonergan (Toronto: University of Toronto Press, 2005), 6:160–82.

[23]Lonergan, "The Mediation of Christ in Prayer," 172.

[24]Robert Doran, "Reflections on Method in Systematic Theology," *Lonergan Workshop Journal* 17 (2002): 45.

tive benefit of campus landscape on student learning.[25] Although most structured learning occurs indoors within traditional instructional classrooms, student-nature encounters help restore attention. The campus landscape is a learning resource that enchants "direct attention," which enables learners to bracket distracting stimuli and focus on an intended activity.[26] By rewilding its green spaces, Catholic higher education draws the learning community's attention to the radical interdependence and fragility of all creation—including the human community. This approach "goes beyond advertising the aesthetic value of the campus open spaces for student recruitment purposes to recognizing the entire campus landscape as a learning space and advertising its educational value—that it emphasizes something deeper than what meets the eye."[27] In the mutual self-mediation of the human community and the local ecosystem, the deep connectivity of all creation is made visible, and the conditions for divine encounter and ongoing conversion flourish. Pope Francis highlights the trinitarian and relational character of ecological conversion. "The human person grows more, matures more and is sanctified more to the extent that he or she enters into relationships, going out from themselves to live in communion with God, with others and with all creatures. . . . Everything is interconnected, and this invites us to develop a spirituality of that global solidarity which flows from the mystery of the Trinity" (no. 240).

There is a growing chorus of theologians that challenge Christians to widen their language of community. Jennifer Ayers asks, "What if communities of faith also understood their ecosystem to be their community, as Aldo Leopold urged, and not just the backdrop against which their human community acts? Such self-understanding is the root of ecological consciousness."[28]

---

[25]Kathleen Scholl and Gowri Betrabet Gulwadi, "Recognizing Campus Landscape as Learning Spaces," *Journal of Learning Spaces* 4, no. 1 (2015): 53–60.

[26]Scholl and Gulwadi, "Recognizing Campus Landscape as Learning Spaces," 55.

[27]Scholl and Gulwadi, "Recognizing Campus Landscape as Learning Spaces," 58.

[28]Jennifer Ayers, *Inhabitance: Ecological Religious Education* (Waco, TX: Baylor University Press, 2019), 57.

Considered by many to be the father of wildlife ecology and the United States wilderness system, Leopold encouraged social ethics discourse to expand its language of community to include nonhuman members of the local ecology. Elizabeth Johnson urges Christians to enlarge the idea of the *communio sanctorum* to "include other living creatures, ecosystems, and the whole of the natural world itself. . . . The communion of holy peoples is intrinsically connected to the community of holy creation, and they stand or fall together."[29] Ecological conversion invites Catholic higher education to include its local ecosystems as vital participants in the conversation that a university is. Thomas Berry urges us to recover a basic and primeval ability to converse with the natural world. "We are talking only to ourselves. We are not talking to the rivers, we are not listening to the wind and stars. We have broken the Great Conversation."[30] A Catholic university is a community of academic conversation specified by charity, that love of friendship for God and for all of creation that bespeaks the influence and teaching of Christ.

Conclusion

In *Laudato Si'*, Pope Francis challenges educators to consider the role of pedagogical aesthetics in educating for ecological conversion. An educational vision of ecological conversion provides an alternative to the death-dealing habits of mind and heart dominant in the technocratic paradigm in our time. Catholic higher education can reimagine its green aesthetics to instigate ecological conversion that invites the university community to participate in a divine love pulling the world toward greater wholeness, depth, and relationality.[31]

[29]Elizabeth A. Johnson, *Friends of God and Prophets: A Feminist Theological Reading of the Communion of Saints* (New York: Continuum, 1998), 240.

[30]Thomas Berry and Thomas Clarke, *Befriending the Earth* (Mystic, CT: Twenty-Third Publications, 1991), 20.

[31]Ilia Delio, *The Unbearable Wholeness of Being: God, Evolution, and the Power of Love* (Maryknoll, NY: Orbis Books, 2013), 78.

Immediate Mediation

Desmond, Williams, and the Silent Image

Ethan Vander Leek

When I look out the window of my study in the library, I immediately encounter diversity. There is a tree, another tree, a building, the ivy crawling up the building, the gray sky. If I focus on a particular tree, I am confronted with further diversity: pinecones of different sizes, different shades of green, diverse length of branches, and more. Should I walk up to the tree, still further diversity presents itself in the detail of the pine needles, the texture of the pinecones. A biologist or chemist or a poet or painter could describe and encounter the tree even more deeply and in more detail.

The world shows itself as a profligate diversity. Before I arrive to behold and encounter this diversity, it is already at work, spreading itself out, giving itself in abundance. I encounter an excess that invites me ever further in. This excess is not empty in itself, waiting for my completing act of mediating perception. The world is over-full, overflowing, and my encounter with the world is a meeting of excess with excess. The world is given as excessiveness, and my minding of the world, my beholding it, is equally an excessiveness, not ultimately resting in this or that emotional or perceptual state, but moving ever further into the depths and diversity of the world. As the Psalmist says, "deep calls to deep in the roar of your waterfalls; all your waves and breakers have swept over me" (Psalm 42:7). The depth of the world offers itself to and invites the depths of my embodied perception, my experience, my dynamically minding activity: deep calls to deep.[1] And, as the Psalmist also suggests, such an encounter between me and the world is given by "you," by a personal God.

The philosophy of William Desmond provides some systematic categories and insights into the question of mediation in philosophical theology. Does God show himself through the mediation of creation? Does the world mediate God to us? Does mediation suggest a fall away from or diminishment of the fullness of the immediate presence of God? Or, alternatively, does immediacy need to be surpassed, overcome by the mediation and self-mediation of the human person or the human community? In what follows, I argue that mediation is neither a fall from primordial immediacy nor an elevation of empty immediacy into the fullness of (self-) mediation. Rather, with Desmond I argue that immediacy is immediately mediated; mediation is the immediate reality. God is immediately present through the mediation of creation. I further argue with Rowan Williams that mediation is not something to avoid, but to engage in ever more fully. For mediation ultimately means dynamic relationship, expressed theologically in God's mediation to us through creation and incarnation.

Metaxological Mediation

Desmond terms his metaphysics as "metaxology." *Metaxu* is the Greek for "middle" or "between," and so metaxology is the wording of the between, giving articulation to the between. To be between is to be in relation, a going out from self to other, dynamically inhabiting the space between self and other. As he writes,

> [Metaxology] puts stress on the mediated community of mind and being, but not in terms of the self-mediation of

[1]See Augustine's similar thought in his exposition of the same verse. He writes, "If 'deep' signifies profundity, surely the human heart is a deep abyss? Could anything be more profound? Human beings can speak, they can be observed as they use their limbs, and heard in their speech; but can we ever get to the bottom of a person's thoughts, or see into anyone's heart?" St. Augustine, *Expositions of the Psalms 33–50*, ed. John E. Rotelle, trans. Maria Boulding (Hyde Park, NY: New City Press, 2000), 251.

> the same. It calls attention to a pluralized mediation, beyond closed self-mediation from the side of the same, and hospitable to the mediation of the other, or transcendent, out of its own otherness. It suggests an intermediation, not a self-mediation. Moreover, the *inter* is shaped plurally by different mediations of mind and being, same and other, mediations not subsumable into one total self-mediation.[2]

Metaxology therefore is not an escape from mediation to immediacy. Neither does metaxology interpret mediation as a tragic fall from some pristine immediacy. Rather, mediation is a plural expression of what Desmond calls "surplus immediacy." The opening description of looking out the window is meant to communicate something of this surplus immediacy. There is immediacy, but it is always surplus, excessive, over-full. The surplus immediacy pluralizes itself into mediated diversity both in being and in mind. As Desmond writes, "Being is given to be as the happening of the between; but this between is *immediately given as mediated* between a plurality of centers of existence, each marked by its own energy of self-transcendence."[3]

In his essay "Surplus Immediacy, Metaphysical Thinking, and the Defect(ion) of Hegel's Concept," Desmond reads Hegel as articulating not a surplus immediacy but a *deficient* immediacy. Hegel's sense of immediacy, for Desmond, is empty and lacking determination. As Desmond summarizes Hegel, immediacy "is nothing in and for itself until the process of mediation, ultimately a self-mediation, articulating the universal form of thought, articulates for us what is there. Immediacy qua immediacy must always be downgraded to a 'mere' beginning, albeit necessary in its own way, but not sufficient, and in fact, absolutely insufficient."[4] This interpretation of Hegel serves to highlight Desmond's own notion

[2]William Desmond, *Being and the Between* (Albany: State University of New York Press, 1995), xii.

[3]William Desmond, "Metaxological Intermediation and the Between," *Metodo: International Studies in Phenomenology and Philosophy* 7, no. 2 (2019): 50; emphasis original.

[4]William Desmond, "Surplus Immediacy, Metaphysical Thinking, and the Defect(ion) of Hegel's Concept," in *The Intimate Strangeness of Being: Metaphysics after Dialectic* (Washington, DC: Catholic University of America Press, 20212), 72.

of "surplus immediacy." Instead of immediacy-as-emptiness *needing* mediation to emerge out of its own deficiency, immediacy-as-surplus invites or summons mediation out of its surplus, its excessiveness. In other words, the surplus immediacy underlies all the plural mediations of the world, both the diversity of beings and the diversity of mediating human activities. While it is true that we are always in some measure mediating the world to ourselves through culture, language, and interpretation, this mediation is dependent, not on defect and lack, but on abundance and over-fullness.

The world that we humans encounter and mediate through experience and through cultural, scientific, and artistic endeavors, is a mediation of the surplus immediacy. Starting from human experience and activity, there are thus three descending steps, each presupposing the next: first, our mediating activity presupposes; second, the mediated reality of the world, which presupposes; third, the surplus immediacy. Desmond willingly brings in theological categories into his philosophy, and here suggests the givenness of *creation*. He writes that creation is a

> primal ontological immediacy: that things are at all: in being and not nothing. This is an ultimate immediacy in that, without it nothing finite, or nothing within finitude, could mediate its being there at all. For this *being there at all* is presupposed by all such mediations; and indeed all such mediations are made possible by it as the primal immediacy of being given to be. . . . "Creation" is an immediate ontological intermediation that brings being to be, enabling the finite between to be, and possibilizing its plurivocal promise. This immediate intermediation of "creation" is a surplus happening presupposed by all intermediations *within the metaxu* of the finite given world.[5]

Our mediations of experience, culture, or anything else, are derivative of the immediate intermediation of creation, a gift, an ultimate relationality. Mediation, then, is not the opposite of immediacy. Immediacy is a surplus immediacy that invites and gives itself in plural mediations.

Now, our mediations can, indeed, cover over or distort surplus

[5]Desmond, "Surplus Immediacy," 76; emphasis original.

immediacy. Spiritual and philosophical disciplines remind us of the derivative nature of our constructions and mediations.[6] These disciplines (prayer, obedience, and silence, for example) awaken us to the astonishment of the surplus immediacy of being, given in the plural mediation of creation. Even our most aggressive or distorting mediations—for example, the environmental violence done to the nonhuman world, or religious and political institutions that exercise violent control over their people—are always derivative of this surplus immediacy. Distortion presupposes plenitude. We can never so fully mediate from our side of power and control that the surplus immediacy of being is absolutely erased. The surplus immediacy is always presupposed. The question is not *whether* we mediate this surplus immediacy, but *how* most faithfully to mediate it. For as surplus, it cannot be approached directly, it is not a determinate object: its immediacy is in the diverse mediations of the world around us: immediate mediation. Writes Desmond: "Our efforts to determine conceptually the meaning of this surplus immediacy call for a fidelity to the fullness of what is communicated in this elemental givenness."[7]

God and Surplus Immediacy

Having described surplus immediacy as that which underlies all mediations of both human activity and the plurality of creation, I now turn to the question of God: How does God relate to surplus immediacy? I suggest that surplus immediacy can fruitfully be interpreted as God himself. God simply is the immediacy of Being itself,[8] showing his excessiveness through the abundant pluralization of finite beings in creation, while never himself a

[6]For Desmond's philosophy as spiritual practice, see Ryan Duns, SJ, *Spiritual Exercises for a Secular Age: Desmond and the Quest for God* (South Bend, IN: Notre Dame University Press, 2020), esp. chap. 3.

[7]Desmond, "Surplus Immediacy," 73.

[8]In Desmond's meditation on God and being he writes: "God is not a being and yet as origin of being is. God is thus Being itself and beyond Being, since Being itself is *huperousia*," *God and the Between*, 287. Being as *huperousia* is God, the over-full excess of Being expressed though not exhausted in any finite thing.

determinate item or thing in creation.[9] "The excess of origin," writes Desmond, "generates the finite excess of plurality."[10] The "agapeic origin" is Desmond's name for God. As origin of creation, the agapeic origin creates, goes out beyond itself for the sake of the other. In this creation out of love, the agapeic origin both shows itself and reserves itself in the plenitude of finite creation. As Desmond writes,

> Though the divine can never be completely encapsulated in created things, through and indirectly in them it can still be approached. As a doubled image, finite being is a to-be-interpreted *poiesis* of the original ground. Finite things have being but are not ultimate or absolute; they image in their intermediate being the ultimate ground. They shimmer in their lack of fixed self-subsistence and make a dance of symbols that tells of something other or more.[11]

This notion of "double image" articulates how mediations both reveal and conceal, both manifest and hide. We must live and inhabit this tension. For we cannot say that images *only* conceal, for this would make them entirely untrue, entirely dissembling; they would not be images *of* anything. The image really connects with or is in a mediating relationship with what it images. But neither does it exhaustively image or show its original. God, as surplus immediacy, is an absolute excessiveness that no specific image or concept or creation can fully capture.

Hence Desmond's invitation to plural intermediations. We draw closer to the immediacy of God by seeing and uncovering the interconnectedness of the mediation of creation, how every finite image of God is involved with other images, so that the

---

[9]Also, even if we Christologically say that God *does* exhaustively identify himself with the man Jesus, Jesus is not an isolated, determinate item, but a dynamic, infinitely expressive relationality, showing the interconnectedness of all things. "He is before all things and in him all things hold together," Colossians 1:17. The excess of Jesus's silence, discussed below, emphasizes how Jesus cannot be circumscribed as a determinate object within a system.

[10]Desmond, *Being and the Between*, 263.

[11]William Desmond, *Philosophy and Its Others: Ways of Being and Mind* (Albany: State University of New York Press, 1990), 138.

whole creation in harmony sings God's praises and manifests his goodness. But any freezing of the isolated image becomes an idol. As Desmond writes, "When an image becomes an idol, it is we who create the change by collapsing an essential metaxological difference; it is not the thing itself that is an idol. An idol is a finite thing worshipped as though infinite."[12] He describes a Hindu practice, where a doll manifests or incarnates the god, but afterward is emptied of divinity and discarded in the Ganges River. "The very destruction of the religious image," he writes, "itself images religious respect for sacred otherness."[13]

"Mystery" is the category Desmond uses to articulate the middle way between a mediation that is an infinite fall from immediacy, and a mediation which fully and exhaustively mediates the divine, thus eliminating the difference between image and original.[14] The religious image is mysterious. The divine is present in the image, yet also entices a deeper and deepening mindfulness. Something not-yet present is made present in the image. Mediation-as-mystery describes that suspension of hiddenness and manifestation.

Everything speaks of God, who is the surplus immediacy that is refracted like white light through a prism into a plurality of colors, of beings, while always retaining his reserve and excessiveness. The surplus immediacy is a principle of unity; finite beings are in community with each other as issues of the surplus; they are not completely disassociated from each other. All beings are plural mediations of the one surplus immediacy. But neither is the surplus something that could be encountered or grasped in-itself. There is immediacy in the mediation of this surplus through diversity of beings, through a diversity of images. We come to know God, to know the surplus immediacy, not so much by stripping away the mediating beings and images, but by recognizing the common gift of being mediated through each of them, both in their singular uniqueness and in their community with each other. In this perspective there is

[12]Desmond, *Philosophy and Its Others*, 140.
[13]Desmond, *Philosophy and Its Others*, 139.
[14]Desmond, *Philosophy and Its Others*, 135–41.

> a pluralization of the event of mediation such that it is impossible to reduce the plurality to one form, namely, that of an encompassing self-mediation. Something escapes this reduction in the immanence of the between. Mediation is so pluralized that there is no singular mediation that will include all others within its own encompassing hold.[15]

Therefore, while the surplus immediacy is a principle of unity, it is not a reductive or totalizing unity. Rather, this unity speaks in profligate plurality, expressed in the diversity of creation. Each being-as-image offers itself as mystery, both showing and concealing the surplus immediacy. The community of beings, too, is mystery, in their constitutive relationality with all others, both showing and concealing the surplus immediacy mediated through the community of creation.

Because God is never exhausted in any one image, or even in the totality of images and beings, various religious and philosophical traditions have developed negative or apophatic theologies. The mystery invites silence, invites the negation of positive statements about or images of God. The practices of silence and negation emphasize the hidden pole in the manifestation-hiddenness dynamic of mystery.[16]

The temptation with negative theology is to think that negative theologies of silence are able to succeed where the positive theologies of images fail. We might think that, since the surplus immediacy is never exhaustively mediated, perhaps silence or negation can approach directly what the mediated image only offers indirectly. However, as Denys Turner says, "Negative signs, for all their negativity, are still signs."[17] Desmond suggests similarly that "silence is an image."[18] So, while negation and silence are indeed crucial, we must not understand them as somehow getting around the inexhaustibility of the surplus immediacy. All our images and words, even negative and silent ones, are mediations.

---

[15]Desmond, "Metaxological Intermediation and the Between," 67.

[16]Desmond, *Philosophy and Its Others,* 141–43.

[17]Denys Turner, *Faith, Reason, and the Existence of God* (Cambridge: Cambridge University Press, 2004), 65.

[18]Desmond, *Philosophy and Its Others,* 140.

Jesus the Silent Image

For further analysis of silence, I turn to Rowan Williams, especially as he relates silence to Jesus. For Williams, silence is always contextual, always in the midst of our working with words and images. There is no pure silence that approaches God directly, without mediation. Silence is an image of the infinite movement and task of mediation. As patiently and carefully as we attend to our mediating images and words, there always remain experiences and events beyond our control. Silence overtakes us when encountering powerful beauty or terrible loss. In these experiences, we know something that is not so much the opposite of mediation, as what exceeds mediation, what establishes mediation: the surplus immediacy. But again, silence is *not,* Williams writes, "a univocal breaking through to some kind of sacred absence."[19] We *must* use language and images. Such mediations are necessary for navigating the world. The image of silence, or the silent image, invites us to engage more deeply in the work of mediation; it does not allow us to run around mediation all together. As Williams writes, "We are not seeking a silence that will deliver us from the specificity of the world we inhabit but one that obliges an ever-deeper attention to it."[20]

Silence does not succeed where speech and images fail. Rather, it is a reminder that our mediations are mediations, are mysteries, not God, not the surplus immediacy "itself." The mysterious insight here is that there is no surplus immediacy "in itself," as if it were a determinate object just out of our reach. Rather, in a trinitarian inflection, we are engaged in an ongoing journey of mediations that participate in that infinite mediation which is the Triune God revealed in Jesus. God is himself immediate mediation, otherness in community with himself, infinite and dynamic relationality, Father and Son infinitely mediated and related in the Holy Spirit. The human work of mediation, of ongoing relation without collapsing into pure identity or dispersing into isolated

[19]Rowan Williams, *The Edge of Words: God and the Habits of Language* (London: Bloomsbury, 2014), 162.

[20]Williams, *The Edge of Words*, 164.

difference, is an ever-deeper participation in God's eternal life. As Williams writes, "Our acts become God's in the process whereby we come to long and love with God's longing and loving; and that can only be realized in us through emptiness, since God desires no 'object' but God, no satisfaction except the eternal continuance of an outpouring into the other."[21] This "emptiness" corresponds to silence: not to be thought as God "immediately" in himself, but an invitation into dynamic movement, further invited into the task of mediation with others and with the world. We encounter God immediately through the endless task of mediating with other people and the world around us, not an enclosed self-mediation, but an inter-mediation, seeking the good of the other without return to self. Such self-divestment is who God is as Trinity, "God's own self as eternal identity in otherness, a self-affirming in giving away."[22]

The diversity of gifts in the Spirit (Romans 12) articulates a plural response to the unity of the history of Jesus, the incarnate Son. Our mediations of the divine in word, image, and act should draw us more deeply into the infinite relationality of God, not seek to freeze it or make it comprehensible and controllable. Jesus, for Williams, is the revelation of this ungraspable dynamism, as he describes Jesus on trial before his death. "Jesus's supreme, eloquent silence before his judges is, in a sense, the moment of supreme revelation in the Gospels. It is where he becomes visibly the mysterious reality that nobody knows how to talk about. . . . What is happening in Jesus is something immeasurably [outside] of the ordinary categories and habits by which people organize the world."[23]

The silence of Jesus, once again, is not the end of a story, but an over-full, excessive beginning. His story and person, beyond

---

[21]Rowan Williams, "The Deflections of Desire: Negative Theology in Trinitarian Disclosure," in *Silence and the Word: Negative Theology and Incarnation,* ed. Oliver Davies and Denys Turner (Cambridge: Cambridge University Press, 2002), 115–35.

[22]Rowan Williams, *On Christian Theology* (Malden, MA: Blackwell, 2000), 74.

[23]Rowan Williams, *Being Human: Bodies, Minds, and Persons* (Grand Rapids, MI: William B. Eerdmans, 2018), 96. See also Rowan Williams, *Christ on Trial: How the Gospel Unsettles Our Judgement* (Grand Rapids, MI: William B. Eerdmans, 2000).

our individual or even communal comprehension, inaugurates a community of diverse gifts in the Spirit and offers an ongoing stimulus for interpreting the world and our relationships afresh. The revelation of God in Christ moves us to silence but then further to an infinite task; silence is not an end in itself. "Revelation," writes Williams,

> is nothing to do with absolute knowledge. It both is and is not completed, "over"; *what* we are interpreting is unquestionably this historical narrative and not another; we are not waiting for a more comprehensive or adequate story, because precisely of the comprehensiveness of the questioning provoked by this story. Yet this is not to say that there is an end to questioning or unclarity. The claims of our foundational story to universal relevance and significance mean that it must constantly be *shown* to be "at home" with all the varying enterprises of giving meaning to the human condition. Thus the "hermeneutical spiral" never reaches a plateau. For the event of Christ to be authentically revelatory, it must be capable of both "fitting" and "extending" any human circumstance; it must be re-presentable, and the form and character of its re-presentation are not necessarily describable in advance.[24]

To blend the discourses of Williams and Desmond, we might say that the surplus immediacy of Jesus, the revelation of his story, continues in the mediations of the church, and negative theology and silence have to do with inspiring and provoking that continued mediation. This is why Williams describes negative theology as an ecclesial practice, where, as he writes, "no single subject possesses the whole or can articulate the whole."[25] The determinate history of Jesus has or is an overdeterminate or surplus significance, and continually summons us to more work, further mediation, deeper interpretation. We are again returned to the ongoing spiritual discipline of mediation, always mediat-

---

[24]Rowan Williams, *On Christian Theology*, 142–43; emphasis original.

[25]Rowan Williams, *Understanding and Misunderstanding "Negative Theology"* (Milwaukee, WI: Marquette University Press, 2021), 26.

ing the excess of creation and the Christ-event. "The discipline of the negative," writes Williams, "is to do with how we find an appropriate imaginative place to inhabit in the face of an abundance which will always be irreducibly other and 'excessive' for us to the extent that the individual thinking subject persistently seeks to replace this abundance with what it can encompass and categorize."[26] Since we are all, in some measure, persistent in just this way, disciplines of silence lead us away from the effort to encompass and categorize, and toward not a pure immediacy but ever-further self-divestment, to image God in our lives and see God's images in creation by becoming more dynamic and less static.

Thus, the philosophical perspective of Desmond converges with the Christological-theological work of Williams. Desmond's surplus immediacy articulates philosophically what Williams's Christology suggests theologically: our ongoing incorporation into the excessiveness of God-in-creation and God-in-Jesus. Further, if the incarnation is God becoming a creature, and if all creatures are immediately mediated in and with each other, then philosophical encounter with the surplus immediacy of creation is also an encounter with the surplus immediacy of the incarnation. From this perspective, philosophy itself, as thoughtful reflection on what is given in the world around us, is only possible because of the incarnation, which establishes, completes, and sums up creation. As David Bentley Hart writes, "All created things are contained within the scope of the incarnation, so much so that one must say that creation *is* the incarnation."[27] As creatures in creation, we are thus immediately caught up in the task of mediating the surplus immediacy of the incarnation. The silent image of Jesus invites an always further, deeper work of mediation: interpreting and engaging with the surplus immediacy of God expressed through creation. The excess of Jesus, imaged in his own silence and provoking the silence of others, is present through creation. By recognizing that we cannot grasp *him* we acknowledge that we

---

[26]Williams, *Understanding and Misunderstanding "Negative Theology,"* 29.

[27]David Bentley Hart, *You Are Gods: On Nature and Supernature* (Notre Dame, IN: University of Notre Dame Press, 2022), 113.

cannot grasp *anyone* or *anything* within the totality of our finite mind and self-mediating activity. We are thus oriented beyond such totality to an infinite journey of mediation, a pilgrimage which does not close in on itself but opens itself to every further diversity and plurality, revolving around the silent, surplus image of Jesus, the Word made flesh.

MEDIATION

AND

ART

"A Medium with a Message"

Corita, Media, and the Catholic 1960s

Tim Dulle

In a playful, poetic preface to Corita Kent's 1967 book *Footnotes and Headlines*, Daniel Berrigan riffed on the famous formulation of media theorist Marshall McLuhan, christening the artist "a medium with a message."[1] A luminary of the Catholic 1960s, when the consumerism and conformity of the postwar United States ran headlong into the reforms of the Second Vatican Council, Corita Kent was internationally renowned for her pop art serigraphs, her socially conscious "advertising for the common good,"[2] and for the innovative pedagogy she developed at Immaculate Heart College in Hollywood. Her silkscreen prints channeled an optimistic strain of Catholic spirituality in an effort to reinvigorate the detritus of US consumer culture, searching for hope in a rapidly changing and often disorienting period of cultural turmoil.

[1]Daniel Berrigan, foreword to *Footnotes and Headlines: A Play-Pray Book* by Corita Kent (New York: Herder and Herder, 1967). Ironically, in a *Newsweek* story for which Corita appeared on the issue's cover, also published in 1967, one Lutheran pastor said of her: "She's sort of a medium without a message—insisting on the changing image, rather than the stable concept, as the proper religious approach." See "The Nun: A Joyous Revolution," *Newsweek*, December 25, 1967, 46.

[2]This text is drawn from one of Corita's silkscreens. See Corita Kent, *yes people like us*, serigraph, 35in. x 28 ¾ in., 1965, corita.org. Note that the titles of all Corita's serigraphs are italicized without capitalization, a practice likely borrowed from e. e. cummings, whom she cited frequently.

Born in Iowa in 1918 and raised in Los Angeles, Corita joined the California branch of the Sisters of the Immaculate Heart of Mary when she graduated from high school in 1936.[3] By the 1950s, she was a practicing artist with a growing reputation, and a beloved art teacher. In the early 1960s, after an encounter with Andy Warhol's *Campbell's Soup Cans*, Corita decided to begin making Catholic pop art. Her bold engagement with the latest artistic and cultural trends won her a wide audience, and by the time she left religious life and Catholicism in 1968, former *New York Times* religion writer John Cogley wrote that she had been "the best known religious in the United States and the walking symbol of the 'new nun.'"[4]

Though the convergences in their thinking have yet to receive much scholarly treatment, Corita also took inspiration from Marshall McLuhan. Her most beloved creations use the manipulation of printed text to explore the possibilities and instabilities of words-in-space (that is, print, or the printed word) to, in her phrase, "take back" words and images from advertisements, "to restore some of their life."[5] In this essay, I show how the work of media theorists, specifically McLuhan and his onetime student Walter J. Ong, provide tools to make sense of many of Corita's 1960s serigraphs. I argue that Corita's work with words stands among the significant media experiments of the Vatican II era, offering insight into an understudied dimension of the *aggiornamento* and its attendant conflicts. More specifically, Corita provides an example of one artist experimenting with media and mediation of the sacred through the cultural vernacular, and her work, I contend, is that of a figure caught between the text-driven visual world of print culture and the emergent setting defined by the instantaneous, unstable character of electronic media. The

---

[3]I note that "Corita" is the proper way to refer to the artist, as per her estate. See Frequently Asked Questions in the "About Corita" section of the Corita Art Center's website, corita.org.

[4]John Cogley, "Corita: Another Symbol Is Gone," *National Catholic Reporter,* December 4, 1968.

[5]Pamela Roth, "A Conversation with Corita Kent," *American Way*, November 1970, 11. Available in "Articles or Interviews by Corita (1950s–1970s)," Box 9.1, Corita collection, Corita Art Center, Immaculate Heart Community.

clash of these two worldviews is an infrequently acknowledged aspect of the conflicts of the Vatican II era, with important implications for understanding trends in religious identity over the past fifty to sixty years.

McLuhan, Ong, and Media Theories

A celebrity scholar beginning in the 1950s, Marshall McLuhan, is famous for memorable and provocative sound bites including "The medium is the message" and the phrase "global village."[6] His major insight, the idea underneath his many slogans, is that the tools humans use to communicate, media, also shape them and rearrange their consciousness. Complementary to McLuhan's is the work of Walter J. Ong, who was McLuhan's student at Saint Louis University. Ong's major project was to trace how new media, especially the development of the alphabet, followed by writing and printing, and then by electronic culture, reshaped users' mental and social worlds, their sensorium and personality structures, with a focus ranging from the early modern period to the late twentieth century.

From the many compelling threads in their vast body of work, most useful here is the transition these thinkers lay out, from (1) an oral-aural world defined by individuals speaking and hearing, largely unaided by additional technology, to (2) the highly visual worlds of manuscript and then print culture, in which words are committed to space through the technology of alphabetic characters, opening the door to, in Ong's words "abstractly sequential, classificatory, explanatory examination of phenomena,"[7] to (3) with the rise of electronic forms of communication such as radio, film, and television, the development of what Ong calls "secondary orality," a situation in which societies re-embrace oral norms, but

[6]The phrase "the medium is the message" appears frequently throughout McLuhan's work but is most prominently explained in the first chapter of his landmark *Understanding Media*. See Marshall McLuhan, *Understanding Media: The Extensions of Man* (1964; Cambridge, MA: MIT Press, 1994), 7–21. The idea of "the global village" is developed in Marshall McLuhan, *The Gutenberg Galaxy* (Toronto: University of Toronto Press, 1962).

[7]Walter J. Ong, *Orality and Literacy: The Technologizing of the Word* (New York: Routledge, 1982), 8.

on a scale impossible for basically oral societies, marked in complex ways by the widespread experience of writing and reading.

It is important, indeed foundational, to remember that the transition between these historical periods does not mean exclusive reliance on either orality or literacy. Ong's primary example here is the discipline of rhetoric, which studies public speaking, but which as an academic subject necessarily relies on writing both for the recording of speeches to be studied and for "making it possible to organize the 'principles' or constituents of oratory into a scientific 'art,' a sequentially ordered body of explanation."[8] Precisely to this point, Corita's work makes visible some of the complex interaction between print culture and secondary orality, or electronic culture, and the impact of this transition on US Catholic culture in the conciliar era and after.

Probably the most important aspect of this transition for this analysis is one of Ong's claims about the interrelationship between word, text, and persons. Namely, he makes a compelling case that the world of oral-aural communication, the world of sound, is also the world of presence, a sense of presence which writing largely fails to convey. This is because sound is always the sound of something happening, in the present tense. In the case of words, in a pre-electronic age, the spoken word is always spoken by another person and is indicative of their being present. A close corollary here is that sound, uniquely among human senses, provides a sense of depth or interiority. To apprehend the world visually, meanwhile, provides access only to surfaces.[9]

Understanding the human sensorium this way has relatively direct implications for thinking about spirituality and religious practice. In *The Presence of the Word*, Ong writes that "the shift of focus from the spoken word and habits of auditory synthesis to the alphabetized written word and visual synthesis . . . devitalizes the universe, weakens the sense of presence in man's life-world, and in doing so tends to render this world profane, to make it an

---

[8]Ong, *Orality and Literacy*, 9.

[9]This is a key insight of the pop art movement more generally. See Hal Foster, *The First Pop Age: Painting and Subjectivity in the Art of Hamilton, Lichtenstein, Warhol, Richter, and Ruscha* (Princeton, NJ: Princeton University Press, 2012).

agglomeration of things."[10] The very fact of writing as a medium carries certain implications, as captured by McLuhan's famous phrase, and this sense of absence is heightened in the transition from writing to printing. If the world of sound is a world of presences, the world of manuscript (handwriting) is less so, and the world of printing, pretty much not at all. Ong notes, "Printed texts look machine made, as they are." In contrast to frequently "ornate, ornamental" manuscripts, "Typographic control typically impresses more by its tidiness and inevitability," giving the impression of "an insistent world of cold, non-human facts."[11] The shift from orality to literacy, on this account, subtly participates in the disenchantment of the universe.

Importantly, Ong also offers insight into something of how style functions relative to its medium. Most notable for print culture is this sense of absence described above, and a few others are worth mentioning. For example, print is generally conducive to a culture of individualism. One might think of the isolated reader, thinking privately in the solitude of their own consciousness, far removed from a situation where knowledge is necessarily dialogical, as is characteristic of oral societies. As McLuhan says, "Print is the technology of individualism."[12] Another implication is that, as Ong writes, "print encourages a sense of closure, a sense that what is found in a text has been finalized, has reached a state of completion."[13] Moreover, "Print creates a sense of closure not only in literary works but also in analytic philosophical and scientific works."[14] In thinking about these media shifts in relationship to Catholic history, one need only note that Tridentine Catholicism arose not long after the printing press, and Vatican II was more or less parallel to the era of Ong's secondary orality, or McLuhan's electronic age.[15]

[10]Walter J. Ong, *The Presence of the Word: Some Prolegomena for Cultural and Religious History* (1967; New York: Simon and Schuster, 1970), 162.

[11]Ong, *Orality and Literacy*, 122.

[12]McLuhan, *Gutenberg Galaxy*, 158.

[13]Ong, *Orality and Literacy*, 132.

[14]Ong, *Orality and Literacy*, 134. Ong highlights catechisms and textbooks as two signature products of this mentality.

[15]McLuhan himself described "the world of Vatican II, where acoustic

Amid the ambiguity and messiness of these large-scale changes, McLuhan identifies a certain sort of figure who is critical for tracking these shifts: the artist. He writes, "The effects of technology do not occur at the level of opinions or concepts, but alter sense ratios or patterns of perception steadily and without any resistance. The serious artist is the only person able to encounter technology with impunity, just because he is an expert aware of the changes in sense perception."[16] McLuhan goes so far as to write that "art is precise advance knowledge of how to cope with the psychic and social consequences of the next technology." Or, similarly, art is "exact information of how to rearrange one's psyche in order to anticipate the next blow from our own extended faculties," meaning newly developed communication media.[17]

Corita Kent, I suggest, was an artist well suited for the Catholic 1960s, an artist who worked to provide this sort of "precise advance knowledge" for how Catholics could adjust their spirituality to the psychic and social consequences to the new media environment under the influence of the American consumer vernacular and Vatican II.

Corita's Work and Her Words

How does Corita's art exist at the juncture of visual culture and electronic culture, and how can her artistic experiments be understood as playing with the possibilities of media in relation to spirituality? Among her hundreds of prints, I limit my examples to work from the mid-1960s, namely serigraphs from the pop art period for which she is best known.[18]

---

man has reappeared in the midst of the great nineteenth-century bureaucracies that still dominate the political, educational, and religious spheres." See Marshall McLuhan, "Liturgy and Media: Do Americans Go to Church to Be Alone?" in *The Medium and the Light: Reflections on Religion*, ed. Eric McLuhan and Jacek Szklarek (Toronto: Stoddart, 1999), 131.

[16]McLuhan, *Understanding Media*, 18.

[17]McLuhan, *Understanding Media*, 66. On the relationship between McLuhan and artists, see Alex Kitnick, *Distant Early Warning: Marshall McLuhan and the Transformation of the Avant-Garde* (Chicago: University of Chicago Press, 2021).

[18]Interested readers can find the works discussed here, and most of Corita's serigraphs from across her entire career, in digital form in the "Collection" section of corita.org.

Here, I include four serigraphs for consideration. First, from 1964, *for eleanor*, which isolates the script G of the General Mills corporation logo, with accompanying text suggesting that "the Big [G] stands for Goodn[ess]."[19] The print relies on the coincidence of consumer abundance, warm domestic sentiment, and the traditional notion of goodness as a divine attribute. The "Big G" stands as a symbol variously signifying the General Mills brand, goodness, or God, in whatever combination one likes. The idea is that reader-viewers can play with the meaning.

[19]Corita Kent, *for eleanor*, 1964, serigraph, 29 5/8 in. x 39 in., corita.org.

Another print from 1964, *mary does laugh*, is a bit more adventurous with text.[20] Market Basket is a chain of supermarkets, and in the 1950s and '60s it had a location in Hollywood, across the street from Corita's campus. In the print, a portion of the company's logo sits in the center, surrounded by words that literally exceed the work's edges, evoking the sort of abundance characteristic of what were then relatively new things, supermarkets. So far as I can tell, the uncontainable words appear to be food-centric, including "burger" and "tomato," implying that this visual information abundance was somehow akin to the consumer abundance newly experienced by many Americans in the postwar era. The central text comes from a letter written by an Immaculate Heart student, Marcia Petty, for the college's Mary's Day, which celebrated the Virgin Mary. Commenting that the women of IHC deserved to understand Mary as relevant to their own lives, the student wrote, "Mary does laugh; and she sings and runs and wears bright orange. Today she'd probably do her shopping at the Market Basket."[21]

A serigraph with similarly manipulated text, from 1966, bears the title *new hope*.[22] Significantly, this work is dedicated to Mildred and Richard Loving, whose marriage violated Virginia's anti-miscegenation laws, and whose case *Loving v. Virginia* was the case by which the US Supreme Court ruled unconstitutional all laws against interracial marriage. In addition to this social commentary, the work illustrates Corita's formal innovations. As Jennifer Roberts has analyzed, in addition to the generally eye-catching style of the main text, the words "new hope" in the upper right are laid out so as to almost read "men hope." On the left of the print, Corita includes words from an e.e. cummings love poem, offered as a sort of inspiration to the couple, and thus also to the reader-viewer.[23]

---

[20]Corita Kent, *mary does laugh*, 1964, serigraph, 29 3/4 in. x 39 ¼ in., corita.org.

[21]For more on the letter which the print's text draws on, see Richard Meyer, "Shop Rite: Corita Kent's Supermarket Poetics," in *Corita Kent and the Language of Pop*, ed. Susan Dackerman (Cambridge, MA: Harvard Art Museums, 2015), 136.

[22]Corita Kent, *new hope*, 1966, serigraph, 30 in x 36 in., corita.org.

[23]Jennifer Roberts, "Backwords: Screenprinting and the Politics of Re-

A final example comes from the prints Corita made for her series *damn everything but the circus*, each depicting one letter of the alphabet. Beyond the visual appeal and the infectious sense of whimsy embodied by these prints, it is notable that Corita made multiple series of alphabets, and her instinctive sense of the importance of individual letters can be a clue to how well her work relates to the theories of McLuhan and Ong, each deeply concerned with alphabetic symbols. As Ong notes, "The alphabet implies . . . that a word is a thing, not an event, that it is present all at once, and that it can be cut up into little pieces." In this, "It represents sound itself as a thing, transforming the evanescent world of sound to the quiescent, quasi-permanent world of space."[24] Corita's "S" in this series bears the accompanying text, "Highly instructive and amusing," and, in smaller text, "My favorite symbols were those which I didn't understand."[25]

In addition to Corita's serigraphs, archival materials show how her art works particularly well in dialogue with the theories laid out above. Corita's self-understanding also reveals an artist whose work reflects her historical position, caught up in the transition from print culture to electronic culture. In a 1970 interview, Corita lays out a few breadcrumbs for taking up this line of inquiry. Asked to describe her own art, she replies, "I also respect the word and like to see it sometimes taken off the printed page or 'illuminated' so to say," which "becomes something between speaking and the typeset page."[26] Ong and McLuhan's theories frequently emphasized writing as the locking of words into visual space, and Corita wanted to resist consigning words to such a fate. She says further, "I have had fun taking back ordinary good words and phrases from ads and trying to restore some of their life to them. Words have life and must be cared for. If they are stolen for ugly uses or careless slang or false promotion work they need to be brought back to their original meanings."[27] In

versal," in *Corita Kent and the Language of Pop*, 68.

[24]Ong, *Orality and Literacy*, 91.

[25]Corita Kent, *s my favorite symbols*, 1968, serigraph, 22 ¾ in. x 22 ¾ in., corita.org.

[26]Roth, "A Conversation," 11.

[27]Roth, "A Conversation," 11.

this sense, Corita makes an important step, one which potentially gestures toward a re-enchantment of the universe which might be possible in an electronic age.

It is also worth noting how Corita conceived of this as a spiritual project. While still a Catholic and a woman religious in 1964, she authored a piece about the relationship between art and human awareness of God's presence. Imploring readers to take up a new way of looking at the world, one informed by the sort of openness and playful spirit illustrated by these serigraphs, Corita wrote, "We all suffer from a kind of deafness to the things of God calling out to us in everyday reality." Therefore, "We need a 'sign language' so as to hear what God is saying to us through them."[28] Moreover, she positions this project as explicitly tied to the ongoing renewal of Vatican II and does so in a way that is suggestive of some of the tensions between media cultures described above. She writes that "many grown-ups of this generation are terribly nervous about the unfinished and the unexpected, about impermanent, growing, changing things." However, "If the grown-ups of the next generation have, as children, done all this opening up and searching and relating and questioning, they will be less nervous about the spelling out of the *aggiornamento*."[29]

Elsewhere, to this point, Corita relies more directly on McLuhan in thinking about cultural tensions and the spiritual dimension of her project. In her contribution to a 1967 magazine symposium, Corita created a distinctive collage of images and text. Splashed across two pages are photos depicting Vietnamese war victims contrasted with pictures of female models whose luxurious hair evokes an ad for haircare products.[30] To this mix, Corita adds

---

[28]Corita Kent, "The Visual Arts," *The Living Light* 1, no. 2 (Summer 1964): 7. Manuscript available in "Manuscripts by Corita (1950s–1960s)," Box 9.2, Corita collection, Corita Art Center, Immaculate Heart Community.

[29]Kent, "The Visual Arts," 9.

[30]The identity of the distressed children in the collage is not specified, but an earlier and similar image in the piece is accompanied by the quote from United Nations secretary-general U Thant, which reads "The War in Vietnam is one of the most barbarous wars in history." Corita Kent, "The Artist as Communicator," *The Critic*, August–September 1967. Available in "Articles or Interviews by Corita (1950s–1970s)," Box 9.1, Corita collection, Corita Art Center, Immaculate Heart Community.

a long quote from McLuhan which states in part that "TV has created within the same young [people] an unconscious demand for depth involvement in all the situations of home and society," which "appears to many parents and teachers as unreal and even outrageous." This, McLuhan concludes, "has awakened spiritual depth in the young."[31] While still writing as a Catholic sister, then, Corita frequently approached catechetical or pastoral work with McLuhan's ideas in mind, an influence that carried across publications in different media.

"A One-Woman *Aggiornamento*"

With good McLuhanesque sensibility, Corita once offered a brief synopsis of what she was up to in bringing text and images together, and in appropriating material from the everyday world around her. "Words are pictures (they have visible forms) as well as carriers-of-concepts (verbal forms)," she wrote, "and with all of the signs that are around us in our manscapes and landscapes, there is a great kind of conversation going on between words and pictures where one beams on the other, illuminating the other as persons do to persons."[32] To those in the business of studying Catholics, this reads as a fairly run-of-the-mill analogical or sacramental worldview, to which I add that Corita's particular application of these principles was a phenomenon of its era, both drawing on and speaking back to the Catholic 1960s.[33] Moreover, the awareness that undergirded Corita's work to "restore some life" to the written words all around her was made possible by her recognition of herself as caught up in the transition between two media cultures, her consciousness indelibly structured by print culture, yet open to the changes affected by developments in radio, film, and television.

---

[31]Kent, "The Artist as Communicator." The quote is attributed to "McLuhan," but includes no additional citation.

[32]Corita Kent, "Choose LIFE or Assign a Sign or Begin a Conversation," *The Living Light* 3, no. 1 (Spring 1966): 2. Available in "Articles or Interviews by Corita (1950s–1970s)," Box 9.1, Corita collection, Corita Art Center, Immaculate Heart Community.

[33]The work which most informs my own thinking here is David Tracy's *The Analogical Imagination: Christian Theology and the Culture of Pluralism* (New York: Crossroad, 1981).

Corita's work is one clue to how the influence of media on the structures of consciousness and on social structure has been an insufficiently understood aspect of the Vatican II era.[34] John O'Malley's masterly work on the distinct style of the conciliar documents does point in this direction, as he examines how their novel genre relative to past councils not only decreed but put into practice the distinctive themes of Vatican II.[35] Likewise, many of the era's conflicts, paradigmatically that between Cardinal McIntyre of Los Angeles and the IHM sisters over the order's experiments in reform, can profitably be understood as clashes between sensibilities and styles informed by the norms of print culture and the emerging personality structures formed by electronic culture.[36]

Ong and McLuhan, as Catholics living and writing during Vatican II, were not inattentive to the council. McLuhan, though he published little directly on the topic, was a keen observer of it, and wrote to Frank Sheed in 1970, "There was nobody at Vatican I or II who showed any understanding of the electro-technical thing in reshaping the psyche or culture of mankind."[37] In a similarly brief fashion, Ong does gesture briefly toward Vatican II in *The Presence of the Word*, noting that the council responded effectively to the "sense of an urgent present in which technological man now lives" by embracing a more dialogical approach marked by spontaneity, and observing, "Public airing of unresolved questions has become a way of life" in the church and in society.[38] However, Ong was not himself a scholar of religious history, and even the work which most frequently discusses religion, as per its subtitle, remains merely "Some Prolegomena for Cultural and Religious History."

Which is to say, while McLuhan and Ong have laid impres-

---

[34]The Vatican II document *Inter Mirifica* does address "the media of social communications," but bears little relationship to the McLuhan-Ong school of analysis.

[35]John W. O'Malley, *What Happened at Vatican II* (Cambridge, MA: Belknap Press of Harvard University Press, 2008).

[36]For a fuller account, see Anita Caspary, *Witness to Integrity: The Crisis of the Immaculate Heart Community* (Collegeville, MN: Liturgical Press, 2003).

[37]Marshall McLuhan, "'Achieving Relevance:' Letters to Mole and Sheed," in *The Medium and the Light*, 140.

[38]Ong, *The Presence of the Word*, 299.

sive and useful groundwork, scholars have yet to capitalize on their advances. Corita Kent, a figure long appreciated but seldom understood in depth by scholars of American Catholicism, helps direct attention to these understudied dimensions of the field. And who better to do so than Corita, the woman whom the *New Yorker* dubbed "a one-woman *aggiornamento*"?[39]

---

[39]James Stevenson, "Peace on Earth," *New Yorker*, January 1, 1966, 23.

Illumination and Sonic Synesthesia

Present and Absent Ornamentation in Hildegard von Bingen

Charles A. Gillespie

Mediation suffuses the synesthetic theology, praxis, and reception of St. Hildegard von Bingen. The twelfth-century Benedictine abbess produced an impressive corpus of visionary writings, supervised illustrated illuminations, song cycles, medicinal treatises, and the Christian world's oldest extant chant-drama: the *Ordo Virtutum*. Hildegard's multimedia conception of the Benedictine *ora et labora* frames ornamentation—what I define as artistic mediation seeking "beautification"—to be a simultaneous playing, praying, and working. The *presence* of ornamentation (like singing, a musical skill for illumination operating on analogy to manuscript images in Hildegard's writing) elevates ordinary words into Trinitarian expressions. So too, imposing the *absence* of ornamentation tempts a turn away from the divine. Knowing God's way (the title of Hildegard's major book, *Scivias*) means learning heavenly melody in contrast to demonic cacophony.

But what might I mean by a phrase like "sonic synesthesia"? Synesthesia describes the gift where certain sensorial experiences manifest complementary sensorial experiences. It is the experience of one sense experience alongside or through another. Synesthesia names that delightful capacity to hear colors and taste sounds. Synesthesia describes *pairings* between experiences. Some report a particular color that goes along with any given letter or number.

Others report the alignment of colors with sounds or numbers.[1] According to the American Psychological Association's *Monitor on Psychology*, research suggests that only about one in two thousand people are "full-fledged synesthetes," but as many as one in three hundred experience some sort of overlapping sensorial sensation.[2] By "sonic synesthesia" I mean to identify the possibility to experience sound, particularly music, through a variety of senses. This gift appears to be rare if we restrict ourselves to material or fleshly interpretation. I want to contend that while a normative anthropology may not presume every human can hear colors and taste sounds, we all might cultivate greater openness to the Holy Spirit uplifting our bodily senses to become synesthetic with our spiritual senses. By "sonic synesthesia" I mean to name how *sound*, via the case of musical sound, mediates spiritual sensation and insight.

Am I claiming that Hildegard was a synesthete? Some scholars try to explain her visions materially via an experience of migraine headaches.[3] Maybe yes, maybe no. But I offer that Hildegard intuits ways for us to hear a spiritual vision, one where the presence and absence of *ornamentation* mediates divinity. This essay treats three ways the presence or absence of music mediates divine knowledge-power for Hildegard. The first section addresses the essential role of sonic and visual illuminations for her theology. Synesthetic experiences are aspects of her spirituality and ground her interpretation of divine presence as "living light." The second section takes up gendered and vocational embodiment in ritual performance(s) of her music-drama *Ordo Virtutum*. The lines of the protagonist soul and the heavenly virtues are sung by

---

[1]See, among many, R. E. Cytowic, *Synesthesia: A Union of the Senses*, 2nd ed. (Cambridge, MA: MIT Press, 2002).

[2]Siri Carpenter, "Everyday Fantasia: The World of Synesthesia," *Monitor on Psychology* 32, no. 3 (March 1, 2001).

[3]The migraine diagnosis was first proposed by Charles Singer in "The Scientific Views and Visions of Saint Hildegard (1098–1180)," in his *Studies in the History and Method of Science* (Oxford: Clarendon Press, 1917). For a discussion of the notion of a "retrospective diagnosis" in dialogue with Hildegard's case, see Katherine Foxhall, "Making Modern Migraine Medieval: Men of Science, Hildegard of Bingen and the Life of a Retrospective Diagnosis," *Medical History* 58, no. 3 (July 2014): 354–74.

women, but the only male character, the devil, *speaks* worldly temptations. The third and final section treats the presence and absence of singing in debates over the role of ornamentation in worship as an expression of Hildegard's authority as abbess in response to hierarchical and patriarchal controls. Hildegard articulates how embodied performance intertwines with other human creative work and generates beauty to be shared. While praying and play do seek their own end, simple praise for their uselessness can miss Hildegard's intervention: to play can become a mode of "praying with."

For this essay, I focus on the presence and absence of ornamentation in Hildegard's musical, artistic, poetic, and theological work. Hildegard can be a premier model for how affective, embodied, entertaining, and sensorial experiences mediate the divinity we study. I reach for the language of ornamentation to subvert one of the anxieties raised by the prominent turn to theological aesthetics in the last half-century. That is, discussions of God encountered via the Beautiful immediately risk the pitfalls of aesthetic theology: experiences of the Beautiful mislabeled *as* God.[4] I aim to retrieve Hildegard's theology of sonic and visual illumination in form and content to interrogate mediated prayer and work, *ora et labora*. Does ornamental prayer or prayerful scholarship imply an indulgent activity, merely pious entertainment? Hildegard's mediated spirituality of *ora et labora* teaches ways to confound the disciplinary classifications that continue to separate spiritual and aesthetic praxis and sensorial mediation from their claim to theological insight.

Ornamentation and Trinity

One opportunity to notice Hildegard's approach to ornamentation is her antiphon for the Solemnity of the Most Holy Trinity: *Laus Trinitati*. In a spirit of multi-sensory mediation, I strongly recommend the reader, here, to pause and listen to a version of the antiphon. There are many freely available online, and I de-

[4]See, among many, the discussion of "aesthetic theology" in Hans Urs von Balthasar, *The Glory of the Lord*, vol. 1: *Seeing the Form, Erasmo Leiva-Merikakis*, trans. Joseph Fessio, SJ; ed. John Riches (San Francisco: Ignatius Press, 1982), 37.

veloped this section working from the rich set of resources and commentary by Nathaniel M. Campbell.[5]

What does it take to sing the Trinity? Commentators identify *Laus Trinitati* as one of Hildegard's weaker antiphons. It appears in the early *Dendermonde* manuscript but is not copied into the celebrated *Risenkodex* of her major works. I am neither a musicologist nor expert in medieval music, nor do I even play one on television, so I hardly have the credentials to support my appreciative opinion that I think this piece does something spiritually lovely. The number of notes for *laus,* praise, equate to the number of notes for *Trinitati.* Music avoids the disasters of Trinitarian mathematics where one plus one plus one equals one. Instead, Hildegard ornaments *musically* what might become spiritually unknown theologically. In song, praising the Trinity *is* knowing the Trinity. To linger with the mystery of the "sound and life and creativity of all within their life" is to praise that mystery. Music gains life when it has sound; creativity means little without expression. A different sort of essay would defend how, for Hildegard, creativity cannot be without a making; at the very least, Hildegard's Christian imaginary makes no room for creationless creativity. Such would have no *life.* The antiphon identifies that living light, the God who, for Hildegard, is creedal light from light but, also, life from life. Praise continues in time. The Trinity can be adequately praised by the heavenly choir whose celestial songs we humans echo. Humanity boasts a temporal condition as embodied creatures that render materiality and flesh into instruments of praise. Angels are not ornamented with a body like humans, yet angels nonetheless praise in such a way that mediates itself to Hildegard *as song*. In singing or listening we join the *angelice turbe*, the crowd of angels, to praise a "wondrous, brilliant splendor hid" that remains ultimately *unknown* to finite humanity. Yet music attests to the Trinitarian life within all life. Music testifies to it, perhaps even *actualizes* it. Ornamentation evokes the living presence of the living light.

There are other ways to illuminate her point about the Trinity. In Hildegard's first major visionary work, *Scivias*, the structure follows the pattern of much medieval mystical writing. First,

[5]A wonderful resource is available from the International Society of Hildegard von Bingen Studies: www.hildegard-society.org.

Hildegard recounts her vision as a kind of verbatim depiction. Hildegard then shares *divine* interpretations of the vision. The living light, her preferred symbol for God, offers an interpretation of the vision's meaning; Hildegard's is spiritual writing. Consider the vision identified to be of the Trinity from *Scivias* Book II. "Then I saw a bright light, and in this light the figure of a man the color of sapphire, which was all blazing with a gentle glowing fire. And that bright light bathed the whole of the glowing fire, and the glowing fire bathed the bright light; and the bright light and the glowing fire poured over the whole human figure, so that the three were one light in one power of potential."[6] The living light goes on to exegete the vision, yet Hildegard *also* supervises the creation of the illumination of this scene. The verbal description has color and light, so too a painted image. According to *Scivias*, the outer "bright light" depicts God the Father who exceeds even the boundaries of the illumination's frame. The sapphire man depicts God the Son. The inner "glowing fire" is the Holy Spirit. The three coinhere: "the three were one light in one power of potential." The living light goes on to provide a series of Trinitarian analogies as intellectual illuminations to grapple with the mystery of the God who is three-and-one.

One such illumination is an analogy to the causes of human words. I want to quote this analogy at some length because it underscores what I believe to be Hildegard's intervention regarding the mediatory power of ornamentation.

> In a word there is sound, force, and breath. It has sound that it may be heard, meaning that it may be understood, and breath that it may be pronounced. In the sound, then, observe the Father, Who manifests all things with ineffable power; in the meaning, the Son, Who was miraculously begotten of the Father; and in the breath, the Holy Spirit, Who sweetly burns in Them. But where no sound is heard, no meaning is used and no breath is lifted, there no word will be understood; so also the Father, Son, and Holy Spirit are not divided from one another, but do Their works together.[7]

---

[6]Hildegard of Bingen, *Scivias*, II.ii.vision, trans. Columba Hart and Jane Bishop (Mahwah, NJ: Paulist Press, 1990), 161.

[7]*Scivias*, II.ii.7, 164.

Here lies a productive theory of *word* that implies communication *ad extra*. Hildegard has differentiated some abstraction of "word" from a phenomenology of words as encountered: *where there is no sound there can be no meaning because there is no breath*. For Hildegard, speech-acts do *more* than translate an inner word into communicative expression. Causing words perform a creative act. Humans mediate our ideas by putting breath and sound to words to share our labor and co-create meaning. The *more* that comes about by mediating with sound—an ornamentation—echoes the medieval Christian monastic tradition generally and Hildegard's Benedictine spirituality in particular. Monastics, including the Sybil of the Rhine, pray and work—*ora et labora*. That work is good for the soul of the monk, and those prayers are efficacious for the good of the souls of the world. Ornate liturgies form a material and spiritual *work of and for the people*. So, too, are the community's musical and artistic ornamentations to prayers and visions of praise.

Performing Virtue[8]

The final book of Hildegard's *Scivias* tells a story—in dialogue form—about a soul tempted by the devil and aided by virtues, but Hildegard also composed a music drama to *perform* it.[9] Rather than rehearse the extensive secondary commentary on Europe's oldest music drama, my aim is to draw attention to the ways Hildegard *does* theology via musical and performance ornamentation.

Ordo Virtutum offers an opportunity to notice many of Hildegard's musical traits and how these elements influence performance and meaning. She assigns particular modal tonalities to

---

[8]Parts of this section were originally developed in close collaboration with Jessica Petrus. My understanding of Hildegard and the *Ordo Virtutum* is greatly indebted to Margot Fassler's scholarship, including *Cosmos, Liturgy, and the Arts in the Tweflth Century: Hildegard's Illuminated "Scivias"* (Philadelphia: University of Pennsylvania Press, 2023).

[9]*Scivias*, III.xiii, 525ff. Many contemporary productions work from Audrey Ekdahl Davidson's performance version first published by Medieval Institute Publications in 1985. All quotations from the *Ordo Virtutum* in this essay derive from Peter Dronke's translation in *Nine Medieval Latin Plays* (New York: Cambridge University Press, 1994).

different characters much in the way later music dramas and film soundtracks might locate particular themes or motives for different characters. The Virtues' first entrance resounds in D mode, and D mode will be their home throughout much of the play. In contrast, Souls in bodies respond in E mode. Hildegard similarly characterizes Anima's sound when she recognizes her humble need for the Virtues' guidance and pleas for their help in E mode. As Anima's own self-image fluctuates between the heavenly Virtues and the temptations of earth, so too does her modal tonality oscillate. The sound of the music ornaments the text.

Range also characterizes. Consider the characters of Humility and Victory. In general, Humility's range remains low and unassuming. Hildegard evokes a quieter and humbler timbre. By contrast, at the plot's high point of conflict, Victory rejoices in the binding of the serpent with the play's highest musical note. Victory's "Gaudete" resounds with a high A two octaves above Humility's low A. The note is a boisterous, triumphant cry. Hildegard evokes a sense of ascent so both Anima and all listening might be swept up in a victory that musically gestures toward the heavens.

But range is not the only musical gesture. Hildegard's chant melodies also vary between two types of text settings: syllabic, where there is one note per syllable, and melismatic where there are multiple notes per syllable. Melismatic chant serves two purposes. First, it encourages textual rumination by quite literally slowing down the time devoted to each word. Second, melismatic chant achieves what we might anachronistically call word painting, a kind of sonic illumination. The last word of the play shows this well. Hildegard sets the word *porrigat* (from *porrigo*, *porrigere*, "to stretch out") to approximately forty notes. The melisma reflects an image of God's hand gesturing over God's people. The music and the image linger. Any triumph over the Devil depends on divine aid. The one who wins, of course, is the Christ. The finale turns everyone's attention toward communal praise of God and an image of the crucified Christ showing his wounds. The chant-drama's final line gives direction: "So now, all you people, bend your knees to the Father, that he may reach you his hand." The hand of Father is the revealed and pierced hand of the Christ, and this reach occurs in melismatic chant on *porrigat* that will "stretch out" to touch the gathered body on sung breath.

Musical techniques, like assigning differing modes to various characters and deploying melismatic chant to emphasize certain words, demonstrate what I mean by ornamentation. Such ornamentation marks a *theologically* significant difference between Hildegard's *Ordo Virtutum* performed and the similar version of this story recounted in the final section of *Scivias*. Musical ornamentation invites embodied reception. This vision *does more* than yet another rather tried and true recounting of Christian virtue's triumph over demonic temptation. Musical and dramatic performance mediate this excess by reaching out to incorporate those listening, watching, experiencing, performing.

Pressed further, many have convincingly argued that the music drama occurred as a liturgical drama.[10] Emerging from a chorus of embodied souls, Anima asks to cast off the shabby "dress of this life" to wear "a radiant robe." But imagine this in the context of a liturgy for a new member's entrance into Hildegard's abbey. The novice requests to abandon secular—that is, worldly—garb for the *habit* and virtuous *habits* of religious life. Yet she is surprised and disappointed to learn that she cannot with a mere sigh join the Virtues in praise of her creator. As they tell her, she must work through the trials of earthly life and its own "grievous toil." Anima longs for the "sweet divinity" and "gentle life" distant from earthly and corporal existence. These Virtues, super heroines of piety, will not abandon her to fight the devil alone; she "must overcome the devil in our midst." Performance becomes an instance of *ora et labora*.

The contest between Virtue and Devil has a familiar plot. The life of even a fallen and tempted creature—once assisted by the grace of heavenly virtues—can glorify God. Indeed, God conquers sin and death precisely through divine time spent in incarnate solidarity with a human life and a human death and resurrection. Following a short prologue featuring the patriarchs and prophets marveling at the array of Virtues, the next scene offers a long meditation on each Virtue. Each one has her own antiphonal chant. If placed in a liturgical context, perhaps these roles were played by the women of Hildegard's community. It is easy to imagine how taking on a dramatic part could become an

[10]See the work of Margot Fassler, Audrey Ekdahl Davidson, Robert Potter, Pamela Sheingorn, and Julia Bolton Holloway.

opportunity to cultivate that virtue. Hildegard may have asked the timid to play Courage or a sister struggling with despair to play Hope. Odds are—and scholars agree—that Hildegard herself most likely sang for Humility. As Margot Fassler poignantly writes, "Hildegard doubtless worked under the influence of the Holy Spirit when she composed, but the Spirit as it guided her hand has a side sensitive to the needs of liturgical practice."[11]

So we see the music drama as an opportunity for ornamentation in the form of embodied encounter for those in her abbey. But what of a congregation or audience? The music gets interrupted by the sound of an unsung character: *Diabolus*. If we examine the *Risenkodex* manuscript, we see the Devil's lines literally run right over the musical staves. *In performance,* the Devil's affect is even more powerful. The Devil has "fallen" to a non-heavenly mode of communication. He does not sing; he does not pray; he does not incline us to live the virtuous life. He is the only character assigned to a male actor. Scholars speculate that Hildegard's priest, Volmar, might have played the Devil. Casting now opens an interesting window into Hildegard's understanding of virtue formation: the *priest* over-performs the temptations of worldly authority and fails to sing along to heavenly music.

Such speech *ornaments*. Rather than *empower* formation by singing, in a way that uplifts, the role of the Devil ornaments with the *absence* of music. His words cut through melody with harsh consonants and guttural delivery. Demonic speech tempts elevated meditation toward disturbed confusion. The priest, who perhaps later in this very liturgy or another time this very day will pray the mass *in persona Christi,* can also fall to temptation. Like any human, he can refuse to sing.

Presence and Absence and Authority

In her visionary writing, Hildegard notes that the choirs of heaven "are singing with marvelous voices all kinds of music about the wonders that God works in blessed souls."[12] The saints and the

[11]Margot Fassler, "Composer and Dramatist," in *Voice of the Living Light: Hildegard of Bingen and Her World*, ed. Barbara Newman (Berkeley: University of California Press, 1999), 160.

[12]*Scivias*, I.vi.vision, 139.

angels *sing* their prayerful praise; music mediates prayer. Moreover, Hildegard connects heavenly song to herself—the visionary as medium of revelatory experience. She says that the angels' "song went through me, so that I understood them perfectly."[13] Music mediates *perfected* knowledge, even if God always transcends total comprehension. Virtuous Knowledge of God sings; it is the devil who speaks in disputed questions. Knowledge of God, for Hildegard, has material, poetic, emotional, and sensual characteristics. Demonic knowledge refuses to sing.

Musical ornamentation accomplishes two theological purposes for praying and working.

1. ORA: *music* provides a way to avoid idolatry; music is virtuous knowledge of God.
2. LABORA: *music* disciplines the monastery's positive dispositions in the soul.

For Hildegard, singing raises us out of ourselves, connects disparate individuals together as one body with one voice, and amplifies the dignity of prayers. Over time, a common musical repertoire becomes a cross-temporal marker of continuity; sung melodies and texts link a community's past to their future. Music, therefore, mediates divine knowledge, virtuous ways of being, and communal identity.

Such communities also have a material place and time. Hildegard commanded two abbeys as a Mother Abbess in Germany's Rhineland. She founded her own monastic community at Rupertsberg and traveled on an unprecedented preaching tour. An example from the end of her life demonstrates the strength of her musico-theological convictions. In 1178, Hildegard's community received an interdict from the local archbishop as the result of an excommunicated nobleman's "improper" burial on Rupertsberg's grounds. The punishment restricted her community's right to prayers in song. Discipline occurred in the apparent taking away of a privilege. To pray is a right and obligation; to *sing* is a privilege for the ecclesially obedient.

But the community was still permitted to *read* prayers aloud. The interdict prohibited Hildegard's beloved singing the Divine

[13] *Scivias*, III.xiii.9, 532.

Office. The community should no longer pray in chant. Here, we see a version of what Talal Asad describes as discipline through punishment; the removal of the *ornamentation* of music as an attempt to restore obedience through humiliation.[14] Hildegard found this to be a great injustice, and she wrote a forceful letter in response to the archbishop. Prayers *in song* are more powerful and proper than prayers only spoken. As Hildegard wrote, "by obeying you we have been celebrating the divine office incorrectly, for from the time of your restriction up to the present, we have ceased to sing the divine office, merely reading it instead."[15] For the abbey to do its work *properly* requires an understanding of ornamentation as *constitutive* of prayer and work. Prayers linked to the heavenly spheres, the music of the angels, the sound of heaven—sung prayers—mediate *spiritual excess*. To invoke an adage of Saint Augustine of Hippo: "When we sing, we pray twice." Hildegard's Trinitarian theology of music might suggest: "To pray virtuously, we *must* sing, because when we sing, we pray *thrice*." The absence of ornamentation, one that labels sonic synesthesia a luxury, confounds the work of prayer.

Hildegard's role in mediating authority in the Church did not end in the twelfth century. In 2012, Pope Benedict XVI promulgated an apostolic letter proclaiming Saint Hildegard of Bingen to hold the title "Doctor of the Universal Church." I wonder where her wisdom about ornamentation leaves us in our *ora et labora*. After the interdict of the COVID-19 pandemic, I submit that Hildegard challenges theologians, teachers, and liturgists to reframe embodied mediation. To pray together *is* to work together. To sing together *is* to work together. There's a reason that lovers of Hildegard also pressed for movements to have liturgical raves. But the creation of psychedelic liturgy or avant-garde feminist performance (like the 2019 Off-Broadway Hildegard musical *In the Green* attempts) miss part of the point. It is not a matter of shaping music and lights and sounds and smells toward who we

---

[14]Talal Asad, *Genealogies of Religion: Discipline and Reasons of Power in Christianity and Islam* (Baltimore: Johns Hopkins University Press, 1993).

[15]Hildegard, "Letter 23: Hildegard to the Prelates at Mainz," in *The Letters of Hildegard of Bingen*, vol. 1, trans. Joseph L. Baird and Radd K. Ehrman (New York: Oxford University Press, 1994), 77.

want God to be. It is a matter of ornamenting what we as the Church do so our shared liturgies might be the sonic synesthesia our Church desperately needs. To say this another way: I want to advocate for more beauty in our spiritual lives, our pedagogy, our prayers through greater ornamentation. But such advocacy, if it is not to join the continuing death-march of white supremacy as an aesthetic program, requires attending to the spiritual lessons of the Visionary Doctor.

A TikTok Theodicy

Using Social Media to Introduce a Christian Approach to Suffering

Jane Sloan Peters

This essay explores how social media mediates the transcendent for members of Generation Z, especially as they attempt to make sense of suffering.[1] When I began teaching Religious Studies at the College of Mount Saint Vincent in the Bronx, I joined TikTok in an effort to understand my students' lives. I soon found that TikTok was not only a valuable way to learn about my students; it was something I wanted to *talk about* with my students. I was especially concerned with the distressing content I encountered over a short period of scrolling. One of my first times on the app, I saw the following videos: a mom cleaning her unhappy toddler's nasal passages, a woman recording herself having a seizure, a man improvising a rap song, and a teenager explaining reasons for her recent suicide attempt while doing the "chopping dance."[2] I was reeling from the sensory emotionally charged bursts.

If such content is what undergraduates consume two hours daily, on average, then it is critical to engage TikTok and other

[1]Members of Generation Z were born beginning in the late 1990s. For more, see Michael Dimock, "Defining Generations: Where Millennials End and Generation Z Begins," *Pew Research Center* (blog), January 17, 2019.

[2]For the viral "chopping dance," see Emerald Pellot, "Here's How to Do TikTok's Chopping Dance," in *In the Know* by yahoo! (July 21, 2021).

social media platforms in theology courses, for two reasons. First, students process life's big questions on social media platforms. The consumption and production of social media content is no mere entertainment or personal expression. However nontraditional or inchoate social media may seem to older generations, young people use apps like TikTok to make sense of their lives, including those experiences and questions that engage the transcendent. Second, good introductory theology courses help students understand the nature of religion and explore their own religious identity. It is commonly accepted that the word "religion" comes from the Latin *religare,* to bind together. Religion helps us make sense of life, that is, helps us understand how elements of human experience come together into a coherent whole. TikTok and other social media sites are sites of meaning-making that appeal to students' religious impulses, broadly construed. One of the most pressing needs of GenZ is to bear witness to their suffering and, as John Paul II said in *Salvifici Doloris*, to grapple with the uniquely human question of *why* we suffer.[3]

In this essay, I will first review how GenZ uses TikTok and explain the issues this raises for theological education. Then, I will describe one way I engaged student use of TikTok to introduce a unit on Buddhist and Christian approaches to suffering—in an assignment in which students documented the suffering they saw on social media. I will explain my pedagogy, which implemented an inquiry-based form of "unlearning" that enables students to assimilate new information. Finally, I will share student responses to the assignment, which show the complex ways GenZ engages the question of suffering on TikTok, and their reasons for doing so.

College Students and TikTok

GenZ spends more time on TikTok than any other app, averaging 12.4 hours per week on this social media platform.[4] Consider-

---

[3]John Paul II, *Salvifici Doloris* (Vatican City: Liberia Editrice Vaticana), February 11, 1984.

[4]Charlie Coombs, "Data by Measure Protocol Has Found the Gen Z Spends the Most Time on TikTok Compared to Any Other App. However, only 83 percent of teens use TikTok compared to 87 percent on Instagram," *thred* (blog), February 16, 2023, https://thred.com/hustle/gen-z-are-spending-more-time-on-tiktok-than-any-other-app/.

ing that a three-credit college course typically requires six hours of outside work each week, the average student's TikTok consumption amounts to taking two college courses each semester. From an educational standpoint, it might be said that undergraduates are all enrolled in the school of social media, where they engage content critically and seriously, content they find meaningful for shaping their lives and worldviews.

In 2022, Pew Research published a survey of teens aged thirteen through seventeen regarding their social media use: this survey gives college educators a good idea of the scrolling habits of incoming undergraduates. Sixty-seven percent of teens use TikTok, and 16 percent of these admit they use it "almost constantly."[5] More women than men, and higher numbers of Black and Hispanic teens, report using TikTok. The same goes for those who say they use TikTok almost constantly.[6]

These numbers are no surprise: educators hardly need to be alerted to the grip social media has on our students. During the pandemic, students sat at home with their phones providing a keyhole view of the outside world. In-person learning has resumed, but not as before. Educators remark that their students still seem to think they are taking classes on Zoom, with students sitting disengaged or just not showing up.[7] Social life has suffered, too: students stand, walk, and even eat with faces buried in their phones, rather than speak to one another. One freshman wrote in an assignment for my class last year, "I'd rather scroll through TikTok than make a friend."

The widespread mental health crisis among young people has been linked to social media use. The Healthy Minds Study, a project dedicated to studying mental health in college-age students, reported in 2021–22 that 44 percent of survey respondents displayed symptoms of major and moderate depression, and 37 percent displayed symptoms of anxiety. The relationship between

---

[5]Emily Vogels, Risa Gelles-Watnick, and Navid Massarat, "Teens, Social Media and Technology 2022," *Pew Research Center* report, August 10, 2022. This study needs nuancing; it gives data not about actual use but about perception of use.

[6]Vogels, Gelles-Watnick, and Massarat, "Teens, Social Media and Technology 2022."

[7]Jonathan Malesic, "My College Students Are Not OK," *New York Times* online, May 13, 2022.

social media use and poor mental health has been documented repeatedly. In the words of one study, social media use among US young adults is "significantly associated with increased depression."[8]

Finally, there is a great deal of distressing content on TikTok. A 2022 article in *Vice* titled "The Rise of #TraumaTok" explored the phenomenon of people posting about their traumatic experiences.[9] The hashtag #trauma currently has 22.4 billion views on TikTok, and #traumatok had 4.2 billion views as of July 3, 2023. While TikTok has explicit content filters in place to shield its users, who can be as young as thirteen, from disturbing content, users can bypass filters with "algo"—words like "seggs" for sex, or "unalive" for suicide.[10] These code words shape the discourse on the app. For example, in 2022 it became trendy to refer to sexual encounters as "wearing mascara." This rapidly evolved into a forum for people to share their experiences with sexual assault, so that incredibly serious and potentially distressing content became interspersed with makeup tutorials and mascara ads.

Not all TikTok is tragedy: much of the content is interesting, inspiring, and downright funny. And TikTok is a space where anyone can belong: a sophomore student remarked that TikTok helped her navigate depression because, unlike Instagram, users show raw, real life. But the quick, disruptive interspersion of suffering among other content is nearly impossible to avoid, since TikTok measures consumer interest based not only on what a user likes or comments on, but on a viewer's subconscious engagement with the app. An investigation from the *Wall Street Journal* concluded that TikTok learns a user's interests by measuring the

---

[8]Liu li Lin et al., "Association between Social Media Use and Depression among US Young Adults," *PubMed Central* 33, no. 4 (April 2016): 323–31. See also M. G. Hunt et al., "No More FOMO: Limiting Social Media Decreases Loneliness and Depression," *Journal of Social Clinical Psychology* 37, no. 10 (2018): 751–68; L. M. Lyall, C. A. Wyse, N. Graham, et al., "Association of Disrupted Circadian Rhythmicity with Mood Disorders, Subjective Wellbeing, and Cognitive Function: A Cross-Sectional Study of 91,105 Participants from the UK Biobank," *Lancet Psychiatry* 5, no. 6 (June 2018): 507–14.

[9]Julie Fenwick, "The Rise of 'TraumaTok': When Does Sharing Trauma Online Become Unhealthy?" *Vice* online, May 19, 2022.

[10]On algo, see Taylor Lorenz, "Internet 'Algospeak' Is Changing Our Language in Real Time," *Washington Post* online, April 8, 2022.

number of times a user views a certain post and even how long she hovers over a post. "Every second you hesitate or rewatch [a video], the app is tracking you. Through this one powerful signal, TikTok learns your most hidden interests and emotions, and drives you deep into rabbit holes of content that are hard to escape."[11] Students might find themselves doomscrolling when all they intended to do was take a study break.[12] This is not a glitch in TikTok's programming, but part of its secret to success.

TikTok Theodicy: The Suffering without the Story

GenZ's encounter with suffering on TikTok is reshaping the human effort to make sense of suffering. Consider how previous generations encountered something distressing: most of these experiences included a narrative arc. With firsthand experience of an event, for example, the terrorist attacks on September 11, 2001, one must live through it, process it, and learn to cope with it: there is an inescapable before, during, and after to be reckoned with. Similarly, in literature like *I Know Why the Caged Bird Sings,* in movies like *My Girl,* or even in songs like Tupac's *Changes* or The Verve Pipe's *The Freshmen*—the intense experience of suffering is integrated into a *story*. Emotions flare and subside; time is devoted to reflecting on the experience; and most important, there is at least some rudimentary teleology—some sense that suffering exists within a bigger picture. Suffering does not have the last word.

This narrative structure is often lost on TikTok, where posts deliver visual and emotional stimulation without resolution. The person producing such content might find this cathartic. Yet the consumer has a different experience: videos play upon the senses

[11] *Wall Street Journal*, "Investigation: How TikTok's Algorithm Figures Out Your Deepest Desires," *Wall Street Journal* Video Series (July 21, 2021); and Hannah Towey, "The Secret Factors That Influence Your TikTok Algorithm and 'For You' Page Were Just Revealed," *Business Insider* online (July 21, 2021).

[12] On "doomscrolling," defined as "the act of consuming large quantities of negative online news in a sitting," see Jane Kelly, "What Is 'Doomscrolling?' Why Do We Do It,a How Can We Stop?" *UVAToday* online (April 14, 2022).

and the subconscious, prompting questions without providing the time or tools to explore the answers. This renders the videos almost meaningless, and yet, paradoxically, these snatches of stories remain embedded in the psyche, data points that demand to be incorporated into the very human act of making sense of life.

It is difficult to systematically discuss the content of TikTok videos because of their diversity and because the techniques used to produce them are constantly evolving. Nevertheless, it is important to give some sense of what one might encounter on the app. The following are examples of videos with distressing content that anyone could encounter on TikTok.

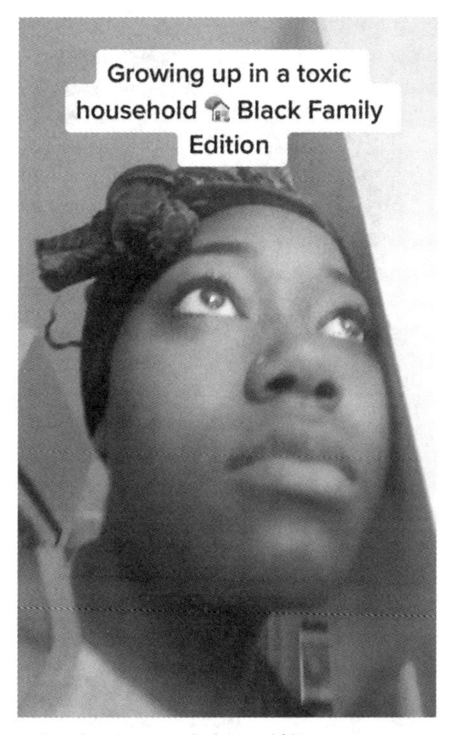

User @genesis_cheri records herself listening, expressionless, to family members arguing in "Growing up in a toxic household Black Family Edition." @genesis_cheri only has 105,000 followers, but this video has been liked almost 600,000 times since it was posted in January 2022. About halfway through the video, her eyes brim with tears and she sets the phone down so the screen goes black.

"Tell you what," a voice says. "At the end of July, if I tell somebody one more time, I'm going to the courthouse and I promise you, y'all gettin' put out of my doggone house." This is Part 5 of a series of posts, but users would have to click on the story to see the other posts: otherwise, this video would appear among unrelated ones.

Many users depict loneliness and mental illness. User @w0kv's post "Lonely under the rain" is one example. A silhouetted man sits, stands, and paces on a dark, rainy street. An eight-second video by @itsfuckingmike with 1 million likes depicts a similar scene with the hashtags #depressed #depressionisreal. In it, a hooded figure sits under a streetlamp on a rainy night. Text superimposed on the image reads, "I'm a man. I'll be fine."

TikTok users can recycle others' sound clips, and it is common to find many videos with the same popular sound overlay. @litfrank, a comedian with 1.2 million followers, posts about his abusive mother and childhood visits from social workers. He imitates his mother's reaction to the departure of a social worker with the caption "POV: My mom 0.5 seconds after our social worker left the driveway." He gesticulates angrily while a viral sound clip from the 2023 movie *The Reading* plays: "Girl, fuck them kids, and fuck you too."[13]

Another popular sound clip critiques the adage, "Everything happens for a reason." Its origins are difficult to trace because it exists in several redactions. In the post originating with @l0nely-bxtch, a woman sobs as a voice says, "You know how people say, 'oh everything happens for a reason' . . . What was the reason? What the fuck was the reason for this? There is none!" Thousands of users have paired this sound with photos depicting illness or loss. It is also common to find selfie videos of tearful users lip-syncing the words but offering little evidence as to what real-life event has prompted the video.

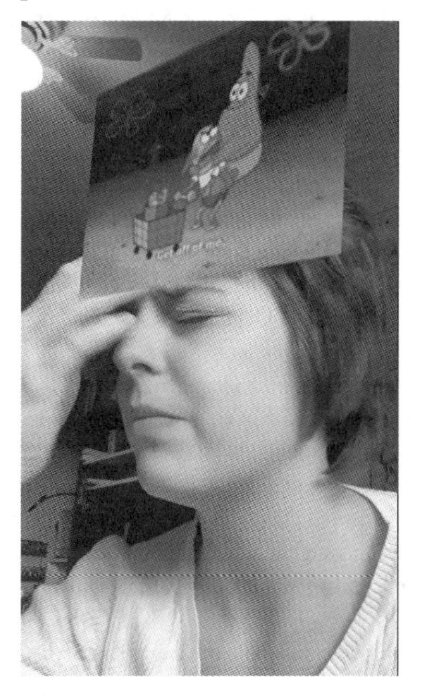

Finally, users post about suffering using TikTok filters. One artificial intelligence filter known as "AI Style" supposedly detects

[13]This sound clip went viral in spring of 2023. See Andrew Lloyd, "Tik-Tokers Want You to Know They Won't Make Sacrifices for Other People's Kids," *Business Insider India* online, March 17, 2023.

illness. The "SpongeBob trauma filter" has 69 million views. Users take a selfie video while pictures from the cartoon *SpongeBob SquarePants* cycle over their foreheads. An algorithm selects one. The most-viewed post depicts @qweer, clearly skeptical of the filter at first, being overcome with emotion as the filter selects an image of Patrick riding piggyback on a fish, who is pushing a cart of groceries, with the caption, "Get off of me." Perhaps this image reminds her of past sexual trauma, although she never clarifies this.

These examples illustrate a paradox of TikTok. On the one hand, people flock to TikTok to bear witness to their suffering, and they do so in a manner that is perhaps more sophisticated than the content first suggests. A user can incorporate features like algo, sound bites, and filters to mediate her experience. Text accompanies image in the form of captions and hashtags. An inventory of likes, comments, bookmarks, and shares shows how popular the post is. This effort to tell a story of suffering might be called a TikTok theodicy. It is not unlike the way a Byzantine catenist borrows a patristic text to make sense of a Scripture passage, or an iconographer amplifies certain facial features to convey sanctity. It is not unlike Christ himself, who uttered a snatch of Psalm 22 from the Cross as he hung beneath an inscription written in Hebrew, Latin, and Greek. TikTok is a place where things come together.

However, the entropic concatenation of videos hardly amounts to a discernible narrative for the viewer. And trends develop so rapidly that one would need to be on the app "almost constantly" to keep up. If there is something inescapably human about how the content is produced, there is something inhuman about how the content is consumed. For both reasons, TikTok could be fruitfully engaged in a religious studies curriculum.

Using TikTok in the Classroom

In RELS 208: "Introduction to Religious Studies," students study how religious traditions treat core elements of human experience. One unit concerns religious engagement with suffering. In a previous unit on religious origin stories, students have identified language in Genesis 1 that indicates that for the Hebrew author, creation is something good, which God intended, and made in an ordered way. For about a quarter of students, this prompts the question of why suffering and death exist at all. How can a world created by a good God, with intention and order, contain suffering? This question leads us naturally into the unit on suffering.

One of the principal goals of this unit is that students be able to explain that, in Jewish and Christian perspectives, suffering is *not* natural, but an aberration, a sign that something has gone wrong with God's created order. Suffering results from evil, an absence or distortion of the good. While some of my undergraduates are ultimately able to speak about suffering in ontological terms, students in RELS 208 must be able to explain the *senselessness* of suffering. God does not cause suffering, but permits it, and God's greatest and most intimate engagement with suffering is in transforming it, through Christ, into something beautiful.

Yet the Christian claim that suffering has redemptive value because of the Cross is not intuitive. Thus, an effective way to approach this concept is to invite students to examine how the world around them tries to make sense of suffering. It is with these goals in mind that I introduce the TikTok assignment. I first refer to previous student questions about God and suffering. I validate their theological intuition that the Genesis narrative presents a problem: The Jewish and Christian creation story does not align with our experience of the world and ourselves.

I then define the term "theodicy," pointing out that they have essentially provided the definition themselves. Theodicy asks why evil and suffering exist in a world created by a good God. I then explain the assignment. Students upload their work the night before class so I have a chance to read them before discussion:

Choose a social media platform (TikTok, Insta, Facebook, YouTube). If you don't have a social media account, you can access a news website like the New York Times or CNN. Scroll for 5 minutes.

1. List the suffering that you see.
2. Categorize the suffering you see using categories of your choice. For example, physical or mental, societal or individual, etc.
3. Three sentences: Why do you think people post about their suffering? In what ways, if any, are they trying to make sense of their suffering?

This assignment helps students become critical consumers of social media content. It also makes students aware of the contemporary narrative surrounding suffering—a kind of "secular theodicy"—so that they do not mistakenly assimilate Christian theodicy into it. It is easy for the Christian message to become so embedded within a cultural narrative that the dominant cultural themes come to masquerade as Christian truisms: one example of this is "everything happens for a reason," a phrase that is not Christian in origin, but is often used as such.

This pedagogical method engages a feature of human memory that is both a strength and a weakness. Memory is associative: it is easier to learn new things when they are linked with material we already know. Yet the brain's ability to incorporate new experiences into previously established cognitive frameworks can lead to false confidence about how much we really know about something. Studies show that those who know the least about a subject tend to be the most confident about their knowledge of it![14] This phenomenon, known as the Dunning-Kruger effect, might be familiar to theology professors whose students process religious ideas through cultural mores that ultimately distort them.

Effective learning involves rupturing preexisting structures in the memory, what neuroscientist Nancy Michael and theologian Ben Wilson call "unlearning." For Michael and Wilson, "Unlearning . . . requires conscious effort to reflect on past learning in order to create the possibility of new future learning that goes beyond our passively formulated, yet operative, mental constructs that undergird how we understand the world, ourselves, and the people around us."[15] The authors associate the term "unlearning" with the Greek term for conversion, *metanoia,* literally, a moving beyond the mind we have. They explain: "The work of unlearning entails actively supporting the creation of new synapses by consciously comparing previous beliefs with information from

[14]See Justin Kruger and David Dunning, "Unskilled and Unaware of It: How Difficulties in Recognizing One's Own Incompetence Lead to Inflated Self-Assessment," *Journal of Personality and Social Psychology* 77, no. 6 (1999): 1121–34.

[15]Nancy Michael and Ben Wilson, "Unlearning Is the New Learning: A Neuroscientific and Theological Case for How and Why to See the World Differently," *Church Life Journal*, March 26, 2021, churchlifejournal.nd.edu.

new experiences, seeking to identify gaps in our experience and misalignments with what we claim to value."[16]

This pedagogical method is not new—at its core, it resembles the rhetorical technique of *aporia*, an expression of doubt, a logical crossroads that prompts deeper consideration. Nor is the method exclusive to the humanities. It is present in the inquiry-based pedagogy of STEM disciplines, in which students learn new concepts by empirically challenging falsely held beliefs about the natural world. Students can find this method difficult: they want the "right answer" for their notes, so they can succeed on the exam and move on with their lives. But fostering "unlearning" creates a rewarding experience in the classroom because it encourages students to engage the material more deeply. Well-catechized students cannot fall back on ready, reliable answers; nor can students unfamiliar with religion keep questions at a safe distance, memorizing material without really engaging it.

Student Responses to the TikTok Study

Students encountered diverse forms of suffering on TikTok: videos about addiction, racism, cultural displacement and "double unbelonging," discrimination based on gender and sexuality, and relationship problems ranging from minor conflicts to serious sexual abuse. Students witnessed mental and physical illness, including miscarriage, eating disorders and recovery, sports injuries, and chronic conditions like Tourette's. One student reported seeing a user documenting his homelessness. Several assignments also mentioned violent posts: for example, fights on public transit and body-cam recordings of violent encounters. Because of how TikTok's algorithm works (see above), this is not only a springboard for conversation, but a window into students' own interests and concerns: what TikTok shows them is often what matters to them most.

Responses to the question, "Why do people post about their suffering?" were varied. Almost all students reasoned that people were, to some extent, seeking attention. "A lot of people today love to seek attention and social media is a great way to do it," one wrote. Another student wrote of a popular account, "It is clear she

[16]Michael and Wilson, "Unlearning Is the New Learning."

posts her suffering for views. . . . This recognition based on her dark humor about her trauma builds her platform as a chance to gain money." The term "dark humor" came up multiple times. Another student reasoned, "People use dark humor . . . to express their emotions in a funny way as a distraction from the actual suffering."

Other students saw more positive reasons for posting. The videos help users connect with others, who post "not because they crave attention but because they want to be heard," one said. Perhaps the posts "raise awareness of a situation," remarked another. Another suggested, "Social media might be the only positive interaction people might have with others." And one student wrote, "TikTok is a community where you can share anything and everything and get someone to reach out and agree. It allows for connections to be made and makes people feel less alone."

Students also offered varied responses to the question, "In what way, if any, are people trying to make sense of their suffering by posting?" "I don't think they're trying to make sense of suffering," one wrote. "It's more so just storytelling." Such responses offer an opportunity to push students to reflect further, to consider how "storytelling" might include a search for meaning.

Other student responses included valuable insights for class discussion. Several students connected meaning-seeking in suffering to coping with, or healing from, suffering:

> A lot of people usually question "why?" especially when the suffering is fresh. I believe no one can make sense to [*sic*] any suffering until they heal, which then won't make it a suffering anymore.
>
> [Posting] can be a way to make sense of their suffering because then they are able to get feedback and advice from other people. . . . Not only can these people help them to understand [their suffering], but they can help figure out ways to cope with their suffering.

Finally, a handful of student responses gestured toward the specific problems raised in Christian theodicy:

> No one really understands why suffering happens to innocent people and is sometimes random. . . . Maybe some people say that everything happens for a reason. . . . But most of the

> time people share how they choose to respond to suffering instead of how they make sense of it.
>
> It's hard to make sense of why anyone is suffering, and I think the reason why they post is because they don't know why. Suffering in my opinion isn't orderly. I think it's random so trying to make sense of it is kind of a waste of time.

Responses like these provide critical points of connection between students' analysis and Jewish and Christian ontology at the root of Christian theodicy.

This assignment represents only one way educators could engage student social media use. While it was not perfect, it was successful insofar as it generated discussion, identified secular "theodicies," and opened avenues for understanding the Christian response to suffering.

Conclusion

I have argued in this essay that theology educators must engage social media in the classroom. GenZ uses TikTok and other social media apps to grapple with complex life questions that touch on the transcendent. The app offers sophisticated, if nontraditional, tools for telling the story of one's own suffering, but the value of this differs for creator and consumer. An assignment asking students to critically engage TikTok succeeded in clarifying what distressing videos students saw as well as their perspectives on why users posted them. The assignment and subsequent discussion prepared students to receive new information they were mostly unfamiliar with, namely, Christian theodicy.

By the time this essay is published, some of its content will be obsolete: new hashtags, filters, and viral trends will have replaced the examples given above. #traumatok may have billions more views. The whirlwind pace at which GenZ's online world changes is so daunting that it seems difficult to engage in the classroom at all: better to stick with primary texts, perhaps, to teach the enduring truths. Yet if we wish to reach our students today, we must do both. For an educator, "putting on the mind of Christ" (Phil 2:8) often means trying to understand the mind of the student.

Natural Law for the Laity

A Case Study in Catholic Education on the Airwaves

Dennis J. Wieboldt III

Natural Law and Catholic Intellectuals

In 1920, the National Catholic Welfare Conference (NCWC)—the American Catholic bishops' official episcopal organization—established the National Council of Catholic Men. At its inception, the council was tasked with supporting the NCWC Social Action Department's mission to inculcate Catholic values within American culture. By sharing the Church's social teaching with Americans of other religious dispositions, the bishops believed that the council's lay members could effectively counter the early twentieth-century anti-Catholic impulse about which American religious historians have written at length.[1] Less than a decade after its establishment, in fact, the council observed in a formal resolution that anti-Catholic "bigotry" was "strong . . . in all sections of" the United States, thus necessitating that the council "undertake a comprehensive program" to "promot[e] truth" about the Church.[2]

[1]On American anti-Catholicism, see, e.g., Mark S. Massa, SJ, *Anti-Catholicism in America: The Last Acceptable Prejudice* (New York: Crossroad, 2003).

[2]*Keynote Resolution of the Eighth Annual Convention of the Nation-*

In 1930, the NCWC approved a partnership between the council and the National Broadcasting Company—known popularly by its acronym, NBC—to launch the *Catholic Hour* radio program. Although the initial impetus for establishing *Catholic Hour* was NBC's desire to fulfill the terms of government licensing agreements, Catholic leaders leveraged this opportunity to present an "elevated and Americanized Catholicism" to NBC's national, multireligious audience.[3] Indeed, then-Archbishop of New York Patrick Joseph Hayes remarked during *Catholic Hour*'s first broadcast that the program was designed as a "service" to "all the people of the United States," Catholic and non-Catholic, insofar as the program presented "the voice of the ancient Church with its historical background" to the nation.[4]

Featuring the likes of renowned Catholic evangelist Fulton J. Sheen, *Catholic Hour* became a prominent medium for the institutional Church's engagement with non-Catholics during its nearly four-decades-long run (1930–1968). At the same time, however, the speakers invited to offer addresses on *Catholic Hour* were well aware that their audience was not exclusively non-Catholic. As the extant evidence suggests, the "education on the airwaves" that the American bishops sought to provide to the nation through *Catholic Hour* had two goals: first, to present Catholic teaching to non-Catholics, and second, to offer Catholic laypeople the vocabulary they would need to dialogue with their Protestant and Jewish neighbors about Catholic teaching themselves. In these ways, *Catholic Hour* media(ted) Catholics' and non-Catholics' exposure to the Church's intellectual class, much of which was composed at this time of vowed religious men.

In their quest to educate everyday Catholics and non-Catholics about the Church, historians have rightly suggested that *Catholic Hour* personalities often situated their addresses over and

---

al Council of Catholic Men, November 18–21, 1929, Box 3, Folder 11, NCWC/USCC Social Action Department Collection, Special Collections of the University Libraries, The Catholic University of America, Washington, DC (hereafter SAD Records).

[3]Alexander Pavuk, "Constructing a Catholic Church Out of Thin Air: *Catholic Hour*'s Early Years on NBC Radio," *American Catholic Studies* 118, no. 4 (2007): 38–42.

[4]"Cardinal Hayes States Purpose of Catholic Hour," in Howard W. Smith, *Law* (Huntington, IN: Our Sunday Visitor, 1940), 35.

against "the rising tide of secularism in American culture in the 1920s."[5] Alexander Pavuk, for instance, has persuasively argued that "influential Catholics in the 1920s and 1930s" believed that "Catholicism could offer the country a philosophical and social tradition that, if applied properly, was actually truer to the American values enshrined at the country's founding than those [secular values] guiding contemporary America."[6] Despite acknowledging that this framing circumscribed many *Catholic Hour* addresses, historians have yet to specifically interrogate a decisive feature of Catholic leaders' early and mid-twentieth-century efforts to confront the perceived "rising tide" of secularism: natural law philosophy. In Pavuk's important 2007 article on *Catholic Hour*, for example, he refers to Fulton Sheen's Neo-Scholastic formation at the Catholic University of Louvain, the centrality of "philosophical complaint[s]" to *Catholic Hour* addresses, and the "loyal[ty]" of popular *Catholic Hour* personalities to Neo-Scholasticism's "deductive mandates."[7] Pavuk leaves unexplored, however, why natural law philosophy was so intimately connected to the NCWC's educational undertakings, aside from the mere fact that Neo-Scholasticism—in which twentieth-century natural law philosophy often found its foundations—was vivifying in "early twentieth[-]century Catholic intellectual life."[8]

Although the Neo-Scholastic education of early and mid-twentieth-century Catholic leaders encouraged their appealing to natural law philosophy *contra* secularism, private correspondence, public statements, and *Catholic Hour* addresses from this period reveal that the American Catholic episcopacy's desire to make natural law philosophy accessible to the laity had another impetus.[9] Indeed, this evidence suggests that Catholic leaders' turning to natural law was motivated, in part, by their conviction that natural law would be the principal agent of American Catholics' reconciliation with

[5]Pavuk, "Constructing a Catholic Church Out of Thin Air," 40–41.

[6]Pavuk, "Constructing a Catholic Church Out of Thin Air," 41.

[7]Pavuk, "Constructing a Catholic Church Out of Thin Air," 51, 57, 59.

[8]Pavuk, "Constructing a Catholic Church Out of Thin Air," 48.

[9]On the formative role of Neo-Scholastic education in Catholic leaders' appealing to natural law, see, e.g., Dennis J. Wieboldt III, "The Natural Law and Interreligious Social Advocacy: The Civil Rights Movement–Era Case of William J. Kenealy, SJ," *American Catholic Studies* 134, no. 1 (2023): 58–63.

non-Catholics. In other words, natural law philosophy appeared to provide a supra-denominational philosophical framework within which Catholics and non-Catholics could share an overarching national identity. Crucially, this sharing of an overarching national identity under the aegis of natural law seemed to facilitate the interreligious cooperation necessary for successful Catholic Action in an increasingly religiously plural nation.[10]

New Media, Old Arguments: Bringing Natural Law to the Laity

American Catholic leaders' emphasis on natural law philosophy's role in interreligious cooperation is especially clear in World War II–era evidence from the NCWC. In June 1943, for instance, John M. Hayes and Edward A. Conway—Catholic priests affiliated with the NCWC Social Action Department—presented at a high-profile conference on interreligiosity.[11] As one newspaper report of the conference observed, "Conway put forward the Natural Law as the basis of agreement between Catholics, Protestants, and Jews. The Natural Law, or Moral Law, is that of which St. Paul speaks as having been written by God in men's hearts. It is the Moral Law which is discoverable and provable by human reason."[12] One month later, the *Irish Catholic* likewise published an article on how Catholics and non-Catholics share a "common law, God's law written on our hearts and conscience . . . [that] provide[s] a working basis for fruitful collaboration of a far-reaching kind."[13] Such contemporaneous articles describing Catholic and non-Catholic clergymen's beliefs about the foundations of interreligious collaboration were collected by and distributed among leaders in the NCWC.

---

[10]As Pavuk has argued, the Catholic Action movement in the United States was "designed to encourage talented lay Catholics to reach out to non-Catholic America in an organized way and, in turn, offer a vision of what American society could be like if it was guided by Catholic ideals." See Pavuk, "Constructing a Catholic Church Out of Thin Air," 40.

[11]Henry Somerville, "Where Do We Go from Here?" *Canadian Register*, June 19, 1943, in Box 7, Folder 25, SAD Records.

[12]Somerville, "Where Do We Go from Here?"

[13]"Collaboration with Non-Catholics," *Irish Catholic*, July 15, 1943, in Box 7, Folder 25, SAD Records.

In addition to participating in conferences and collecting and distributing material internally about how natural law philosophy could facilitate cooperation between Catholics and non-Catholics, leaders in the NCWC actively published written work for the laity on natural law's central role in constructive interreligiosity. In August 1943, for example, the famed American Jesuit and Neo-Scholastic political philosopher John Courtney Murray corresponded with Hayes about the NCWC's interest in adapting one of Murray's scholarly articles on interreligious cooperation for a Catholic Peace Association pamphlet.[14] Only one month after Murray's article was published, the NCWC collaborated with the Protestant Federal Council of the Churches of Christ in America and the Jewish Synagogue Council of America to issue a statement on preconditions for world peace.[15] In this statement, the NCWC and its collaborating Protestant and Jewish organizations asserted that peace "depends upon practical recognition of the fact" that all individuals are "subject to the sovereignty of God and to the moral law which comes from God."[16]

In the mid-1940s, as in the postwar period, American Catholic leaders continually emphasized how adhering to the dictates of natural law philosophy could catalyze constructive relationships with non-Catholics and remedy the ills of (secular) modernity. To make natural law philosophy accessible to the laity, the NCWC not only published written articles on this topic, but also turned to *Catholic Hour*. Indeed, wartime and postwar *Catholic Hour* addresses were frequently used as vehicles for Catholic leaders' attempted inculcation of natural law philosophy within the laity. Using the new medium of the radio, Catholic leaders attempted to make old arguments about natural law accessible to the laity; in other words, they tried to render abstract intellectual ideas about natural law present in the homes of everyday Catholics.

Of the many different ways that *Catholic Hour* personalities

---

[14]Murray to Hayes, August 14, 1943, Box 10, Folder 65, SAD Records. For Murray's original article, see John Courtney Murray, SJ, "Intercredal Co-Operation: Its Theory and Its Organization," *Theological Studies* 4, no. 1 (June 1943): 257–86.

[15]See "Religious Groups Set Forth Minimum Needs for Just World Peace," *NCWC News Service*, October 4, 1943, in Box 10, Folder 65, SAD Records.

[16]"Religious Groups Set Forth Minimum Needs for Just World Peace."

incorporated natural law into the NCWC's education on the airwaves, few were as direct as in *Catholic Hour* addresses on the philosophical foundations of the American legal tradition. In fact, perhaps the most striking demonstration of natural law philosophy's prominent role in Catholic intellectuals' early and mid-twentieth-century educational efforts can be found in a series of *Catholic Hour* addresses delivered in May 1940 by Howard W. Smith—a Catholic priest and canon lawyer at Our Lady of the Lake Seminary in Cleveland, Ohio.[17]

In four addresses over the course of the month, Smith attempted to make accessible to a lay audience many of the natural law–informed ideas about the philosophical foundations of the American legal tradition that were being articulated in more complex ways by university-level Catholic philosophers and legal scholars at this time.[18] Indeed, Smith's first address gave expression to central dimensions of early and mid-twentieth-century Catholic thinking about legal philosophy, beginning with the foundational presupposition that the "real source of law . . . comes from God."[19] By closely analyzing the text of Smith's address and placing it in its historical context, it will become clear that Smith not only presented natural law as the remedy to secularism's discontents, but also asserted that natural law could offer an intellectual bridge between Catholics and non-Catholics in the United States. As has been suggested, this two-part approach to making natural law accessible to the laity was part and parcel of the NCWC's broader approach to Catholic education on (and off) the airwaves.

Articulating Foundations: Natural Law and the American Legal Tradition

After articulating the premise of his first address—that God is the "real source of law"—Smith channeled the nation's experience of the Second World War to suggest that the "social and

[17]See Smith, *Law*.

[18]On natural law philosophy's role in Catholic legal education during this period, see, generally, John M. Breen and Lee J. Strang, "The Road Not Taken: Catholic Legal Education at the Middle of the Twentieth Century," *American Journal of Legal History* 51, no. 4 (2011): 553–637.

[19]Smith, *Law*, 4.

political chaos" around him arose out of "contempt for law."[20] In Smith's view, this contempt for the true nature of law was a product of the then-popular belief that law is merely posited by human persons and need not be reconciled with the ordinances of a higher legislator. This positivist conception of law, Smith claimed, "supplanted the genuine Christian and Catholic concept of law" because academic writers—especially Jean-Jacques Rousseau, Karl Marx, Thomas Hobbes, and Oswald Spengler—had effectively captured the "academic worlds" with their positivist philosophies.[21]

Quite unsurprisingly, Catholic legal scholars of this period likewise labeled these European thinkers as progenitors of an intellectual movement to undermine traditional views about the American legal tradition's philosophical foundations. For example, the year after Smith's address was delivered on *Catholic Hour*, Jesuit priest and Boston College Law School dean William J. Kenealy argued that secular and positivist legal philosophies which repudiate natural law are "irreligious" and "essential[ly] un-American."[22] Tellingly, Kenealy moreover asserted that these alternative legal philosophies had been theorized by many of the same European figures that Smith critiqued, including Hobbes, Rousseau, Kant, Marx, and Spengler.[23]

Having given exposition to the view that God is the ultimate source of law, Smith continued in his address to highlight other defining characteristics of early and mid-twentieth-century Catholic thinking about the relationship between natural law and the American legal tradition. These other characteristics were set out in exceedingly clear terms: "A Catholic always starts with certain principles—the existence of God, the Creator and Designer of all things; the existence in man of an intelligent and spiritual principle called the soul. For us God is an intelligent being—not a blind force—and in His creation of the universe there must be a

[20]Smith, *Law*, 4.

[21]Smith, *Law*, 5.

[22]See the reproduction of Kenealy's sermon at the 1941 Red Mass in Boston in William J. Kenealy, SJ, "The Majesty of the Law," *Loyola Law Review* 5, no. 2 (1950): 105.

[23]Kenealy, "The Majesty of the Law," *Loyola Law Review* 5, no. 2 (1950): 106.

design and plan."[24] In other words, Smith argued that a Catholic's approach to understanding the American legal tradition's philosophical foundations must not only be predicated on a belief in God's ultimate sovereignty over positive (i.e., human-made) laws, but also on the belief that individuals have eternal souls situated within a divine plan.

Though these beliefs might have been easily intelligible to an audience of Catholic philosophers or legal scholars, they were likely not as readily understandable to a lay Catholic listener of *Catholic Hour* with little to no extensive philosophical education.[25] Similarly, while a Catholic philosopher or legal scholar of this period would likely have been able to communicate these beliefs to a non-Catholic interlocutor with relative ease, the lay Catholic asked about his or her perspective on a recent legislative enactment by a Protestant or Jewish neighbor would have been more troubled in his or her communication of these beliefs. These practical challenges of transmission between Church leaders and lay Catholics undoubtedly encouraged the Church's intellectual class to subsume these various dimensions of the Church's apparent teaching on legal philosophy under the abstract heading of "the Natural Law." In Smith's words, "The reflection of God in His Creation—man—is called the Natural Law. Man, by the light of his reason, comes to know of this plan and this eternal ordering of things as reflected in his own being."[26]

In attempting to make natural law philosophy accessible to his lay audience, Smith noted that "men of all times have known" about natural law, citing the writings of Aristotle, Cicero, and Thomas Aquinas.[27] Alongside these three figures, however, Smith also placed "the Supreme Court of the United States."[28] While a

---

[24]Smith, *Law*, 5–6.

[25]Though not referencing addresses on natural law in particular, Pavuk has helpfully emphasized that listeners made "regular complaints . . . that *Catholic Hour* speeches were too academic and high-toned." "In fact," Pavuk has moreover argued, "a listener needed to possess a more than passing sense of historical and theological ideas, along with a fair vocabulary, to understand the full implications of many talks." See Pavuk, "Constructing a Catholic Church Out of Thin Air," 48.

[26]Smith, *Law*, 7.

[27]Smith, *Law*, 7.

[28]Smith, *Law*, 7.

Catholic priest and canon lawyer's interest in discussing Aristotle, Cicero, and Aquinas vis-à-vis natural law during this period is unsurprising, what should be striking is this inclusion of the Supreme Court on Smith's list of those individuals and entities who recognize natural law's foundational position in the American legal tradition.

Smith's decision to place the Supreme Court alongside Aquinas and his Greco-Roman predecessors reflects the widespread view among early and mid-twentieth-century Catholic leaders that natural law philosophy is inextricable from the American legal tradition. This was a claim that John Courtney Murray famously articulated two decades after Smith in his seminal *We Hold These Truths*, but it was also a claim, during this earlier period, that seemed to offer lay Catholics a way to constructively position themselves in a nation once overtly hostile to the Church. Indeed, implicit in Smith's assertion about the Supreme Court was a syllogism that found more prominent expression in Murray's later writings: if Catholics know something about natural law philosophy through Aquinas, and if natural law philosophy is a constitutive facet of the American legal tradition, then Catholics can be Americans and have a unique ability to articulate what "being American" really means. This was a profoundly important view for the Catholic episcopacy to inculcate within the laity, particularly during wartime.

Extending Natural Law's Reach: A Catholic Idea with Universal Implications

After delivering his first *Catholic Hour* address on May 5, Smith delivered a second lecture on the "Meaning of Law" on May 12. In this second lecture, Smith again channeled the experience of wartime by beginning his address with references to modern totalitarianism and absolutism. Recalling the kingship of James I and Otto von Bismarck, Smith claimed that these men were "totalitarians and the Church was forced to resist their despotism as she is now resisting that of Hitler and Stalin."[29] Such a claim—that the Church is a primary opponent of totalitarianism because it rejects the secular, positivist belief that positive laws

[29]Smith, *Law*, 11.

need not be reconciled with a higher law—was incredibly influential in early and mid-twentieth-century Catholic intellectual circles.[30] Consequently, Smith sought to provide his audience of lay Catholic lawyers, doctors, teachers, nurses, and politicians with the vocabulary they would need to explain to their Protestant and Jewish neighbors why Catholics were allied with the nation writ large in its opposition to totalitarianism. Importantly, this vocabulary remained closely connected to a Thomistic understanding of natural law philosophy.

Toward the conclusion of this second address, Smith specifically articulated how the Church's Thomistic intellectual tradition should inform a Catholic's approach to understanding the American legal tradition's philosophical foundations. Characteristically turning to Aquinas, Smith first reiterated Aquinas's definition of law as a "mandate of reason having for its aim the public good and promulgated by him who has the care of the society."[31] Despite citing an authority whom Smith himself described as the "great philosopher and teacher of the Catholic Church," he used Aquinas to assert natural law's supra-denominational catholicity (i.e., universality).[32] Indeed, Smith so much as claimed that "when a Jew is deprived of his possessions, barred from business and the professions, simply because he is a Jew, we have a violation of Natural Law."[33] As he moreover indicated in the concluding sentence of this second address, Smith hoped that all "civilized men may again be happily united by a Catholic philosophy of law."[34] As has been suggested, this emphasis on natural law's simultaneous Catholicity and catholicity was common among Catholic leaders of this period. Informed by the long-standing memory of American anti-Catholicism, perceived interwar and wartime threat of secularism, and evident suspicion about Catholics' sympathy to totalitarianism, those tasked with media(ting) between the Church's leaders and laity turned to natural law.

---

[30]For further discussion, see, e.g., Dennis J. Wieboldt III, "Natural Law Appeals as Method of American-Catholic Reconciliation: Catholic Legal Thought and the Red Mass in Boston, 1941–1944," *US Catholic Historian* 41, no. 4 (Fall 2023): 27–52.

[31]Smith, *Law*, 15.

[32]Smith, *Law*, 15.

[33]Smith, *Law*, 15–16.

[34]Smith, *Law*, 17.

In his third *Catholic Hour* address, Smith continued to make claims about the American legal tradition's philosophical foundations that reflected dominant themes in early and mid-twentieth-century Catholic intellectual life. Perhaps none of these claims was more important than that with which this third address began: namely, that the Declaration of Independence demonstrates how Americans' civil rights "flow from the creative plan in God . . . [known as] the Natural Law."[35] As the political scientist Ken I. Kersch has argued in other contexts, this was but one discursive formulation of twentieth-century Declarationism—a popular type of politico-legal thought in the United States which frames the Declaration (and especially its discussion of the "Laws of Nature and of Nature's God") as the creedal expression of American ideals.[36]

Smith's explicit invocation of the Declaration alongside "the Natural Law" attempted to demonstrate that the Founding Fathers' formative articulation of American ideals was, in one crucial sense, Catholic. Likewise, Smith's employment of Declarationist rhetoric also attempted to demonstrate to his lay *Catholic Hour* audience that the politico-legal tradition which followed the Declaration—precisely because of its foundations in natural law—was catholic. Smith's discussion of the historical roots of "universality in law," in fact, was immediately followed by a popular passage from Galatians emphasizing the fundamental unity of all human persons: "There is neither Jew nor Greek; there is neither bond nor free; there is neither male nor female. For you are all one in Christ Jesus" (3:28).[37]

Situated in the broader context of this third address, Smith's argument that legal universality had been championed by the Church since the Middle Ages implicitly communicated that the Church's philosophical tradition had something distinctive to contribute to the United States' understanding of the Declaration's

[35] Smith, *Law*, 18.

[36] On Declarationism generally, see Ken I. Kersch, "Beyond Originalism: Conservative Declarationism and Constitutional Redemption," *Maryland Law Review* 71, no. 1 (2011): 229–82. On Catholics' specific employment of Declarationist rhetoric, see Ken I. Kersch, *Conservatives and the Constitution: Imagining Constitutional Restoration in the Heyday of American Liberalism* (Cambridge, UK: Cambridge University Press, 2019), 297–359.

[37] Smith, *Law*, 21.

supra-denominational ideals. Consequently, Smith was able to frame Catholics in the United States as authentically American because their Church and state shared a philosophical foundation in the "creative plan of God reflected in the soul and being of His creature, man . . . what is called the Natural Law."[38]

Ideas for a (Catholic) Nation: Natural Law and American Radio

As in his first three addresses on *Catholic Hour*, Smith's fourth and final address continued to expound upon how natural law should inform a Catholic's approach to understanding the American legal tradition's philosophical foundations. Thus, this case study of Catholic education on the airwaves suggests that early and mid-twentieth-century Catholic leaders leveraged natural law philosophy to communicate how Catholics in the United States could be both Catholic and American. Although natural law philosophy may have initially seemed ripe to remedy the transnational crises spurred by secularism, Catholic leaders in and working for the NCWC used appeals to natural law to catalyze constructive relationships between Catholics and non-Catholics in an increasingly religiously plural nation. Put more directly, Catholic intellectuals like Smith employed natural law as a medium of understanding between themselves and the laity, and likewise framed natural law as a medium of understanding between Catholics and non-Catholics.

Just as scholars have recognized natural law philosophy's importance to John Courtney Murray's interreligious undertakings, so too should the history of this earlier period encourage renewed scholarly interest in how natural law shaped Catholics' engagement with non-Catholics during the early and mid-twentieth century. Indeed, understanding Catholic leaders' employment of natural law during the Civil Rights Movement to facilitate interreligious dialogue (for Catholic Action) must account for these earlier efforts to appeal to natural law.[39] Similarly, making sense

---

[38]Smith, *Law*, 20.

[39]On natural law philosophy's role in the Civil Rights Movement–era history of the NCWC, see, briefly, Wieboldt, "The Natural Law and Interreligious Social Advocacy," 77–80.

of Catholic leaders' largely ineffective employment of natural law during emerging debates about contraception in the latter half of the twentieth century must make sense of this interwar and wartime discursive history.[40]

These outstanding questions about the practical effectiveness of natural law appeals notwithstanding, the scene from *Catholic Hour*'s history introduced in this essay suggests that scholars of American Catholicism should also consider anew how emerging forms of twentieth-century media—including and especially the radio—facilitated Catholic intellectuals' engagement with the laity and non-Catholics. In the particular context of legal philosophy, there is abundant evidence that Catholic intellectuals leveraged other radio programs (in addition to *Catholic Hour*) to render abstract ideas about natural law philosophy present for millions of Americans. In 1949, for example, the University of Notre Dame's Natural Law Institute—an academic institute devoted to exploring the relationship between natural law and American jurisprudence—successfully lobbied the Columbia Broadcasting System (CBS) to air an institute-sponsored address on natural law philosophy's supra-denominational and supra-national universality.[41] Likewise, between 1948 and 1951, the university's public information director prepared radio scripts about natural law that Notre Dame alumni read on local radio stations across the country to increase interest in natural law within local communities.[42] The institute's founder, Clarence E. Manion, dean of Notre Dame College of Law, established a popular radio program after his retirement to expose everyday men and women to many of the ideas that initially motivated his founding of the Natural Law Institute.

As has been suggested, even a cursory review of the history of *Catholic Hour* (and the Natural Law Institute) illustrates that novel questions remain unanswered about how Catholic intellec-

---

[40]On natural law philosophy's role in Catholic debates about contraception, see, generally, Mark S. Massa, SJ, *The Structure of Theological Revolutions: How the Fight over Birth Control Transformed American Catholicism* (New York: Oxford University Press, 2018).

[41]Helen J. Sioussat to Raymond J. Donovan, November 23, 1949, UDIS 020/03, University of Notre Dame Archives (hereafter UNDA).

[42]See, e.g., John V. Hinkel to Notre Dame Club Presidents, November 30, 1948, UDIS 020/01, UNDA.

tuals and institutions used new forms of media to render certain abstract ideas present for lay Catholics and their non-Catholic neighbors. By considering these questions anew, historians and theologians are well poised to uncover how Catholics came to understand the potential (dis)advantages of these new mediums of communication, how the practical limits of these mediums themselves shaped the substantive and discursive articulation of Catholic ideas during the twentieth century, and what the consequences of these limits were for twentieth-century Catholic intellectual life.

The Art of Sammy Chong as a Revelatory and Symbolic Mediation of a Servant God

Vicente Chong

Many Christians believe that we can find God in all things. Indeed, for some believers, art is an event in which we can discern some kind of divine presence because God is revealing God's self in and through such an experience. In this regard, the concept of symbol can help us understand the reality of art as a mediation of God's revelation. This article explores the experience of art as a symbolic mediation of God's revelation to human beings, employing especially Karl Rahner's theological notion of symbol. In this sense, I will analyze some artworks of Sammy Chong's as an example of the revelatory and symbolic power of art, especially as a manifestation of a servant God. Thus, in terms of method, first, I will present some of his paintings. Then, as a second step, I will reflect theologically upon these works of art.

Sammy Chong's "Them" Series

Sammy Chong is an artist who explores a variety of topics in his work, such as the disconnectedness in modern societies, the ecological crisis, and the spiritual search. In his series "Them," he depicts the reality of migrant workers in a symbolic way.[1] These

[1]Sammy Chong, ""THEM" Series," sammychong.com/section/439212-THEM-Series.html.

paintings present some human figures doing types of work that are generally considered "humble jobs," such as the work of trash collectors, housemaids, and construction workers. For instance, the paintings *A Great Fence* and *Food of the Earth* depict the reality of Latin American migrants who work as landscapers and agricultural laborers. This is a first level of reality that is shown in these paintings.

There is more than this first level. If we pay close attention, we realize that the solid depictions of these figures do not cover the whole canvas. Some parts are transparent, like a colored glass that allows us to see beyond or beneath the surface. In those transparent areas, we see some black-and-white images printed on the canvas. They represent elements of the histories, families, and cultures of these people. This is a second level of reality revealed in these paintings.

There is more than this second level. Perhaps one of the most striking elements of these paintings is that the persons depicted have the faces of mythological, divine, or spiritual figures. For example, the head shape of the figure in *A Great Fence* is that of Inti, a divinity of the Incas, and the model in *Food of the Earth* has the face of Tlaloc, a deity of the Aztecs. These heads represent the religious dimension of migrant workers. This is a third level of reality. All these three levels of reality are present at the same time in these artworks.

These paintings express the real situation of migrant workers in our world. On the one hand, these artworks invite migrant workers to be proud of their own cultural and religious identities, and to appreciate their own contribution to society. On the other hand, these paintings invite us to see the humanity of migrant workers. They are not objects that can be used and exploited. They are human beings who have dignity, and whose rights should be respected. Their "humble jobs" are not less important than any other work in our society, and as such, they should be appreciated.

The title of the series is also significant. "Them" could mean the segregationist attitude toward migrants. "We are not them" is the common belief of racist and xenophobic people who consider themselves superior to others. The "us vs. them" mentality reflects and produces social divisions. These artworks challenge that mentality. They invite us to recognize that "they"—namely, migrant workers—have the same human dignity that "we" have. These paintings raise the question, what if these human figures are not "them," but "us"? What if we remember that maybe we are also migrants or descendants of migrants? What if we recognize that there are some things that distinguish us from them, but there are also some things that we all have in common? These artworks invite us to dream of a society where there is unity in diversity, i.e., an inclusive society where all human beings are accepted as equal in dignity but also where their differences are respected.

Thus, Chong's "Them" series shows the complexity of the human and social reality of migrant workers. I suggest that those works of art that express the complexity and depth of our human reality are mediations of God's self-communication to human beings. Following Karl Rahner's theology, I will explain this theological interpretation of art as follows.

Art as Mediation of God's Self-Communication to Human Beings

According to Rahner, God reveals God's self to human beings in and through our human reality. Rahner explains first the event of God's revelation from the perspective of human transcendence.[2] According to Rahner, we all have the experience of transcendence. We experience ourselves as finite beings. However, we are always trying to transcend that finiteness to reach the infinite. We are always longing for the infinite.

We have this experience of transcendence in different ways. For example, at the cognitive level, we experience that we have the capacity to ask questions to overcome our limited knowledge. And when we get answers, we have new questions. Therefore, as we experience ourselves as finite beings at the level of knowledge, we are always moving toward infinite knowledge, although we will never achieve such a goal in our earthly life. We also have the experience of transcendence at the level of freedom. Here, we understand freedom as the possibility of being who we really are as individuals and as a people. In this sense, we often experience that our freedom is finite. We are limited by internal and external factors. However, we are constantly striving to liberate ourselves from those elements that constrain our freedom. Thus, as we experience ourselves as finite beings at the level of freedom, we are always moving toward infinite freedom, although we will never achieve such a goal during our life in this world.

The experience of transcendence always occurs in and through a concrete and historical reality. It is mediated through our own

---

[2]See Karl Rahner, *Foundations of Christian Faith: An Introduction to the Idea of Christianity*, trans. William V. Dych (New York: Crossroad, 2005), 20–23, 31–39, 51–66.

human existence and through the world around us. Thus, art, as an essential element of our human lives, can be a mediation of transcendental experience. Art can express our human finiteness and, at the same time, our longing for the infinite. Art can provoke an experience of transcendence in its recipients.[3]

Therefore, the origin and the aim of the experience of transcendence is ultimately the infinite reality, which in Christian terms we call "God," who is revealing God's self to us and who is inviting us to participate in God's life. God's revelation is what makes possible transcendental experience. Rahner understands the event of divine revelation as the self-communication of God to human beings.[4] God's self-communication takes place in history and through the mediation of concrete reality. First, God communicates God's self in and through our own human reality, that is, our own bodies, emotions, ideas, moral conscience, and hopes. Second, God communicates God's self in and through other people. Indeed, our interaction in freedom and love with other people is a mediation of our relationship with God. Especially, our relationship with the poor and the excluded from society is an important mediation of our relationship with God. Finally, God communicates God's self in and through the world around us, that is, through nature, the world, and society. Thus, art, as

---

[3]See Karl Rahner, "Art against the Horizon of Theology and Piety," in *Theological Investigations*, trans. Joseph Donceel and Hugh M. Riley (London: Darton, Longman and Todd, 1992), 12:165–66. Art includes three elements—the artistic object, the artist, and the recipient. We can add a fourth element, which is the world presented by the artwork. Art can be an experience of transcendence vis-à-vis these three or four elements. When I say that art can express an experience of transcendence, I am talking about the artistic object and the world that it presents. When I say that art can provoke an experience of transcendence, I am paying more attention to the recipient. However, art can be an experience of transcendence for the artist as well. For instance, artists can have an experience of freedom in the way they use their creative imagination. See Vicente Chong, *A Theological Aesthetics of Liberation: God, Art, and the Social Outcasts* (Eugene, OR: Pickwick Publications, 2019), 126–27, 137–38, 144–53.

[4]See Rahner, *Foundations of Christian Faith*, 116–33. According to Rahner, God communicates God's self to human beings in two modes: in Jesus Christ, i.e., through the incarnation of the Son, and in grace, that is, through the Spirit that has been poured out in every human heart. Here we are paying more attention to the event of God's self-communication in grace.

an essential element of our lives, can be a mediation of God's self-communication to human beings.

Art can be a mediation of God's revelation in different ways.[5] According to Rahner, art has the potential of being a mediation of God's self-communication as it expresses the complexity of our human reality. By doing so, art can provoke in its recipients an experience of transcendence, which is implicitly or explicitly an experience of God. Thus, when art expresses the joys, sufferings, loves, dreams, and struggles of human beings, the recipients of such an art can experience the complexity and depth of our humanity, that is, they can experience the mystery of our human existence. In this way, maybe they will open themselves to the possibility of recognizing the mysterious ground of our human existence, which is God. Therefore, art can be a mediation of God's self-communication to human beings as long as art provokes an experience of transcendence in its recipients, and by doing so, it evokes the origin and the aim of such an experience, which is God.[6]

Therefore, Chong's "Them" series can be a mediation of God's revelation as long as such works of art express and provoke a transcendental experience in their recipients. On the one hand, these paintings express the experience of transcendence of migrant workers. These artworks show the reality of people who did not experience the conditions necessary to thrive in their own land, and who wanted to overcome such a situation by migrating to

---

[5]See Rahner, "Art against the Horizon," 163; Karl Rahner, "Priest and Poet," in *Theological Investigations*, trans. Karl-H. Kruger and Boniface Kruger (London: Darton, Longman and Todd, 1967), 3:316–17.

[6]For Rahner, art does not need to present an explicit Christian religious object or theme—such as Jesus and the saints—to be a mediation of God's revelation. Some works of art with explicit religious themes have been made for the decoration of churches and for liturgical purposes, but they do not necessarily produce any experience of transcendence in their recipients. This kind of artwork can be called "religious" simply because it presents explicit religious themes, but it is not a mediation of God's communication. However, Rahner also recognizes that some works of art with explicit religious themes can provoke a transcendental experience in their recipients. See Rahner, "Art against the Horizon," 167; Karl Rahner, "The Theology of the Religious Meaning of Images," in *Theological Investigations*, trans. Joseph Donceel and Hugh M. Riley (London: Darton, Longman and Todd, 1992), 13:159; Karl Rahner, "On the Theology of Books," in *Mission and Grace*, trans. Cecily Hastings (London: Sheed and Ward, 1966), 3:121–22.

another country. On the other hand, these works of art invite their recipients to see the humanity of migrant workers. They challenge viewers to transcend and overcome their own biases against foreigners. If a viewer of Chong's artworks experiences such an invitation and such a challenge, he or she is having an experience of transcendence. However, it is God's self-communication that makes possible the transcendental experience in and through art. Thus, through these works of art, it is God who reveals God's self as a God who cares for migrant workers. It is the Spirit of God who invites us to see the reality of migrant workers, and who calls us to be in solidarity with them by building a more welcoming and inclusive society.

Art as a Symbolic Mediation of God's Self-Communication

The reality and concept of symbols can help us understand the phenomenon of art as a mediation of God's revelation. I will explain some aspects of a theology of symbols—especially Rahner's—that will help us understand the reality of art as a symbolic mediation of God's self-communication.

Symbols include three aspects: a symbol, the reality symbolized, and the recipients of symbols. The relationship among these three elements produces a dynamic phenomenon. Let us explore first the relationship between a symbol and the reality symbolized. From the perspective of a symbol, we can say that a symbol is a reality that makes present or re-presents another reality, that is, a reality symbolized.[7] To be clear, when we use the words "representation" or "representing," we mean "making the other really present." Thus, a symbol is something concrete and perceptible through the senses that makes present "the other," i.e., another reality, which can be concrete and perceptible as well, or can be non-perceptible in or by itself.

From the perspective of the realities symbolized, we can say that some beings realize and communicate themselves in and

[7] See Karl Rahner, "The Theology of the Symbol," in *Theological Investigations*, trans. Kevin Smyth (London: Darton, Longman and Todd, 1966), 4:225.

through the other, that is, through a symbol.[8] Rahner sometimes uses the words "expression" and "expressing" to explain this relationship between a symbol and a reality symbolized. A symbol is an expression of a reality symbolized. And vice versa, a reality symbolized expresses itself in and through a symbol.[9]

Now let us explore the relationship between a symbol and its recipients. According to Avery Dulles, symbols imply "participatory knowledge."[10] That is, the recipients of a symbol can know the reality symbolized if they participate in the world of such a symbol. Participatory knowledge means that the recipients need to be open in order to know and be moved by a symbol. Symbols have the power to affect the whole person. Symbols give us new ideas. They touch our emotions and stimulate our imagination. They move our will; hence, they influence our actions. Indeed, symbols evoke and provoke. However, symbols can "do something to us"[11] if the recipients are willing to enter the worlds that symbols open for us.

Now let us focus on religious symbols. A religious symbol is a concrete and perceptible reality that makes present a divine real-

[8]See Rahner, "Theology of the Symbol," 234.

[9]See Rahner, "Theology of the Symbol," 224. Some authors distinguish between symbols and signs. On the one hand, a sign is a pointer that refers to the reality signified. The relationship between a sign and the reality signified is extrinsic, artificial, and socially agreed upon. On the other hand, the relationship between a symbol and the reality symbolized is intrinsic. To express this idea, Rahner says that a symbol is constituted by the reality symbolized, and Tillich asserts that a symbol participates in the reality symbolized. However, some authors point out that sometimes it is difficult to distinguish a symbol from a sign because, in reality, the distinction between sign and symbol is not clear-cut, but fluid. Furthermore, there are different understandings of the symbolic reality. For some authors, a symbol calls our attention to the symbol itself in order to make present the reality symbolized. For other authors, on the contrary, a symbol effaces itself or becomes transparent, as it were, to refer to the reality symbolized. Probably, these different notions of signs and symbols, and the tension between them, will exist for a long time in academic discussions. See Rahner, "Theology of the Symbol," 224–26; Paul Tillich, *Dynamics of Faith* (New York: Harper Torchbooks, 1957), 41–42.

[10]See Avery Dulles, *Models of Revelation* (Maryknoll, NY: Orbis Books, 1992), 136–37.

[11]Avery Dulles, *The Craft of Theology: From Symbol to System* (New York: Crossroad, 1995), 65.

ity. As I said above, some symbols have the power to represent a reality that is not perceptible in or by itself. For this reason, symbols are appropriate mediations to represent a divine reality since such a reality is transcendent. In this sense, symbols are mediations of God's revelation.[12] Anything in the world has the potential of being a symbol of God's presence. For instance, a beautiful sunset, the love of our parents, and those who defend human rights, can be symbols of God's love for human beings. In this sense, art—including art that does not present an explicit religious object or theme—can be a symbolic mediation of God's self-communication.[13]

Therefore, Chong's "Them" series can be a symbolic mediation of God's revelation. As a symbol, these paintings open levels of reality.[14] They not only depict the reality of migrant workers, but also show other dimensions such as their histories, families, and cultures. As symbols, these artworks can provoke an experience of transcendence if their recipients enter the world that they open for us. Moreover, these artworks can be a mediation of God's self-communication because, as symbols, they can represent a God who loves and serves those who suffer from social injustice.

The Symbol of a Servant God

A striking feature of Chong's "Them" series is its portrayal of deities and other spiritual figures not in a position of power, but in a situation of service. Perhaps the artist did not intend to express anything about divine beings. However, art, as symbolic, has a "surplus of meaning," and such is the case with these artworks.

---

[12]See Dulles, *Models of Revelation*, 131–33.

[13]In his theological analysis of symbols, Rahner wonders whether sacred images—such as religious paintings and statues—can be considered primordial symbols (that is, symbols that make present the reality of God) or secondary symbols (that is, signs that point to divine reality). However, in this analysis, Rahner does not talk about "secular" art as a symbolic mediation of God's presence. In other articles though, Rahner explains that secular art can be a mediation of transcendental experience, and as such, it can be a mediation of God's self-communication (see note 6 in this article). Thus, when I say that art, even secular art, can be a symbolic mediation of God's self-revelation, I am connecting Rahner's theology of symbols and his theological understanding of art. See Rahner, "Theology of the Symbol," 243.

[14]See Tillich, *Dynamics of Faith*, 42.

In these paintings, we see deities and other religious figures doing "humble jobs." The idea or the image of a servant divinity might be shocking for those who think that a divine being is, by definition, omnipotent. However, this image is not and should not be strange for Christians, since one of the most important symbols of God that is revealed in Jesus Christ is that of a servant God. In the Gospel of Mark, Jesus says, "The Son of Man came not to be served but to serve, and to give his life as a ransom for many" (Mk 10:45), which is reminiscent of the symbolic figure of the Suffering Servant in the book of Isaiah (Is 52:13–53:12). Likewise, in his letter to the Philippians, Paul speaks of the *kenosis* of the Son, who "emptied himself, taking the form of a slave" (Phil 2:7). However, God's attitude of service is born out of love. Indeed, when Paul talks about the kenosis of the Son, the apostle is exhorting the Philippians to love and serve one another as Jesus did (Phil 2:2–5). This understanding of love as service is symbolically expressed in the Gospel of John, when Jesus washes his disciples' feet: "If I, your Lord and Teacher, have washed your feet, you also ought to wash one another's feet" (Jn 13:14).

The Christian symbol of a servant God is subversive because it goes against the grain in a world that glorifies power. On the one hand, such a symbol expresses that God is not an authoritarian being, but a loving God. It shows that the way of God is not that of power, but of loving service. If God has a power, then it is the power of love, because "God is love" (1 Jn 4:8). On the other hand, the symbol of a servant God reminds us that Christians are called to love and serve one another as Christ did.[15]

Elizabeth Johnson says, "The symbol of God functions."[16] Indeed, different symbolic images of God influence how human beings understand God and humanity. Such images affect how human beings act in accordance with their notion of God. If human beings believe in a divinity that uses power in an authoritarian way, they will imitate such a divine figure by looking for economic, social, and political power in order to dominate

---

[15]The beautiful musical composition "The Servant Song" by Richard Gillard talks about Jesus's call to serve one another. I recommend praying with and reflecting upon its lyrics.

[16]Elizabeth A. Johnson, *She Who Is: The Mystery of God in Feminist Theological Discourse* (New York: Crossroad, 1992), 4, 5, 38.

others. But if they believe in a loving and serving God, they will likewise love and serve.

However, the symbol of a servant God—like any other symbol of God—has the danger of being distorted by those who want to dominate others. Those who have economic, social, and political power can use the symbol of a servant God to tell the oppressed that they should serve those in power because that is God's will. To avoid this distortion of the symbol of a servant God, it is necessary to look at other symbols of God that are part of our Christian faith, such as the symbol of a liberating God.[17] Indeed, God is a God who loves the poor and the excluded from society. God wants to liberate them from their situation of poverty and social exclusion. If God has a power, then it is a power at the service of their liberation, that is, a divine power that works in and through concrete and historical mediations. In this sense, the symbol of a liberating God is an empowering symbol. It invites the poor and the excluded from society to work for their own liberation. Therefore, the symbol of a servant God and the symbol of a liberating God are in a dialectical and complementary relation.

The symbol of a servant God can also correct the misuse of the symbol of a liberating God. The symbol of a servant God reminds the poor and the oppressed that if they ever come to have some power, they should stay alert to the misuse of power, lest they become as authoritarian as their oppressors. Moreover, Jesus says: "I do not call you servants any longer . . . , but I have called you friends" (Jn 15:15). Indeed, the true aim of the process of liberation is a society without masters and servants, that is, a world of fellowship among human beings and communion with the environment.

Thus, Chong's "Them" series is a symbolic mediation of a servant God. To be clear, I am not saying that the religious figures in these paintings are a portrayal of our Christian God. Rather, these artworks invite us to use our "analogical imagination."[18] By

[17]We need different symbols of God to have a deeper understanding of the mystery of God, while knowing that divine mystery will always be beyond our grasp.

[18]David Tracy coined the expression "analogical imagination." See David Tracy, *The Analogical Imagination: Christian Theology and the Culture of Pluralism* (New York: Crossroad, 1981), 405–55.

showing deities and other spiritual figures in a situation of service, these paintings remind us that we Christians have a similar image of God. They help us to remember that the symbol of a servant God is part of our Christian faith, and by doing so, they remind us that we are called to love and serve others, especially those who are poor and excluded from society.

In conclusion, Chong's "Them" series is a symbolic mediation of God's self-communication to human beings. These paintings represent and express the longing of migrant workers for a worthy and fulfilled life, a movement that is originated by and aims at the infinite mystery of God, who loves and serves the poor and the excluded from society, and who invites us to do likewise.

MEDIATION

AND

RESPONSIBILITY

Religion(s) in the Ruins of the Temples

Robert A. Orsi

> *Conjuring a future full of pasts, a ghost ridden freedom is both a way to move on and a way to remember.*
>
> —Anna Tsing[1]

> *For indeed it cannot be foreseen, where and in what form in our world the tradition of the sacred can find expression.*
>
> —Gershom Scholem[2]

We live in a time of multiple and multiplying crises. *We* being citizens of the United States; *we* also being humans on this planet. I will have the climate crisis in view for the most part, but it is not possible to separate one contemporary crisis from another, climate catastrophe, for example, from the rise of neofascist political movements. The crises magnify and exacerbate each other. As these extreme and entwined dangers proliferate, the problem of hope presents itself with increasing urgency. Hope is a complicated subject in any context. I will define it for my purposes here as the capacity to imagine an otherwise to reality

---

[1]Anna Lownenhaupt Tsing, *The Mushroom at the End of the World: On the Possibility of Life in Capitalist Ruins* (Princeton, NJ: Princeton University Press, 2015), 79.

[2]Scholem cited in Peter E. Gordon, *Migrants in the Profane: Critical Theory and the Question of Secularization* (New Haven, CT: Yale University Press, 2020), 103.

as given. In our present circumstances, what and where are the resources for hope?

The question of hope, in turn, entails the political imagination. Are humans in particular times and places capable—intellectually and emotionally, as well as politically—of attaining sufficient distance from the dire contingency of their circumstances to envision a possible (or even an impossible) future beyond the limits set by the imperatives and constraints of those circumstances? In the case of the climate crisis, this would be a future beyond the one envisioned within the terms of the Anthropocene, the current geological age. "The stakes are enormous," climate activist Daniel Sherrell writes, "and the odds are lengthening, and the prospect of fighting against them can seem daunting if not Sisyphean." To fight against these odds, Sherrell says, requires "acting in the play of politics."[3] But this is the rub: how to find the wherewithal to enter this space of political play? Sober climate scientists tell us it is too late; we have already lost. Others imagine more or less dystopian futures. Nearly 70 percent of animal populations have been destroyed since 1970.[4] Now what? This is a matter at once political and intimate, epistemological and ontological. It affects relationships, troubles memory, (re)arranges temporalities; it determines small choices as well as big ones. The prospects for resilience, endurance, even survival are at stake; so is the possibility of resistance.

There are many alternatives to hope—hopelessness being the most obvious. Another is violence. In a recent treatise, *How to Blow Up a Pipeline*, Swedish climate activist and theorist Andreas Malm argues that "the irresponsiveness to the [climate] crisis" among world leaders in business and government has "exceeded expectations."[5] At this juncture, Malm says, sabotage is a morally

[3]Daniel Sherrell, *Warmth: Coming of Age at the End of Our World* (New York: Penguin Books, 2021), 120.

[4]Rosamunde Almond, Monique Grooten, Diego Juffe Bignoli, and Tanya Petersen, eds., World Wildlife Fund, *Living Planet Report 2022: Building a Nature-Positive Society* (Gland, Switzerland, 2022). This document was very widely cited in the international press. For a critical examination of the term "Anthropocene," see Eileen Crist, "On the Poverty of Our Nomenclature," *Environmental Humanities* 3 (November 2013): 129–47.

[5]Andreas Malm, *How to Blow Up a Pipeline: Learning to Fight in a World on Fire* (London: Verso, 2021), 65.

legitimate option. "Here is what this movement of millions [of people concerned about the climate crisis] should do, for a start," he writes. "Damage and destroy new CO2-emitting devices. Put them out of commission, pick them apart, demolish them, burn them, blow them up."[6] But even sabotage, as Malm presents it, is about something like hope. "The question is not if sabotage from a militant wing of the climate movement will solve the crisis on its own," he writes, "but if the disruptive commotion for shaking business-as-usual out of the ruts *can come about without it* [italics in orig.]."[7] The issue is always how to nourish the capacity of humans to look beyond that to which they have acclimated themselves to figure out how to generate the disruptive commotion of hope.

One of the primary domains of human experience in which such imagining-beyond has taken place is religion. But religion's usefulness as an ally in challenging structures of oppression is a contested matter within secular forums of political critique. Religious versions of possible alternative futures are often seen as a distraction from real world struggles and solutions or as compensation for present-day distress. End-time visions encourage pessimism and resignation. (I am careful not to use the language of "apocalypse" in reference to the climate crisis, for example, because conservative Christian eschatology offers only the sourest vision of hope, and then only for the saved.) Classical social scientific approaches to religion theorized its primary functions to be the sacralization and normalization of the social order. It is axiomatic to secular critical theorists that "we have no sources for our critical leverage against the social world we inhabit other than the resources that belong to this same world."[8] Commenting on this tradition in her introduction to the 2009 symposium on the question "Is critique secular?" philosopher Wendy Brown speaks of the "intensity with which critique attaches itself to secularism, articulates itself as a secularizing project, and identifies itself with the dethroning of God."[9]

---

[6]Malm, *How to Blow Up a Pipeline*, 67.

[7]Malm, *How to Blow Up a Pipeline*, 69–70.

[8]Peter E. Gordon, *Migrants in the Profane: Critical Theory and the Question of Secularization* (New Haven, CT: Yale University Press, 2020), 103.

[9]Wendy Brown, Introduction to *Is Critique Secular: Blasphemy, Injury,*

Reading through the literature on the climate crisis recently for a course I was preparing, however, I encountered the growing conviction among climate theorists that an effective response to the crisis could precisely *not* come from the "inhibiting ideologies" of the carbon-modern or from the lifeways it fueled.[10] This sense of a theoretical dead end in secular critique is a significant development in what has become a crucial area of contemporary critical and cultural theory. As anthropologist Arturo Escobar articulates a widely shared sentiment, "We cannot emerge from the crisis with the categories of the world that created the crisis (development, growth, markets, competitiveness, the individual, and so on)."[11] Critique in the face of climate catastrophe cannot be secular, or it cannot be only secular. Many climate theorists are searching urgently for some point of transcendence outside and beyond the constraints of the carbon-modern from which humans might reimagine their circumstances and discover as yet unforeseen pathways forward. Theorist Donna Haraway describes this as "an elsewhere and an elsewhen that was, still is, and yet might be."[12] Escobar proposes "pluriversal politics" to replace politics as usual. Whereas the carbon-modern "has managed to universalize its own idea of the world, which only modern science can know," he writes, "the notion of the pluriverse inverts this seductive formula, suggesting pluriversality as a shared project based on a multiplicity of worlds and ways of worlding life."[13]

Given this imperative toward a transmundane other, many climate activists have been turning to religion(s) for a vision of an elsewhere. (I do not think the doxological cadence of Haraway's language was unintentional.) Toward the end of *The Great De-*

---

and Free Speech, by Talal Asad, Wendy Brown, Judith Butler, and Saba Mahmood (Berkeley: The Townsend Center for the Humanities, University of California Berkeley; distributed by the University of California Press, Berkeley, CA, 2009), 7–19, "intensity" on 11.

[10]Naomi Oreskes and Erik M. Conway, *The Collapse of Western Civilization: A View from the Future* (New York: Columbia University Press, 2014), 35.

[11]Arturo Escobar, *Pluriversal Politics: The Real and the Possible* (Durham, NC: Duke University Press, 2020), 26.

[12]Donna J. Haraway, *Staying with the Trouble: Making Kin in the Chthulucene* (Durham, NC: Duke University Press, 2016), 31.

[13]Escobar, *Pluriversal Politics,* 27.

rangement: Climate Change and the Unthinkable, for instance, Indian novelist and climate writer Amitav Ghosh points to the "increasing involvement of religious groups and leaders in the politics of climate change" as one of "the most promising development[s]" in recent decades.[14] Since its publication in 2016, Ghosh's extended essay has become a key text in the critical analysis of the climate crisis. Ghosh was among the first to argue that the cultural forms characteristic of the Anthropocene could not adequately represent the changed realities of life on earth today, let alone offer a vision of life beyond them. His case in point is the modern novel, preoccupied as it is with the proprieties, sensibilities, and discontents of the bourgeois social world. In religion(s) that *predate the carbon-modern*, on the other hand—this temporality is crucial for him, *pre-carbon-modern*—Ghosh and other climate writers believe that humans may find ways of living in time and space unconstrained by the metaphysics and ontologies of the Anthropocene. Mostly, these writers have in mind Indigenous religions, but Ghosh turns at the end of *The Great Derangement* to Catholicism, finding in Pope Francis's 2016 encyclical, *Laudato Si'*, and more generally, in Catholicism itself, a preeminent example of the elsewhere and elsewhen: metaphysically, in its rich pre-carbon-modern theological and spiritual traditions; politically, in its institutional presence across the globe.

I devoutly wish I were able to share Ghosh's vision, and his hope. But it is precisely here, in a secular climate theorist's identification of Catholicism as an option for hope in a burning world, that the work I have been doing on the history of the Catholic sexual abuse crisis in the United States and around the world intrudes. I have seen absolutely nothing in the many documents produced by the clergy sexual abuse crisis over the past decade that gives any evidence among Catholic leaders of intergenerational responsibility, which Ghosh identifies as one of the preeminent contributions of pre-carbon religions to the climate challenge, and even less any capacity to transcend the narrow privileges and prerogatives of the institution on behalf of greater goods. If there is one incontrovertible conclusion to be drawn from these grim and dispiriting sources it is this: unfailingly, Catholic authorities

[14]Amitav Ghosh, *The Great Derangement: Climate Change and the Unthinkable* (Chicago: University of Chicago Press, 2016), 159.

took their primary responsibility to be the maintenance of the prestige and power of the Catholic Church. How could it be otherwise? Diocesan websites in the United States affirm that the Catholic Church is holy because it was instituted by Christ, that Christ gave his church the gift of the Spirit, and that the church's doctrine and way of life are the same today as in the time of the Apostles. This is catechesis. What greater value is there than the defense and protection of this institution? The logic governing Catholic decision-making was thoroughly ecclesiological, thoroughly institutional, hermetic, and completely unyielding.

We know now, for example, that John Paul II, who is widely celebrated as the "pope of youth," protected and supported throughout his long papacy the serial rapist and pedophile, Father Marcial Maciel, whose crimes and sins were as prodigious as his financial contributions to the church. Young people "chanted John Paul II, we love you," at the annual World Youth Day rallies he initiated, a Catholic writer much charmed by this pope recalls, and "he responded in that wonderful baritone voice, 'Perhaps I love you more.' "[15] But John Paul II's love for youth was apparently neither capacious nor concrete enough to include the very many boys and girls Maciel raped, among them Maciel's own children. Maciel founded a religious order of men, the Legion of Christ, among whom he trolled for victims. Karol Wojtyla was raised to the honors of the altar in 2014. Asking people to honor him as Saint Karol makes them complicit in his silence and in his betrayal of the vulnerable. If it is true that John Paul II was "fond of saying that young people are the future of the church," then in the disregard he showed for Maciel's victims the pope gave clear proof of what he believed the church owed the future.[16]

---

[15]Mary Beth Bonacci, "The Pope of the Youth," *Crisis* 23, no. 5 (May 2005).

[16]There is a vast online literature on the subject of John Paul II and Marcial Maciel. See, for example, Gerald Renner and Jason Berry, "Head of Worldwide Catholic Order Accused of History of Abuse," *Hartford Courant,* February 23, 1997; Jason Berry, "Legion of Secrets: Jason Berry's Saga Ends," *The Gambit*, March 9, 2009; Jason Berry, "Francis Inherits Decades of Abuse Cover-Up," *National Catholic Reporter*, February 9, 2019; Jason Berry, "Institutional Lying at the Heart of the Crisis," *National Catholic Reporter,* February 20, 2019; Jason Berry, "Francis Must Fix Cover-Up Culture that John Paul II Enabled," *National Catholic Reporter*, February 21,

As did priests and prelates around the world, who intimidated and humiliated victims of sexually abusive priests, often ordering them to confess their alleged sin of calumny against the church for speaking out about what a priest or priests had done to them, even when they had told their stories in the privacy of a bishop's office, or in the confessional, or to a nun they had (usually mistakenly) trusted. Sometimes they were made to confess to the men who had sexually abused them or to a fraternal ally of his. Rather than withdrawing serial abusers from active ministry—as many victims and their families pleaded with them to do—church authorities moved them around the national and international landscape of Catholic ecclesial, charitable, and educational institutions; never explaining the reason for these reassignments, they all but ensured that more lives would be broken. All of this was consistent with orthodox Catholic ecclesiology.[17] (I acknowledge there are competing ecclesiologies among Catholic theologians; I am also aware that these alternatives find little welcome in the centers of church power.) The Catholic theology of the priesthood determined the hierarchy of human worth. In his June 16, 2009, letter announcing the "Year for Priests" set to commence three days later on the feast of St. Jean-Marie Vianney, the Curé of Ars, patron saint of priests, Pope Benedict XVI quotes Vianney: "Without the priest, the passion and death of our Lord would be of no

---

2019; Jason Berry, "Cardinal Pironio Now on Sainthood Path, Received Money from Notorious Abuser Maciel," *National Catholic Reporter*, March 4, 2022; on the curial culture of silence and complicity, see Jason Berry, "The Last Bull: Cardinal Sodano Goes Out," *National Catholic Reporter,* December 27, 2019. *National Catholic Reporter* published a helpful guide to Jason Berry's early reporting on Marcial Maciel and the Legion of Christ, see https://www.ncronline.org/feature-series/legion-christ-investigation/stories. See also Alma Guillermoprieto, "Father Maciel, John Paul II, and the Vatican Sex Crisis, *New York Review of Books,* May 17, 2010; for a contrary view, see Andres Beltramo Álvarez, "John Paul II Knew about the Vatican's Investigation into the Maciel Case," *La Stampa,* April 25, 2014; see also the thoughtful opinion piece by Eric Sammons, "Did Pope John Paul II Cover Up Abuse?" *Crisis,* December 12, 2022.

[17]On the dominance of what I am calling "orthodox Catholic ecclesiology," see Susan Bigelow Reynolds, *People Get Ready: Ritual, Solidarity, and Lived Ecclesiology in Catholic Roxbury* (New York: Fordham University Press, 2023), 14.

avail."[18] As stories of clerical criminality and ecclesial complicity continued to surface around the world, the year-long solemnity in honor of ordained men was surely intended to remind the laity of their rightful place in the church and of the mortal danger to their souls if they stepped outside it by holding accountable the ontologically elevated figures who, again in the words of the Curé of Ars, as quoted by the pope, "continue [Christ's] work of redemption on earth."

How church authorities responded to clerical sexual abuse was also in line with church law. In 1962, the year of the first session of the Second Vatican Council, Pope John XXIII, who has also been canonized—in the context of the clergy sexual abuse crisis, the institution seems determined to prove the holiness of its administrative ranks—reissued the secret directive threatening bishops with excommunication if they turned clerical sexual criminals over to secular authorities. This coincided with this beloved pope's insistence that the church's windows be opened to the light and fresh air of a new day, just as Pope John Paul II's protection of Maciel coincided with his presence at rapturous youth rallies. Such sexual hypocrisy is constitutive of the religious and political history of modern Catholicism. Throughout the twentieth and twenty-first centuries, Catholic authorities have made common cause with fascist and authoritarian regimes around the world to guard the sanctity of "the reproductive family" against democratic popular movements for reproductive choice, legal divorce, contraception, and women's and gay rights, while doing nothing to rein in the sexual crimes and misdemeanors of clergy. These included, we know now, the rape of Indigenous women by missionaries and priests, and priests forcing women they impregnated, including nuns, to have abortions. The powers in the church indulged the sexual license of politically powerful Catholics. The sexual, sacramental, and political are not distinct in modern Catholicism. The documents of the crisis allow us to see more clearly how this system works.[19]

---

[18]"Letter of His Holiness Pope Benedict XVI Proclaiming a Year for Priests on the 150th Anniversary of the 'Dies Natalis' of the Curé of Ars," June 16, 2009.

[19]On John XXIII's approval of *De Modo Procedendi in Causis Solicitationis,* see Thomas P. Doyle, A.W.R. (Richard) Sipe, and Patrick J. Wall, *Sex,*

What does it mean, then, to live with this knowledge, with what has been suspected but is now disclosed and documented? In the early 2010s, I did ethnographic fieldwork in Chicago among adult survivors of clerical sexual abuse. Most were in their late sixties and early seventies; they had all been deeply formed in Catholic sacramental practice, theology, and devotions. One of the topics we returned to often was their on-again, off-again relationship with Catholicism as an institution. In this context, a number of survivors referenced a scene in the 1939 film *The Wizard of Oz* that spoke powerfully to their experience. After an arduous journey filled with terrible dangers (not unlike the survivors' own lives), Dorothy, her little dog, Toto, and their three companions, the Scarecrow, the Tin Man, and the Cowardly Lion, have arrived at the throne room in the Emerald City. Their aim is to present the Wizard with their most fervently held desires in the hope—with the confidence, even—that he will grant them. He is, after all, the "great and powerful Oz." The Scarecrow wants a brain; the Tin Man, emotions; the Cowardly Lion, courage; Dorothy and Toto, to return home to Kansas. What happens next, I am sure you know. A majestic and terrifying vision of the Wizard's face appears amid flashing lights above the supplicants, his mighty voice echoing in the chamber, but as he proceeds to scold and bully them, Toto, with the unfailing sense dogs have when something is not quite right, pulls back a curtain to reveal that the Wizard is in reality a frightened little man, standing at a console, mechanically creating the illusion of his grandeur with levers and pulleys.

A priest among the survivors—I call him "Frank" in *History*

Priests, and Secret Codes: The Catholic Church's 2,000-Year Paper Trail of Sexual Abuse (Los Angeles: Volt Press, 2006), 47–53. The story of the collusion of Catholic prelates and priests with reactionary regimes must be examined in the histories of various modern nations, but a useful introduction is James Chappel, *Catholic Modern: The Challenge of Totalitarianism and the Remaking of the Church* (Cambridge, MA: Harvard University Press, 2018). For an introduction to the subject—and crime—of priests compelling women and girls they have impregnated to have abortions, see Doris Reisinger, "Reproductive Abuse in the Context of Clergy Sexual Abuse in the Catholic Church," published in 2022 in the international open-access online journal *Religions*, special issue on "Sexual and Spiritual Violence against Adult Men and Women in the Catholic Church."

and Presence, and will do so here too—interpreted the scene for me.[20] At the end of the movie, Frank says, the good witch, Glinda, asks Dorothy, "What have you learned?" "This is the key question," Frank emphasizes. He repeats it three times to make sure I understand: "What have you learned? What have you learned? What have you learned?" Frank was sexually assaulted by two priests in his childhood parish in New Jersey and by another in the seminary. In the early 2000s, Frank's bishop chastised him for going public with his story, which Frank chose to do in solidarity with other victims. He was removed from his parish, stripped of his pension, and essentially left homeless. No such punishment is meted out to criminal priests, who are almost always allowed to retire with dignity and full financial support. "These guys get to stay," as Frank says, whereas he had to go.

What have you learned once the curtain has been pulled back, the illusion pierced? That Frank believes there is something to be learned from the still accumulating evidence of clerical sexual crimes and ecclesiastical complicity is the first and perhaps the most important lesson to be taken from his and other survivors' witness. Remembering preserves knowledge of something that ought not, must not, be forgotten; to forget what has come to light poses a grave risk to the living. I emphasize memory in this context as a *process—remembering*—rather than as a *conclusion*: the answer to Frank's question, "what have you learned," or one answer, is that we are still discovering what there is to know and what it means.

This is an ongoing task. Historian Jan T. Gross writes that the Holocaust is "a point of departure rather than a point of arrival in humankind's ceaseless efforts to draw lessons from its own experience."[21] The revelations of a pervasive and permissive culture of sexual misconduct and crimes in the Catholic clergy (and by Catholic nuns, too) is like this for Catholics (and for scholars of Catholicism, and of religion, too), *a point of departure.* Gross

---

[20]For more on Frank in the broader context of my fieldwork among survivors of clergy sexual abuse in Chicago and elsewhere, see Robert A. Orsi, *History and Presence* (Cambridge, MA: The Belknap Press of Harvard University Press, 2016), esp. Chapter 7, "Events of Abundant Evil," 215–48.

[21]Jan T. Gross, *Neighbors: The Destruction of the Jewish Community in Jedwabne, Poland* (Princeton, NJ: Princeton University Press, 2001), 13.

again: "While we may never 'understand' why [the Holocaust] happened," by which I understand him to mean never grasp a reality of this magnitude in all its multiplicity of causes, "we must clearly understand the implications of its having taken place."[22]

There is an ethical dimension to remembering, of course—a question of what some call "memory-justice"—but there is an ontological one as well. The implications of its *having taken place: the point of departure is also a point of rupture.* The world was one way before the events that are remembered occurred, another way afterward. Remembering marks, and more, maintains this line of demarcation: before knowing/after knowing. Sitting beside their fellow Catholics in their churches—sitting astride this line, in other words, that their presence in the pews inscribes in the really-realness of the sanctuary—survivors are unwelcome reminders of the brokenness of their sacred world, of the new temporality of Catholicism. For this reason, as survivors well know, many, perhaps most, of their fellow Catholics want them to disappear (as Frank's bishop wanted him to disappear). In one suburban Illinois church, the congregation literally held a rite of exorcism to rid itself of the survivors and their allies among them who were insisting their fellow parishioners not forget that one of their own parish priests had been identified as an abuser of a young woman. This ritualization of the imperative to forget underscores the metaphysical and ontological stakes in remembering. Catholics hoping to exorcise the truth refused to be "bruised by history," in Lauren Berlant's powerful phrase. Berlant calls neoliberal subjects who insist on maintaining their innocence of the violence done in their names as "infantile citizens."[23] In this sense, Catholics who insist on forgetting are "infantile Catholics," or as survivors call them, "the 'sheeple' of God." What have you learned? Will you be bruised by history? Or rather, you *will be* bruised by history, and what will you learn from the bruising?

Religious "traditions" (what Ghosh calls "religious world-views") do not come down through the years in some sort of cocoon of metaphysical quarantine, as Ghosh seems to suggest

---

[22]Gross, *Neighbors: The Destruction of the Jewish Community in Jedwabne*, 13.

[23]Lauren Berlant, *The Queen of America Goes to Washington: Essays on Sex and Citizenship* (Durham, NC: Duke University Press, 1997), 6.

with his language of "pre-carbon modern." Religious traditions are not isolated from the selfish and self-aggrandizing ambitions of the historical entities whose most profound values such traditions allegedly express and preserve. Catholic spiritual and devotional traditions, theologies, even the sacraments, have been mobilized on behalf of the schemes, crimes, and fears of the men throughout history and in different places who stood behind the ecclesiastical curtain. Catholic ritual and theology are fully implicated in their misdeeds and remain haunted by them. This is well known, but it is consistently forgotten. What Frank calls "the blindly sentimental love affair with [the] illusion" ("the great and powerful Oz") is preferable to the reality survivors reveal and recall. What is more constitutive of the ideal, allure, and power of the Tridentine priesthood, for instance, than the understanding of the priest as participating in Christ's redemptive sacrifice? The priest reenacts Christ's sacrifice in the Mass; the priest recapitulates Christ's sacrifice in the gift of himself to God in his vocation and to his congregation in his service. Yes, and here we ought to remember that the theology of redemptive sacrifice was fully mobilized by rapacious priests who offered themselves as sacrificial victims willing to take upon themselves the sinfulness of their victim's sexual needs and desires. They used the theology of the Eucharist as the metaphysical dynamic of their seductions. Clergy sexual abuse was deeply situated in Catholic history, theology, and practice.[24]

Ghosh seemingly ignored, in other words, the past fifty years

[24]Again, Benedict quoting Vianney, in the June 16, 2009, letter, "What a good thing it is for a priest each morning [at the celebration of the Eucharist] to offer himself to God in sacrifice." Noting that the Curé of Ars "did . . . not avoid self-mortification" (a mild way of describing the priest's ardent and bloody use of the lash against himself), Benedict quotes the saint's regular practice in confession, "I give sinners a small penance and the rest I do in their place." The pope adds, "The core of his teaching remains valid for each of us [priests]: souls have been won at the price of Jesus's own blood, and a priest cannot devote himself to their salvation if he refuses to share personally in the 'precious cost' of their redemption.' " On priests using Christian soteriology to ensnare their younger victims in the confessional, see, for instance, Robert A. Orsi, "The Study of Religion on the Other Side of Disgust," *Harvard Divinity Bulletin* 47, nos. 1 and 2 (2019): 20–30, about Boston's Father Paul Shanley's practice of offering to take the sin of boys' masturbation onto himself by masturbating them.

of global Catholic history in confecting his sense of hope from the Catholic pre-carbon-modern "tradition." Survivors cannot. Catholicism ought to have been a "moral beacon" for this broken world, Frank told me, "but that moral beacon is all but extinguished by [the church's] own work." The Catholic Church is the largest non-governmental landowner on the planet, in possession of an estimated 177 million acres of land. Given this extraordinary religious/political fact, a number of climate activists have recently expressed the hope that Catholic authorities might put these vast holdings to the service of life on the planet. With the cooperation of Vatican officials, for example, Molly Burhans, founder of the organization Goodlands, has been at work developing a geographical database of the church's real-estate holdings (the first such attempt since the time of the Holy Roman Empire). Burhans encourages Catholic authorities to make "sustainable land management decisions—for example, to conserve forested land that can absorb and store carbon." The more desperate and hopeless we become in the face of climate catastrophe, the more compelling such a prospect becomes, and the more understandable. No wonder Ghosh overlooks the past fifty years of Catholic history. The result, though, is a shallow vision of hope. If a child was solemnly, intentionally left by her bishop to be raped by a priest, what grounds are there for thinking that these same men will take good care of the earth's common future?[25]

I understand that cynicism is not a critical or theoretical position, or a theological one, but then again, hope that runs utterly counter to the evidence of history and contemporary events is not an enlargement of the political imagination—it is another form of denial. As anthropologist Anna Tsing puts the dilemma, "Neither tales of progress nor of ruin tell how to think about collaborative survival."[26] *Laudato Si´* is a magnificent document, but the world

---

[25]On Molly Burhans's work, and for more information about the Catholic Church's global landownership, see Timothy Schuler, "Mapping One of the World's Largest Landowners," October 18, 2017, at *Longform*; see also David Owen, "How a Young Activist Is Helping Pope Francis Battle Climate Change," *New Yorker,* February 8, 2021; "sustainable land management decisions" from *Yale Climate Connections,* YCC Team, "The Catholic Church's Vast Landholdings Could Help Protect the Climate," June 24, 2021

[26]Tsing, *Mushroom at the End of the World*, 19.

has reason to be—or, as Frank would say, the world has learned to be—deeply suspicious of the Catholic Church as a point of transcendence in a burning world. Where does this leave us?

I often heard it said at meetings of survivors—sometimes by survivors themselves, sometimes by their friends and supporters—that *here* was the real church, that this time and this place where survivors came together to share their lives with each other was the authentic sacrament of modern Catholicism and its true sacred space, not the Eucharist celebrated in parish churches, which the sexual crimes of the clergy and their cynical cover-up by Catholic authorities had so obscenely profaned. The sacred was outside the sanctuary. The statement that here is the real church is metaphysical and ontological in the Catholic context; it is also profoundly subversive. Catholicism's institutional authority from the earliest centuries onward has been grounded in the laity's disciplined absorption of the shock of the dreadful contradiction in their lived experience between the beauty and sustenance of the faith, on the one hand, and the venality, sexual rapacity, and moral corruption of the institution and its power brokers, on the other. "Most of us could walk like circus performers across tightropes that were strung between private knowledge and public acknowledgement," historian Fintan O'Toole describes the relationship of Catholics to the church in mid-twentieth-century Ireland, at the time when the institution was at the height of its moral and political power in the country and its behavior most corrupt and unaccountable.[27]

Maybe this is Catholicism's hard and ancient realism. It is precisely amid such existential horrors—good people doing dreadful things, bad people behaving with kindness and generosity—that humans may catch a glimpse of what an elderly priest in Graham Greene's *Brighton Rock* calls "the appalling . . . strangeness of the mercy of God."[28] But *remember* here bishops commanding

---

[27]Fintan O'Toole, *We Don't Know Ourselves: A Personal History of Modern Ireland* (New York: Liveright, 2021), 197.

[28]Graham Greene, *Brighton Rock*, with an introduction by J. M. Coetzee (New York: Penguin Books, 2004), 268. Greene is describing in this passage the life of the French poet Charles Péguy. Richard Greene calls "the mercy of God" one of the great themes in Graham Greene's fiction (Richard Greene, *The Unquiet Englishman: A Life of Graham Greene* [New York: W. W. Norton, 2020], 105).

children who had been sexually abused by priests to go to confession to these same priests: doing as they were told, the children went. The capacity to walk the tightrope was not innate. It was formed in Catholic bodies and souls by the multiplication of such incidents of walking anxiously between emotional, physical, and ontological violence on one end of the tightrope, and consolation, grace, and forgiveness on the other. For many survivors, at the end of the twentieth century and the beginning of the twenty-first, walking the tightrope became impossible, and finally, and perhaps most importantly, meaningless. To say, "Here is the *real* church," is to relocate the ground of Catholic truth and authority and to claim it for oneself. "It's not that it's all a lie," Gary, one of the survivors, says about the church. "There's a lot of truth in the illusion" and "the truth isn't gone" when things turn from the dazzling Technicolor of the illusion to the black and white of everyday life. But "the curtain has to be drawn back"—Gary here is talking as if to other survivors—because "you've got to learn." O'Toole's tightrope is strung today for all Catholics between knowing and not-knowing, remembering and forgetting.

"If you want that love and acceptance that you felt in the illusion," Gary says, "you're going to have to provide that" for yourself and others. "It was probably not a good thing to have it provided [for you by others] in the first place." Gary refers to the time before the illusion is unveiled as "Truthville." "We've done all the thinking for you," the authorities in Truthville say, "because you don't know anything." But in the gospels, Jesus invites others to speak, and he listens when they respond. When Jesus asks, "Who do *you* say I am?" Gary says, "It is important that you answer that question yourself." It's like the masses Jesus fed miraculously with bread and fish, he goes on. When they come back the next day to see another miracle, Jesus says to them, in Gary's telling of the story, "you've come back for the wrong reasons. You're going to have to learn how to feed yourself and each other," he imagines Jesus saying to the crowds, "and if you don't do this for yourself, you're going to go back to starving."

The monthly meetings of Chicago-area survivors I attended for two years had a distinctive ethos, carefully cultivated and sustained by participants, at once Catholic and something other-than-Catholic. The meetings resembled now and then, in tone and sensibility, the feeling of secular self-help groups, to which many of the survivors had belonged (some still did). At the same time, they were informed at a deep level by the participants' Catholicism, as well as by their shared disillusionment with the church. They were familiar with each other's often quite difficult personal histories, their respective periods of sexual and emotional chaos, substance abuse, broken family relations, and professional disasters, and open about their present-day struggles as well. And in their exchanges during these evening sessions—which were not always nice and polite—they offered *each other* the "appalling strangeness" of mercy beyond orthodox notions of good and bad, sin and virtue. The survivors were committed to each other, at the meetings and outside them. Their relationship with God, in contrast, was more tentative, fluid, and ambivalent. God came in and out of focus. Mostly, they tended to keep God at arm's length. God, whoever or whatever God was, was not to intrude on or diminish their capacities for surviving. God was irrelevant to their empathy for each other. God was a source of strength, survivors often explained to me, or God was nothing to them. They mostly stayed out of Catholic churches, although now and then they attended services for reasons of friendship and family. The survivors I knew were polymorphous in their spiritual curiosity and creative in religious syntheses. They took wisdom where they found it. What mattered most was that they had survived the God given them by the church.

Climate activists will be better served in their search for transcendence by turning to men and women like these survivors practicing religion(s) in the ruins, where there is no longer any attempt to purify the sacred from history or lived experience. Catholicism is not the only religion in ruins in the early twenty-first century. The Orthodox Church in post-Soviet Russia is fully implicated in Putin's war; government Islam in Iran authorizes a brutal regime of violent misogyny; Buddhism is compromised in Myanmar, where monks have aligned themselves with the genocidal agenda of the state; Orthodoxy and Ultra-Orthodoxy in Israel; Hinduism in Modi's India; white Christian evangelism and far-right Catholicism in the United States. It seems that what were once called the "world religions" are all in some state of ruin. The designation "world religion" was a colonial and racist invention that served to mark off the religions not included in the category as fit for conquest and extermination.[29] Perhaps, the contemporary alignment of "world religions" with fascist and authoritarian regimes is a sign of their isolation from the lived experience of their peoples, signaling the beginning of the end of them and the emergence of new religious formations and institutions, new forms of religious consciousness and imaginations. It may be only in the ruins of temples that humans learn necessary arts of survival for these dangerous times, ways of being together and attending to each other and to their shared planet. It is in the ruins that new moral visions may emerge, new ways of understanding the world, and new ways of being religious, beyond the good/bad religion binary and beyond the intentions of power. What arises in the ruins will not necessarily always be positive or benign (religion being what it is). Nevertheless, it is to what is happening in the ruins that we ought to pay attention, because it may be in ruins that we will find the allies we are looking for in our current predicament, rather than in the temples.

[29]On the subject of world religions, see Tomoko Masuzawa, *The Invention of World Religions; or, How European Universalism Was Preserved in the Language of Pluralism* (Chicago: University of Chicago Press, 2005); see also David Chidester, *The Empire of Religion: Imperialism and Comparative Religion* (Chicago: University of Chicago Press, 2014).

Contributors

Vicente Chong, SJ, is a visiting assistant professor of systematic theology in the School of Theology and Ministry at Boston College. He received his PhD from Heythrop College, University of London, and worked as a professor of systematic theology at the Pontificia Universidad Católica del Ecuador. His research interests include theological aesthetics, liberation theology, Trinity, and creation. His current work focuses on the theology of symbols.

Christopher Denny is an associate professor in the Department of Theology and Religious Studies at St. John's University in New York, where since 2004 he has taught as a historical theologian in undergraduate and graduate classes. Denny has been an Associate editor of the College Theology Society journal *Horizons* since 2016, after a previous term as a book review editor for the journal. In addition to serving as a member of the CTS board, he has also served on the board of the American Academy of Religion and as the executive director of the AAR's Mid-Atlantic Region. In 2017, he was a distinguished visiting professor at the University of Dayton. Denny is the author of *A Generous Symphony: Hans Urs von Balthasar's Literary Revelations* (2016), and the co-editor of three books: *A Realist's Church* (with Patrick Hayes and Nicholas Rademacher—2015); *Empowering the People of God: Catholic Action before and after Vatican II* (with Jeremy Bonner and Mary Beth Fraser Connolly, 2014); and *Finding Salvation in Christ* (with Christopher McMahon, 2011). His recent published essays have appeared in the *Journal of Interreligious Studies, Christianity and Literature,* and the *Journal of Hindu-Christian Studies.*

Tim Dulle Jr. is a Manresa Postdoctoral Fellow in the Center for Ignatian Service at Saint Louis University. He works as a cultural historian of American Catholicism, with an emphasis on Catholic identity and practice since the Second Vatican Council. His primary research project has focused on the American Pop artist and longtime Roman Catholic nun Corita Kent, and he has taught courses in American religious history, the Catholic intellectual tradition, and Ignatian spirituality.

Joseph S. Flipper is the Mary Ann Spearin Chair of Catholic Theology at the University of Dayton with appointments in the Department of Religious Studies and the Race and Ethnic Studies Program. Formerly, he was associate professor of theology at Bellarmine University in Louisville, Kentucky, where he also served as the associate director of the Ethics and Social Justice Center. He was awarded a Ford Foundation fellowship in 2019–2020, and he was in residence as a Visiting Scholar at the McGrath Institute for Church Life at the University of Notre Dame. He was the recipient of a 2011 Ford Foundation Dissertation Fellowship and a doctoral fellowship from the Forum for Theological Exploration. Dr. Flipper's research intersects three areas: Black Catholicism in the United States, race and religion, and twentieth-century Catholic theology. He is the author of *Between Apocalypse and Eschaton: History and Eternity in Henri de Lubac* (2015), which examines the French Jesuit Henri de Lubac's theological account of history in the context of the broad revival of eschatological thinking in the twentieth century. He is currently working on his second book, *Theological Terrain: Geography and Ecclesiology in Twentieth-Century Catholicism*, which will examine geography in Catholic ecclesiology across transnational contexts.

Charles Gillespie is assistant professor of Catholic studies at Sacred Heart University where he also serves as director of the Pioneer Journey. He studied at Villanova University, the Yale Institute of Sacred Music and Yale Divinity School, and the University of Virginia. His research and teaching investigate religions, the arts, and culture focused on the Catholic Intellectual Tradition (especially Hans Urs von Balthasar), phenomenology and interpretation theory, systematic and fundamental theology, spirituality and ecology (especially the Irish mystic, John Moriarty), and theatre and performance studies. His scholarly writing can be found in *Logos, Labyrinth*, *The Other Journal, Religions,* and as chapters in edited volumes. He will soon complete his first monograph, *God on Broadway*.

Matthew Gummess is a Carmelite friar with roots in southeastern New Mexico and Chicago. He is a PhD candidate in history and philosophy of science and systematic theology at the University of Notre Dame. His current interests include the place of gender and human sexuality in the field of theological anthropology, the history of liberation theologies, foundational theology, and the integration of the sciences into theology as *ancilla theologiae*. His dissertation, "The Science of the Cross: Towards a Cross-Disciplinary Theology of Desire," serves as a case study in how to do science-engaged theology. It develops a method for Catholic theologians to engage scientific research on sexual desire, based on a comparative epistemological analysis of twentieth-century research programs in psychiatry and theological anthropology.

Timothy Hanchin is associate professor of theological and religious education in the Department of Theology and Religious Studies at Villanova University. He also serves as director of the Heart of Teaching, a pedagogical formation program integrated into graduate theological education at Villanova University. His scholarship addresses theological pedagogy, mission and identity in Catholic education, trinitarian theology, and Lonergan studies.

Jacob M. Kohlhaas, is an associate professor of moral theology at Loras College (Dubuque, Iowa). He teaches a range of courses in theology, ethics, and general education and directs the Loras College Honors Program and the Catholic Studies minor. His research centers on theological anthropology, ethics, and relationships. His work has been published in *Theological Studies, Journal of Religious Ethics, Journal of Moral Theology, America,* and *US Catholic*. He is the author of *Beyond Biology: Rethinking Parenthood in the Catholic Tradition* (2021), and co-editor with Mary Doyle Roche of the 2020 Annual Volume of the College Theology Society, *Human Families: Identities, Relationships, and Responsibilities* (2021) as well as *Catholic Family Teaching: Commentaries and Interpretations* (2024).

Amy Maxey is an assistant professor of spirituality at the Oblate School of Theology in San Antonio, Texas. Her research interests include Christian mystical traditions (especially from the medieval period), contemporary feminist and womanist theologies, and twentieth-century Catholic systematic theology. She is currently working on a book which develops a feminist understanding of mystical consciousness by integrating womanist understandings of eros with contemporary historical and theological work on Christian mysticism.

Stephen Okey is an associate professor of theology at Saint Leo University in Saint Leo, Florida, where he teaches courses in Catholic theology and ethics. He earned his master's degree in theology from the University of Chicago Divinity School and his PhD in Systematic Theology from Boston College. He is the author of *A Theology of Conversation: An Introduction to David Tracy* (2018). He has published scholarly essays in *Political Theology* and *International Journal of Public Theology*. His research interests are in public theology, Catholic social teaching, and technology.

Robert A. Orsi is the first holder of the Grace Craddock Nagle Chair in Catholic Studies in the religion department at Northwestern University in Evanston, Illinois, where he also holds a joint appointment in history. He earned his BA from Trinity College in Hartford, Connecticut, and his PhD in religious studies from Yale. He was president of the American Academy of Religion in 2002–2003. His research has included historical and ethnographic work in American Catholicism and studies in theory and method in the study of religion. He is the author of numerous books, including *The Madonna of 115th Street: Faith and Community in Italian Harlem, 1880–1950* (1985; 2nd ed. 2002), which received the John Gilmary Shea Prize from the American Catholic Historical Association and the Jesuit National Book Award; *Thank You, Saint Jude: Women's Devotion to the Patron Saint of Hopeless Causes* (1996), which won the Merle Curti Award in American Social History from the Organization of American Historians; and *Between Heaven and Earth: The Religious Worlds People Make and the Scholars Who Study Them* (2004), which received an Award for Excellence in the Study of Religion from the American Academy of Religion.

Deepan Rajaratnam is a doctoral candidate at Saint Louis University where he researches the intersection of ecclesiology and pneumatology with a particular interest in the laity. Building on the work of Yves Congar and Ormond Rush, Rajaratnam focuses on the sense of the faithful through the lens of local church to advance a synodal reception of Vatican II. Accordingly, Rajaratnam creates space for a stronger consideration of culture and place in Catholicism as it is lived. Rajaratnam was selected as the 2019–2020 Religion & Public Life Fellow for the Lived Religion in the Digital Age initiative. In 2019, he earned the Susan Perry Award for the Best Graduate Essay from the College Theology Society.

Hanna Reichel is associate professor of reformed theology at Princeton Theological Seminary. Reichel earned a Dr. theol. (~ PhD) in systematic theology from Heidelberg University, Germany, after an MDiv in theology and a BS in economics. Prior to coming to Princeton in 2018, Reichel taught at Heidelberg University and Halle-Wittenberg University. Reichel has co-edited six volumes on themed journal issues and has authored more than two dozen peer-reviewed articles or chapters as well as two monographs including *Theologie als Bekenntnis: Karl Barths kontextuelle Lek¬türe des Heidelberger Katechismus* (2015), which received the Lautenschläger Award for Theological Promise and the Ernst Wolf Award, and *After Method: Queer Grace, Conceptual Design, and the Possibility of Theology* (2023).

Katherine G. Schmidt is an associate professor in the Department of Theology and Religious Studies at Molloy University (New York). She received her PhD in 2016 from the University of Dayton. Her work focuses on the relationship between theology and digital culture, as well as questions of technology and media more broadly.

Jane Sloan Peters is an assistant professor of religious studies at the College of Mount Saint Vincent.

Laura Taylor is an associate professor of theology and the director of the Center for Teaching and Learning at the College of St. Benedict and St. John's University in Central Minnesota. Her teaching and research interests include feminist and liberation theologies, as well as the Scholarship of Teaching and Learning (SoTL), especially as it relates to theology.

Ethan Vander Leek is a doctoral student in religious studies at Marquette University. His doctoral research focuses on the implications of William Desmond's philosophy for Christian theology and spirituality, especially Rowan Williams and the Christian mystical tradition.

Dennis J. Wieboldt III is a JD/PhD student in history at the University of Notre Dame, where he is a Richard and Peggy Notebaert Premier Fellow at the Graduate School and Edward J. Murphy Fellow at the Law School. His research explores the relationship between law, politics, and religion in the twentieth-century United States. Dennis's refereed scholarship has been published or is forthcoming in *American Catholic Studies*, *US Catholic Historian*, *Horizons,* and the *Journal of Catholic Social Thought*, among other venues.

Trevor Williams is a doctoral candidate in theology at Villanova University with a concentration in historical and systematic theology. He is writing his dissertation on the French philosopher Emmanuel Falque with attention to animality and the liturgy. His research interests are in fundamental theology, liturgical theology, biblical interpretation, the reception of Vatican II, Catholic social teaching, and theology in popular culture. Williams recently won the Founders' Circle Prize by the Society for the Study of Christian Spirituality and published articles in *Logos*, *Spiritus*, and *The Heythrop Journal*. He is also co-editing the book *Theological Discourses on Social Media* with Christopher B. Barnett and Clark J. Elliston.